CULTURAL HISTORIES OF CINEMA

This new book series examines the relationship between cinema and culture. It will feature interdisciplinary scholarship that focuses on the national and transnational trajectories of cinema as a network of institutions, representations, practices and technologies. Of primary concern is analysing cinema's expansive role in the complex social, economic and political dynamics of the twentieth and twenty-first centuries.

SERIES EDITORS
Lee Grieveson and Haidee Wasson

ALSO PUBLISHED
Cinema Beyond Territory: Inflight Entertainment and
Atmospheres of Globalisation, *Stephen Groening*
Empire and Film, *edited by Lee Grieveson and Colin MacCabe*
Film and the End of Empire, *edited by Lee Grieveson and Colin MacCabe*
Global Mexican Cinema: Its Golden Age, *edited by Robert McKee Irwin and
Maricruz Castro Ricalde*
The Grierson Effect: Tracing Documentary's International Movement,
edited by Zoë Druick and Deane Williams
Shadow Economies of Cinema: Mapping Informal Film Distribution, *Ramon Lobato*

Making Movies into Art

Picture Craft from the Magic Lantern to Early Hollywood

Kaveh Askari

•

A BFI book published by Palgrave

For Kristin

First published in 2014 by
PALGRAVE

on behalf of the

BRITISH FILM INSTITUTE
21 Stephen Street, London W1T 1LN
www.bfi.org.uk

There's more to discover about film and television through the BFI.
Our world-renowned archive, cinemas, festivals, films, publications and learning resources are here to inspire you.

Palgrave in the UK is an imprint of Macmillan Publishers Limited, registered in England, company number 785998, of 4 Crinan Street, London N1 9XW. Palgrave Macmillan in the US is a division of St Martin's Press LLC, 175 Fifth Avenue, New York, NY 10010. Palgrave is a global imprint of the above companies and is represented throughout the world. Palgrave® and Macmillan® are registered trademarks in the United States, the United Kingdom, Europe and other countries.

Cover image: *The Blue Bird* (Maurice Tourneur, 1918), Famous Players-Lasky Corporation/Artcraft Pictures Corporation, courtesy of George Eastman House.
Designed by couch
Set by Cambrian Typesetters, Camberley, Surrey
Printed in China

This book is printed on paper suitable for recycling and made from fully managed and sustained forest sources. Logging, pulping and manufacturing processes are expected to conform to the environmental regulations of the country of origin.

British Library Cataloguing-in-Publication Data
A catalogue record for this book is available from the British Library
A catalog record for this book is available from the Library of Congress

ISBN 978–1–84457–695–1 (pb)
ISBN 978–1–84457–696–8 (hb)

Contents

Acknowledgments

This project began at the University of Chicago, where I was lucky to land in an engaged and collegial cohort during the early years of the Committee on Cinema and Media Studies. Ken Eisenstein, Doron Galili, Sarah Keller, Chika Kinoshita, Dan Morgan, Jennifer Peterson, Rob Spadoni, Charles Tepperman and Allison Whitney discussed this work in its earliest stages. Chicago faculty who workshopped early drafts include James Lastra, Joel Snyder and Jacqueline Stewart. Yuri Tsivian gave me my first lessons in archival research and my first in-depth tours through the landscape of 1910s cinema. Miriam Hansen was an exceptional mentor for so many because, as practical and specific as her recommendations were, one never left her office uncertain about the larger reasons why this work matters. We all really miss her. Tom Gunning's profound commitment to this project has continued through its transformations in recent years. The pleasure that he takes in new research has motivated me to extend my investigation in ways I would not otherwise have done. He encouraged me to pursue what appeared to be the project's impasses and to realise that these were actually its most exciting opportunities.

Much of the research for this book was made possible by two Mellon fellowships. The first was awarded by the Council on Library and Information Resources, and the second by the University of California, Berkeley. During the travels associated with these fellowships, I came to depend on the knowledge and enthusiasm of several archivists in the USA and Europe. I would specifically like to thank Paula Entin at the Princeton University Library, Barbara Hall at the Margaret Herrick Library, Jenn Libby at the Visual Studies Workshop, Mark McMurray at St Lawrence University Special Collections, Claudy op den Kamp and Simona Monizza at the Netherlands Film Museum, Zoran Sinobad and Mike Mashon at the Library of Congress, Caroline Yeager and Joe Struble at the George Eastman House and Charles Silver at the Museum of Modern Art. Christophe Gauthier helped me to navigate the collections at the Bibliothèque de l'Arsenal in Paris. At Berkeley, I had the unique opportunity to work with the Pacific Film Archive to preserve and present material from the Black family collection. This would not have been possible without the work of Mona Nagai, Kathy Geritz and, especially, Jon Shibata. Thanks to the National Film Preservation Foundation for supporting the effort and to Carl and Annetta Black for their commitment to preserving their family archive. Working through this material with them has been a rare treat.

I have benefited from input, usually while exploring dining options around conferences and archives, from Richard Abel, Giorgio Bertellini, Vincent Bohlinger,

Marta Braun, Jon Burrows, Ian Christie, Mark Garrett Cooper, Donald Crafton, Patrizia diBello, Allyson Field, Jennifer Horne, Jane Gaines, Philippe Gauthier, Miranda Hofelt, Richard Koszarski, Murray Pomerance, Simon Popple, Lauren Rabinovitz, Matthew Solomon, Dan Streible, Brigitta Wagner, Tami Williams, Artemis Willis and Mike Zryd. Scott Curtis read multiple drafts of the first chapter. Charlie Keil edited two satellite articles that helped me with the introduction and conclusion. Laura Marcus and Dana Polan read the third chapter and helped me to understand Freeburg and Patterson in broader contexts. Simon Popple, Vanessa Toulmin and John Plunkett edited material that was used in the first chapter. This material appeared previously as 'Alexander Black's Detective Lectures and the Motion Studies of Eadweard Muybridge and Thomas Eakins', in *Early Popular Visual Culture* vol. 3 no. 1 and 'Photographed Tableaux and Motion Picture Aesthetics: Alexander Black's Picture Plays', in *Multimedia Histories: From the Magic Lantern to the Internet*. Rob King and Gregory Waller provided meticulous commentary on the article version of Chapter 5, which appeared in *Film History* vol. 26 no. 2 as 'Art School Cinema: Rex Ingram and the Lessons of the Studio'. That chapter also benefited from Ruth Barton's generosity and knowledge of Rex Ingram's career.

During my two years at Berkeley I revised the manuscript with advice from Scott Combs, Laura Horak, Jean Ma, Zhivka Valiavicharska, Kristen Whissel and Linda Williams. Now in the Pacific Northwest, I am happy to have had the opportunity to finish this work in community with Michael Allan, Michael Falter, Katharina Loew, Christopher Pavsek and Andrew Ritchey. Eric Ames, Sudhir Mahadevan, Leigh Mercer and James Tweedie have been welcoming at the Moving Image Research Group at the University of Washington. Jennifer Bean found time to carefully read my work and to mentor me through the adjustments to a new regional film culture and a new assistant professorship. At my home institution gratitude is due to Marc Geisler, World's Greatest Department Chair, and to Provost Brent Carbajal for their support. Two summer research grants and two grants from the Office of Research and Sponsored Programs allowed me to wrap up this research at archives in New York and Washington, DC. In the Department of English, Dawn Dietrich, Kathleen Lundeen, Brenda Miller, Douglas Park, Lysa Rivera and, especially, Bill Smith helped me to think through some of the final decisions. Students in my seminars, including Nat Barr, Zach Furste, Matt Holtmeier, Maia Melton, Amos Stailey-Young and Chelsea Wessels, offered valuable perspective on some of the central questions of the book. Nat's curiosity for the material was evident in the extra attention he gave to the project as a research assistant.

Haidee Wasson and Lee Grieveson have been great series editors, for their extensive knowledge of the topic as well as their prompt, effective and good-humoured handling of the project. Jenni Burnell, Sophia Contento and Joy Tucker took care with many details of its production. Thanks to the two readers for their wise appraisals of the text and their suggestions for tightening its frame.

Gifts of hospitality and the bonds of kinship sustain the everyday work of any lengthy project. Those who offered this type of sustenance during the research and writing of this book include Marcus Aurin, Rich Brown, Claude Burgers, Kendall Dodd, Monika Gehlawat, Elise Geltman, Max Harless, Noël Herpe, Michael Kunichika, Bregtje Lameris, Kelly Nichols, Jessica Spivey and dozens of relatives in North America and Iran. I know I am not alone in admiring Joshua Yumibe's insight and generosity as a close colleague. I am truly lucky to have him as one of my closest friends. Brian Whitener has been an inspiring travelling companion since we were just kids. He and I have fallen naturally into productive living and writing situations for weeks, months and years at a time. Finally, I should probably thank Kristin Mahoney for persuading me sometime during our first year of college – maybe it was deep April – to enroll with her in a course on aesthetics. In the twenty years between that course and this book, Kristin has braved and enjoyed all of the risks and rewards of building intellectual lives in collaboration.

Introduction

As to the relation of the stage player to the photodrama – Michael Angelo painted pictures. He also molded statues, expressing himself in paint or putty with equal zest, and so did Benvenuto Cellini. I consider the cases parallel.

Herbert Tree, 'The Worthy Cinema', 1916

In 1916, Sir Herbert Beerbohm Tree was both too early and too late for art cinema. The founder of the Royal Academy of Dramatic Art and one of the best-known Shakespearean actors in the world wrote an article for the *New York Times* after finding himself lured to Hollywood with the promise of celluloid posterity and a six-figure pay-cheque. In his view, American cinema lagged behind the stage-friendly traditions of the *film d'art* in France and related movements in Italy and England, and he hoped to correct this deficiency with his work at the newly formed Triangle Film Corporation. In his manifesto for 'Worthy Cinema' he defined an art cinema that combined moving pictures with educational imperatives and serious historical theatre. Alongside his discussion of aesthetics, he wrote, 'I am told that the motion picture is already an established institution in your western schools. This is a surprise and a gratification to me, for I have long realized the extraordinary value of the picture lesson and advocated such an extension of its use.'[1] Tree addresses several different constituencies – painterly, educational, civic, historical – in his brief public appeal to a more artistically valuable cinema. These stowaway discourses of art, more so than Tree's rather straightforward goal of ushering in a new wave of stage-star performances in early Hollywood, provoke a series of questions that deserve more attention in historical film studies. What does it mean to 'consider the cases parallel'? How can we situate his accompanying definition of art cinema within the film industry's ambitions, and how exactly has he gone about seeking cross-media alliances? To these ends, what can his reference to Michelangelo's and Cellini's expressions in paint and putty indicate about the traditions he uses to define art cinema? Tree's mix of artistic and educational imperatives typifies a period that was too early for institutionalised art cinema and too late for cinema to function merely as a technical extension, or publicity engine, of established arts. This period of uncertain exchange between emergent American cinema and the other arts, when film-makers and critics did not know whether to look forward or to look back for art cinema, and when they turned to discourses of painting and sculpture, even in cases when theatre's influence seemed most conspicuous, is the subject of this book.

REWINDING ART CINEMA

I begin with the term 'art cinema' here instead of the more historically situated 'better films', 'quality films', 'exceptional photoplays', 'cinema compositions', or 'worthy cinema' because of its value as a broader category that still means something to most film viewers. It is a term of distinction, or a marker of ambition, that can immediately generate discussion about the latest art-house release or about the long history of cinema's artistic ambitions.[2] I have been asking undergraduate students to define art cinema since I began working on this project, and the most common consensus is that the term describes a contemporary niche for films that diverge from mainstream commercial tastes. The films are usually described as being 'slower' in some way, with the expectation that they will reward attention with provocative, hip and even beautiful imagery. Most examples come from post-1990s American indie films and contemporary world cinema. Students' favourite directors typically come from this category and have included David Lynch, Gus van Sant, Julian Schnabel, Kelly Reichardt, Paul Thomas Anderson, Todd Haynes, Sofia Coppola, Wong Kar-Wai, Jean-Pierre Jeunet and Nicholas Winding Refn. Their interests are mostly contemporary, save an occasional interjection from a Godard or Ozu fan who has discovered the Criterion Collection. The niche marketing of contemporary art cinema, its economics of prestige, come easily to groups of liberal-arts students. They are already aware that the majority of their examples come from films produced or distributed by art-house divisions of major studios, and they encounter these films in an age when even small art-house cinemas are shifting to the model of more screens/fewer seats to target niche audiences.[3] It usually takes a little more time to contextualise art cinema beyond the recent past, to outline other economies of prestige and to frame the aesthetic as its contested terrain.

The first step in contextualising art cinema's contested historical terrain involves showing how the term most commonly refers to movements after World War II. The foundational works on postwar art cinema have defined it as an institutional and aesthetic response to Hollywood's global ubiquity, and they have primarily located this response in the new waves of Western Europe in the 1960s.[4] These institutional networks differ from contemporary niche marketing in their reliance on state support (particularly in Italy and France) and a different kind of international festival, which created the space for production and circulation in the face of Hollywood's domination of world markets. Aesthetically, these films built upon principles of reflection on the medium, of authorship as a primary means of understanding a group of films and of cinematographic realism over both Hollywood-style storytelling and the designed images that please the eye. New-wave art cinemas were globalised, but not in the same way as current niche productions. They showcased their languages and national contexts worldwide through festival networks accommodating to their subtitles and familiar styles.[5] To talk about art cinema in reference to this, most established, historical context is to choose the approaches to authorship and the unadorned aesthetics of 1960s new waves as a point of reference for new cinemas that continue through the 90s. It opens up analysis of a broad range of global new waves, from South America to Asia, which employed shared modes of production, networks of circulation and aesthetic concerns.[6]

Making Movies into Art

But art cinema in any age is full of crosscurrents, outmoded forms and cross-contaminations from the other arts that contribute to its texture. Rosalind Galt and Karl Schoonover define art cinema as a category characterised by a productive impurity.[7] It is neither mainstream nor avant-garde, and it corrupts generic categories. It courts viewers who are ambitious, but who also seek an equal measure of impure aesthetic pleasure in their serious films. This is clearly the case with the films on the roster of contemporary art-house exhibition, but it also applies to some new waves. Considering the category of art cinema as one of productive impurity means re-evaluating those ambitious films, or aspects of films, that might otherwise seem out of place. The Iranian new wave, for example, is often noted for its aesthetic minimalism and austerity despite having an aesthetic range, including strong interests in colour, poetic traditions and richly composed pictures, that often runs counter to these assumptions. Looking back even further, these questions of what is included or omitted by the categories that have defined art cinema help to frame the stakes of a history of early art cinema in the USA. The task in locating early art cinema is to search for diverse networks and institutions of art that structure and lend meaning to an earlier group of films' ambitions, but also to recognise the persistence of questions about the position of cinema as an art medium in relation to aesthetic traditions that have long preceded and continue to develop alongside it.

The challenges of definition increase as one looks back at early art cinema because its institutions, as well as the institutions it opposed, were far less established. If a student of film history were to ask about an early art cinema in the USA before the new waves, before the international festivals and even before World War II, one might guide that student to recent scholarship on the 1930s: to the Museum of Modern Art film library, to the work of educators like Frederick Thrasher, to film criticism in influential periodicals from the *New York Times* to *Close-up* and *Experimental Cinema*. One might point back a little earlier to 1920s ciné-clubs or to films of the historical avant-garde in France or Germany, scarce as they were at first on the American scene. The Little Cinema movement of the late 20s, or the moment when Fox brought F. W. Murnau to Hollywood and paired him with pictorialist photographer Karl Struss, might provide more American context. But whether one defines early American art cinema in terms of emerging directors' styles, strategies of exhibition, or discussion of the topic in dedicated periodicals, these practices resolve towards the end of the silent era into the 30s. Before this coming-into-focus at the end of the silent period, 'art cinema' casts wider circles of confusion, blurring but not erasing its ambitions.

To look back, then, at the earliest encounters between movies and art requires analysis that does not trace successes strictly in terms of commercial stability (of niche production and exhibition) or even influence in the typical sense.[8] Cinema from the beginning was conceived in relation to the arts of literature, theatre, painting and sculpture, but this environment of possibility is necessarily also rife with hybrid and awkward works, with dead ends and false starts. The *film d'art* productions in France are the best-known efforts to link stage and screen, both for their ambitions for French national theatre and for their influence across national borders.[9] Similar appropriations of theatre's status took place in the USA, where American film entrepreneurs in the 1910s imported the famous performances of Sarah Bernhardt and contracted celebrity performers like Herbert Beerbohm Tree. Alongside these efforts to preserve the eloquent gestures of stage stars, silent American moving pictures regularly staged fictions within the painter's studio where audiences could watch compositions unfold. Magic lanternists attached cinematograph demonstrations to art lectures, and films explored the aesthetics of performers' bodies, from fitness pioneers creating living sculpture in the 1890s to prestige productions of early Hollywood.[10] Museums, ateliers and courses in art appreciation aided in the process of making movies into an art. As numerous as they were evanescent, these test cases of early art cinema betray a continuing set of ambitions, even if they rarely took lasting root within a single institution. Many early 'artistic' films pay homage to the idea of the masterpiece in painting and sculpture, but most of them are too eccentric to fit within the grand 'white elephant art' famously decried by Manny Farber as gilded and bombastic, increasingly out of place with each subsequent decade of the twentieth century. A more appropriate, if irreverent, animal metaphor might be the 'camel' as described by the designer Alec Issigonis, in *Vogue*, a few years before Farber's essay: 'a horse that was planned by a committee'.[11] To a certain colonialist eye, a camel might indeed recall a kind of mongrel horse, comically misshapen by its impure pedigree and thus a perfect metaphor for a design born of the awkward collaboration of multiple interests.[12] Educational, civic and entrepreneurial organisations overlapped in their ambitions for moving-picture art, providing continual opportunities for these often ill-fated collaborations. The industrial designer and the Hollywood producer may live in fear of such awkward 'camels' as Tree's work with Triangle, but they provide some of the richest material for the media historian. What the aesthetically ambitious moving pictures from this early period may lack in financial (and sometimes even critical) success or stability, they make up for in their promiscuous experimentation and kaleidoscopic possibility.

This book seeks continuities among these efforts, and thus a frame for early American art cinema, by arguing three basic points: that its products should not be tracked as events within single companies or organisations, but as a pattern of collaborations between organisations; that questions of art-film technique in this period were really attempts to search for an artistic medium-reflexivity for cinema and thus should be framed by intellectual history; and, most distinctly, that theories of picture composition and craft underpinned this intellectual history. The early motion picture made contact with the other arts in moments of experimental collaboration among different business and cultural interests. One finds examples in an auditorium when a lantern lecturer painstakingly corrected the jerky movements of the cinematograph, when a mass producer of Arts-and-Crafts-inspired home décor like Louis C. Tiffany recommended paintings to a commercial photographer dabbling in adapting paintings for the screen, and when a film director wrote a preface for a book by a theatre professor defining film art as first and foremost an art of picture composition. The products of these remarkable collaborations – Alexander Black's *Miss Jerry*, Lejaren à Hiller's *The Young Painter* and Rex Ingram's preface to Victor Freeburg's *Pictorial Beauty on the Screen* – questioned and theorised moving-image art. These projects proliferated on the periphery of good film business, in minor configurations and repetitions. A historical approach that seeks out the myriad committees that planned art/cinema collaborations like these can locate, in their cluttered archival detail, the many points of contact among a range of ambitious projects that might otherwise appear isolated. An intellectual-historical approach can identify the traditions that link these projects as they search for common aesthetic terms. Together, the material and intellectual history of these projects can address their persistent reliance on the visual arts. Pictorial definitions of moving-image art thrive from 1890s magic lantern experiments through the first art films and film theories of the 1910s. Uncovering this neglected early history may offer perspective on some of the roads not taken, the aesthetic alternatives and the continuing pleasures and provocations of films that have come to define art cinema.

SITUATING CINEMA AMONG THE OTHER ARTS

The tactic of linking educators, film-makers, critics and arts organisations complements two currently vital developments in film studies. It contributes to an intermedial turn witnessed across film studies, and it adds to the growing body of historical studies of film institutions. The term 'intermedial' has emerged in recent scholarship on film, literature, theatre and cultural history to orient film history towards multi-media questions.[13] The emergence of early cinema studies over the past decades (roughly simultaneous with the emergence of new media) has certainly played its part in catalysing this broader transformation. In shifting focus away from notions of a 'prehistory' of cinema, and in no longer seeing the magic lantern and other devices merely as incomplete manifestations of the moving image, current studies have revealed a media ecology in which fluid conceptions of image and address persist or re-emerge as one early moving-image technology replaces or reimagines another.[14] Indeed, one of the benefits of this shift in perspective is that it emphasises connections among media technologies, not only within a given period but also across periods of media history.[15] In either case, a cross-media approach attends, not simply to the proliferation of media formats, but specifically to the points where one medium recycles, augments, or jumps out of the frame of another. In the study of art cinema, an intermedial approach examines moments when the motion picture borrows from another art medium to claim its own legitimacy, or its own exceptional qualities.

Intermedial approaches focus on the dynamics of encounter among media, and attend to the institutions that stage these encounters. One point that recent film historiography has made clear is that institutions play a role in defining media at least as much as do those media's mechanisms, emulsions and production techniques. Each aspect of the medium cannot exist without the other. Thus, a cross-media emphasis contributes to a revitalised institutional approach that has proven influential within film studies of late. This approach is particularly important for a study of art cinema since it often relies on institutional support beyond the entertainment market. *Making Movies into Art* joins recent institutional histories such as those by Dana Polan (2007) on the history of university film study, Peter Decherney (2005) on *Hollywood and the Culture Elite* and Haidee Wasson (2005) on the Museum of Modern Art.[16] The book excavates intellectual histories of cultural institutions, such as the Brooklyn Institute of Arts and Sciences, the Society of Illustrators and Columbia University, focusing specifically on how these institutions helped generate cinema's cultural value by borrowing from the visual arts. Remember that cinema was not just a new art form, but also a means of visual publicity. Cinema functioned as medium for the negotiation of the public reception of art at a time when there was an increasing sense that American collectors could leverage the nation's prosperity to counteract a perceived exclusion from European aesthetic traditions. Whether through the practice of buying up old masters, or using the Kodak camera to extend painterly traditions, or circulating 1890s European teaching studio traditions on an accelerated scale in American art pedagogy, Americans increasingly defined their relationship to art as one of entitlement. Moving-image technology played a key role in providing access to art. Early art cinema was just as much about seeing moving pictures as a medium for negotiating the public relation to art as it was about defining the medium itself as art in relation to the neighbouring arts. Each intermedial exchange relied on the other.

These films, lantern shows, tableaux and lecture-hall performances – these encounters of an unseen cinema – established the intellectual networks that tested moving-picture aesthetics. The archival research that undergirds the project marks some of the material contours of the various institutions in question, and then folds them into discussions about aesthetics. *Making Movies into Art* places Vachel Lindsay in an art-school classroom in 1905 lecturing about the impression of movement in painting; it places the American Impressionist painter (and Lindsay's art teacher) William Merritt Chase, along with novelist William Dean Howells and New York intellectual Seth Low at 1890s magic lantern lectures by Alexander Black, the 'inventor of the picture play'; it describes the way publicity stills from Paramount turned into lecture slides in a Columbia University classroom. In each case, the institutional connections and the archival record link up with a history of ideas about moving picture aesthetics. This broader history of art cinema encompasses aesthetic theorists of spectatorship and the aesthetics of movement like Paul Souriau and Vernon Lee as well as the figures who explicitly theorised film art like Lindsay, Hugo Münsterberg, Victor Freeburg and Frances Taylor Patterson. Each of these cases uncovers intellectual networks and intersections, not previously known or seen, which aligned the moving picture with the visual arts. What is at issue here are the moments of encounter, when nineteenth-century aesthetic education reached to accommodate moving images, and when early cinema reflexively took part in the American public reception of art.

The pressing issue is not in finding examples of early art cinema, but in framing historiographical questions adequate to this variegated body of work. This book offers one way: by linking moving pictures with the educational traditions of teaching the public how to appreciate fine art as pictorial workmanship. The presence of this undercurrent in so many of the efforts to define moving-picture aesthetics, even those better-known practices that sought to align the cinema with the legitimate stage, is why I began with Herbert Tree. In what one would expect to be a relatively straightforward case for more highbrow drama on screen there is instead a complex rhetoric of the visual arts and education. He lauds cinema as an educational extension, not merely as a classroom visual aid but as having a more lasting aesthetic impact.[17] Most importantly for my argument here, Tree aligns this move from one medium to another, in his case between theatre and cinema with Michelangelo and Benvenuto Cellini. Michelangelo signalled the elevation of public taste, but a different nineteenth-century discourse found inspiration in the intermedial nature of his projects. Michelangelo's expressions in materials like paint or putty signalled the admiration for workmanship of the kind that Ralph Waldo Emerson praised, the artist's 'carrying steadily onward, with the heat and determination of manhood, his poetic conceptions into progressive execution'.[18] Discussed next to Cellini, this link with craft is even clearer, as Cellini's memoir was by far the best-known literary account of artisanship from the mid-nineteenth century through the early decades of the twentieth.[19] John Addington Symonds' introduction to his best-selling translation of the memoir made Cellini's name, for Tree and the rest of the English and American reading public, synonymous with aesthetic craft.[20] Tree's techniques, as with many quality films, may come clearly from the stage, but he makes his case for the translation of these techniques by keying into discourses of education and craft. This promotional rhetoric becomes a relevant part of intellectual history when it reflects persistent strategies that writers used to relate cinema to the other arts. An intellectual-history approach takes these claims seriously – considering, for example, how the publishing history of Cellini's autobiography overlapped with the projects of turn-of-the-century educators. Discourses of the visual arts permeated these projects, and this influence is all the more significant because in many cases, not only Tree's brief stint in Hollywood, the promotional rhetoric circulated more widely than the productions themselves.

CRAFT, PICTURE, MOVEMENT

American crafts traditions, including the Arts and Crafts movement most prominently among them, are not typically understood to have had a major influence on cinema. A direct influence can certainly be found among art directors such as Hugo Ballin, and designers of title cards for silent films, but even there, if we consider only the borrowing of styles, Arts and Crafts remained more or less a minor mode. And yet, so often the aesthetic questions posed by craft practitioners and educators resurface among American film-makers and film critics. Lanternists drew from craft rhetoric to sell the magic lantern as a tool for producing composed transitions and handmade movement over mechanised motion pictures.[21] *The Craftsman* magazine ran articles about the craftsmanship of pictures by photographer/film-maker Edward Curtis. Film advertisers used Arts and Crafts design clichés in the trade press for prestige companies like Universal's Bluebird label, even when the films themselves bore none of the traces of this style. Critical writing on motion pictures mobilised discourse on craft, beginning with early articles in the *Moving Picture World* by Louis Reeves Harrison. This tendency reached a high point in the 1910s and early 20s with book-length manuals with titles like *Screencraft*, *The Technique of the Photoplay* and *Cinema Craftsmanship* by Harrison, Epes Winthrop Sargent and Frances Taylor Patterson.[22] These instances of deploying the idea of craft, often for promotional ends, warrant consideration as a coherent phenomenon. By shifting focus from the borrowing of styles in actual films to intellectual history, the influence of the movement becomes much more significant. This approach is only fair when considering movements, which, in addition to providing a battery of recognisable styles, were often more about posing philosophical questions about the role of aesthetics in democracy and the function of craft labour in modernity. In other words, the influence of craft traditions in film promotion and education advocated less for one narrow set of stylistic traits than as an intellectual frame for mediating a range of stylised films.

There was something particularly useful in the colloquial sense of the word 'craft' for thinking about film as an everyday vernacular medium. But this application was also problematic. Craft redefined labour in response to an industrial age by emphasising the knowledge of processes and technologies specific to a medium. Such a model suited moving pictures' search for a medium identity, but had to contend with the fact that film technology exemplified, to many people, the destruction of that very knowledge. The labour of the moving-image-maker, as work, was a vexed issue in part because of film's connection to the very mechanisation of art that craft movements rejected. Thus the discourse of craft in moving pictures had the paradoxical task of defining aesthetic work within a medium that threatened to take it away. To do this, it turned, not on the question of cinema's radical newness, but instead on cinema's intermedial connections to the work of other artists and artisans. Ideas of craft established one set of coordinates whereby cinematic technologies could fit into longer histories of printing technologies or education in design. Moving pictures could make a claim for a medium identity expressed like other craft media: in terms of effort, executed through mastered processes, over time.

It is no coincidence that much of the early craft discussion of art cinema took place in how-to movie literature. The how-to texts of early art cinema take their cue from a moment when art educators adapted craft's textual traditions to their own pedagogical innovations. As craft historian Glenn Adamson has noted, the modern how-to instructional text emerged in the eighteenth century as the literature particular to craft became a genre devoted as much to philosophical claims about art and craft as to disseminating norms of practice.[23] By the end of the nineteenth century, progressive education in the USA adopted the how-to text and produced a steady stream of art texts and lectures in this mode. But these mitigated how-to texts verged away from the hands-on specificity of a trade manual. Mastery of trade technique was still too practical a principle to have broad pedagogical appeal within the aesthetic tradition of Arts and Crafts. Turn-of-the-century educators needed a broader theory of technique, itself translatable across a variety of media. They found this in the study of composed pictures.

The themes of intermediality and craft in cinema converge in this book in the intellectual history of picture composition. Composition was on many art educators' minds at the turn of the century, and had distinct advantages for cinema. First, anchoring education in the fundamentals of pictorial design facilitated interchange among media, and thus between cinema and the other arts. Pictorial traditions linked otherwise divergent styles of theatre, tableau performance, illustration, painting, photography and the cinema in the nineteenth and early twentieth centuries. Pictures had a common set of formal cues, temporalities and modes of address that were translatable across a variety of media. If storytelling offered one means of exchange between cinema and the other arts, picture composition offered an equally viable alternative. The second, equally beneficial advantage of composition for moving pictures was that it maintained a sense of art as applied skill. Composition, while more abstract than specific techniques, still registered as the execution of skilled labour. The link between picture composition and craft is particularly strong in the theories of 'picture study', one of the main pedagogical traditions that energised American art education at the turn of the century. Picture study integrated ideas of picture and craft as a means to break down some of the aesthetic hierarchies carried over from nineteenth-century schools. Historians of art education like Mary Ann Stankiewicz have provided detailed maps of the picture-study tradition and its influences in North America by the turn of the century.[24] They have shown how American picture-study lectures had, since the 1880s, appropriated John Ruskin's and William Morris's principles of craft labour.[25] Picture study took an intermedial approach to the labour of art. Its how-to methods integrated the appreciation and production components of an art education not confined to a single medium.

The most influential of these picture-study educators, Arthur Wesley Dow, developed a method that shaped even the first courses in motion-picture study (Chapter 3) in the 1910s. Dow's composition-based pedagogy revamped the more compartmentalised approaches to teaching art that predominated in his day. Drawing from his colleagues in art education, Ernest Fenollosa and Denman Ross, Dow defined composition as a content-free and non-medium-specific paradigm that reconciled divergences among artistic practices. He taught that the same basic principles of line, shading and colour could apply to work from any nation and in any pictorial medium. Dow and his colleagues addressed what they saw as tired divisions and imbalances between the representational arts and the decorative arts. Instead of inculcating the value of a hallowed work, picture study sought out the abstracted principles of composition inherent in any (possibly quotidian) object or scene. The adaptability of this composition-focused approach was, indeed, its greatest strength. Educators and students could now freely adapt their basic methods of analysis to discuss media and works as far-reaching as Persian rugs, Arts and Crafts furniture and even modernist paintings, so long as they taught aesthetics as a basic arrangement of line, shading and colour. The method gained momentum between Dow's 1899 first edition of his *Composition* textbook and the 1910s.[26] Influence in the USA ranged from higher and secondary education training programmes like Columbia University's Teachers College, to public extension-course lectures. Pictorial composition offered a model by which educational institutions could effectively cooperate, by which lantern slide collections could be put to work predictably and by which (even its more conservative proponents had to admit) art education remained open to new media technologies. In other words, composed pictures facilitated an abundant culture of exchange between mediums, and theories of picture composition allowed a common language for discussing multi-media art.

Picture study and theories of composition streamlined art education, but, for motion pictures, the cross-media reach of these theories also anchored the new medium in the field of art history. Media historians have often described the advent of motion pictures as a moment in which traditions of representation were radically cast aside, but upon closer inspection it is often hard to disentangle aesthetic rupture from aesthetic continuity. Centuries-long pictorial traditions energised motion pictures. Nineteenth-century notions of craft, pictorial contemplation, empathy and the picturesque intertwined in the dynamic energy of the medium.[27]

Nowhere is this intertwining more evident than in the question of *movement* in discussions of early art cinema. That the moving image could be discussed in terms of tradition and craft at all is a testament to the adaptability of conceptions of picture composition. Movement, beginning at least with modernist writing on the cinema, often marked the radical rupture of filmic representation. Movement also was perceived to be more automated, thus further outside of artists' control, than even the mechanically reproduced still image of which so much was made in debates about early photography. But movement's mechanism and dynamism notwithstanding, critics and film-makers repeatedly related it to composition. If the dance of reds and greens in early hand-coloured moving pictures inspired awe, the magic of the new mechanical medium was not the only reason. The careful attention to colouring could compel viewers, not only with the novelty of moving colour, but also because the colourist's work evoked the labours of the master printer, carefully constructing an animated image through the application of exacting skill and patience with the medium.[28] The first twenty-five years of American cinema history are filled with writing by people who saw movement as something that could be crafted and composed as a picture, from the often downplayed aesthetic (even decorative) content of Eadweard Muybridge's illustrated motion-study lectures to the early 1920s musings on the aesthetics of movement in *Life* magazine by film critic Robert Emmet Sherwood. The relationships between the still and moving image proved a productive site of enquiry and experimentation – one that welcomed pictorial traditions and their definitions of beauty, but which at the same time remained aware of the ways that these traditions began to mean something different once they were adapted to accommodate cinema.

Writers and image-makers addressed the question of composition, and the relation between still and moving pictures, with similar analogies. By far the most common among these was the term 'tableau', which reappears in each chapter of this book in different historical and metaphorical iterations. The tableau's modern definition as 'a pictorial grouping' developed in eighteenth-century France and England. By the end of the eighteenth century and throughout the nineteenth, it became associated with a family of performance traditions that employ a pictorial approach to staging. As I discuss the distinct performance traditions that make use of staged pictures throughout this book, I refer to them by their distinct names. However, I also use terms like 'tableau culture' to reinforce the notion that these divergent practices have intermedial concerns in common.[29] If critics in the 1890s often did not make the distinction between the end-of-scene tableau and the tableau vivant, then we must explore the common aesthetic concerns that caused these critics to collapse distinctions between these divergent practices. The relation between movement and the static picture stands out among these common aesthetic concerns, enabling early amateur theorists of moving images to understand them as inciting contemplation in the manner of composed pictures. Drawing from tableau culture's preoccupation with the aesthetics of movement and stasis, moving-image-makers and critics found ready-made solutions to the new aesthetic conundrums brought about by instantaneous photography and the photography of motion. The linked cases in each chapter offer glimpses into this process of appropriation, oscillating between pictorial aesthetic traditions and moving-image technology.

In each case the tableau, conceived less as a technique than as a trope in intellectual history, defined a possible early art cinema by linking the moving image with picture craft. The tableau analogy linked performance and the study of pictures – composed pictures, offered for contemplation. It helped critics like Victor Freeburg imagine composition in moving forms as related to composition in static forms. Alexander Black referenced the tableau when he described his decade-long project to create an alternative motion picture, one in which he crafted the 'movement' frame-by-frame. The tableau made paintings come to life in early films about the artist's studio, and the tableau analogy made early film critics see paintings in the scenes of their favourite directors. The tableau technique may have been a holdover from theatrical performance before cinema, but, in many cases, tableau-heavy film performances (like Herbert Beerbohm Tree's) did not simply remind critics of the more legitimate medium. They fed into more dynamic how-to definitions of moving-picture art through which many began to understand moving pictures in terms of workmanship.

AESTHETIC APPRECIATION AND THE MODERNITY OF PICTURE CRAFT

The modernity of picture craft is not readily apparent to say the least; at first glance these artsy productions seem more aligned with the old guard than the avant-garde. But present in each of the chapters of this book are examples of why it is inappropriate to characterise these productions as simply Victorian nostalgia. If the confrontation between moving-image technology and pictorial traditions forms one of the broadest arcs of the book, the debates about how to compose movement vividly stage the problem of the modernity of early art cinema. In the aesthetic problem of pictured movement, traditions of aesthetic thought traceable back to Diderot and Lessing come into direct contact with discussions about instantaneous photography's and film's tendency to fragment time and record ephemeral moments. In the films, magic lantern shows and tableau performances in each of my chapters, this interest in fragmentation paradoxically merges with aesthetic traditions that would appear to oppose it. I do not argue against the modernity of these developments so much as take caution about connecting these traditions in purely formalist terms.

The style of these productions is only central to this project insofar as it points outward to two significant forces of change in the American consumption of art images in this period. The first is the professional streamlining that corporatised artistic production and linked the applied arts with the fine arts, and the second is modern expansion of art education in the effort to make aesthetic appreciation a pillar of the formation of the democratic citizenry. These transformations in American aesthetic culture were not simply simultaneous. They complemented each other, even as they moved in the seemingly contradictory directions of professional specialisation and general education. One of the ways we can see how these two forces interrelate is to trace in them the odd trajectory of notions of craft labour.

Craft movements in the USA had a precocious ability to reconnect with the commercial efficiency they originally sought to reject. North America certainly had its share of enduring anti-modern applied-arts communities influenced by the British Arts and Crafts movement, notably on the West Coast where assorted factors, including perhaps, geography, encouraged them to pursue more eccentric, anarchist, socialist, or occult inflections of the movement. But these outliers and fundamentalists proved far less influential in advocating craft than those who abstracted craft rhetoric for the managerial class and for genteel publications. The Stickley and Tiffany companies, for example, brought design within reach, if at the cost of harshly reinterpreting the labour politics that originally inspired the movement.[30] These companies used the rapidly expanding market for magazines to promote their abstracted version of craft. From general magazines like *Cosmopolitan* and *Ladies' Home Journal* to the more specialised pages of *Applied Arts Book, Arts and Decoration* and Stickley's *The Craftsman*, the salaried worker engaged with questions of aesthetics and craft through domestic consumption. By locating aesthetics in the private home, these magazines integrated fine and applied arts. *Arts and Decoration*'s editorial choices are particularly revealing in this regard as they put equal emphasis on gossip from the salons and the art schools, and advice on interior decoration. The magazine's pages swelled in the first decade of the twentieth century with advertisements by companies selling craft furniture or reproductions of famous artworks, and by companies selling (with splashy full-page ads) the locks and vaults needed to secure this newly acquired private property.

The market demands put on artists by these changes led to significant efforts to professionalise within each medium or genre of work. New organisations rapidly appeared, from the National Sculpture Society, begun in the 1890s by Charles C. French and Robert Aitken, to the National Society of Illustrators, founded in 1901 by professional illustrators including Charles Dana Gibson and N. C. Wyeth. These trade organisations, in addition to their immediately practical functions of creating networks and organising exhibitions, involved themselves deeply with efforts to promote their mediums. In this way they aligned with the arts magazines, which devoted significant advertising space to the various art schools and summer art programmes around the country. The societies sought to increase their educational as well as their commercial presence. Education provided some of the best publicity, and most members of these organisations taught at art schools like the New York School of Art and the Art Student's League, even when they did not need to do so for financial reasons. The public relations campaigns for their mediums made these growing arts societies amenable to collaborations with other institutions, including the cinema.

This idea of a modernised approach to aesthetic work that unified the fine and applied arts took hold just as rapidly through the new approach to pedagogy. Picture study may have emphasised restraint and contemplation, but in the schools it was a decidedly modern phenomenon. If educators in this tradition taught old masters and ancient sculpture, it was not to encourage rote, reverential copying or really even to instill a sense of their historical traditions. Useful or fine, ancient or modern, the composition of these objects found a new purchase in an integrated general-education theory of pictorial design. This process of integration welcomed the newly specialised artists working in different mediums into a progressive curriculum of art appreciation. General education and professional specialisation could complement one another.

To enhance the efforts of schools and reach some of the magazine readership another way, educational publishing programmes by companies such as Prang in Boston published a range of texts – each teaching appreciation for a slightly different audience.[31] University and museum lecturers like John Van Dyke and John LaFarge compiled their lectures as textbooks, which extended the reach of these lectures enough to earn a reputation for Van Dyke and LaFarge as two of the primary authors of art-education textbooks of the period.[32] A third was Mabel Emery, who saw it as her mission to bring picture study into primary and secondary education. In her *How to Enjoy Pictures*, which organised paintings by subject, as did many educational lantern slide companies, she suggests ways to integrate picture study principles, not only into the art curriculum, but also with the study of subjects like reading, writing and geography.[33] Emery's book with Prang marks an early stage in the arguments that the visual education movement would develop more than a decade later.

For these art editors, educators and textbook authors, appreciating pictures was a new kind of work taught in the same how-to spirit of earlier craft texts. But while art educators depended on craft principles, the way their lectures transformed these traditions speaks directly to interests central to cinema and media studies. Picture-study educators did not necessarily hold up craft as a means of resistance to the changes taking place in the world of art and design. Through a subtle sleight of hand, picture study actually revitalised craft ideals by transforming them into a modernised programme of art appreciation. It appears that, in some cases, the didactic composition redirected some of those earlier craft-based notions of work so prevalent in the preceding decades.[34] While art educators' craft rhetoric often resembled that of traditionalist reformers, ultimately they reversed the anti-modern goals of earlier proponents of American craft by redefining how and why students should contemplate the basic pictorial components of line and shape. There is a real irony to this move because they indirectly diminished craft labour in the design industries that their courses inevitably supported. But rather than abandon thoughtful, individual work, they migrated the craft ideal to the domain of contemplation. In other words, as craft labour receded in aesthetic production, it re-emerged as an abstracted ideal in the theories of composition and appreciation. When proponents of early art cinema appropriated craft traditions, they preferred them in this abstracted form.

A contributor to a 1910 issue of the *School Arts* book, an influential Arts and Crafts periodical first published in 1901 as the *Applied Arts Book*, illustrates how this modern transformation of craft labour could work in an everyday classroom.

Appreciation
A dextrous line, the work is done.
That work a million eyes hath won!
But few see the weary years
Of struggle 'mid a mist of tears.
That lay enshrouded in that line.
And fewer trace
Through realms of space,
The yearning of the spirit fine
That grasped the potencies of line.[35]

This piece of amateur verse recycles language found in abundance in art-education periodicals and textbooks. It would be easy to imagine it written on a classroom wall.

The poem breaks down an artwork, a composition, into one of its fundamental components. Romantic sentiments notwithstanding, the poem describes a line as an expression of work. But the real work moves to the domain of appreciation and the cultivation of aesthetic desire that Dow institutionalised at places like Pratt and the Teachers College at Columbia. This stanza and many others like it functioned as motivational aides for classroom exercises. Looking at these projected pictures was work, but not necessarily work as a form of self-denial promoted by the anti-modern critics who saw the lyceum lecture and moving images as another component of the chromo civilisation. It was abstracted work. Picture study, from its initial theorisation to its broad circulation in schools and educational arts magazines, retooled art education by casting composition, and therefore its appreciation, as a kind of modernised craft labour. The educational lantern and motion pictures complemented these efforts.

Understanding the effects of appreciation-based education in this way explains the wildly eclectic assortment of moving-picture styles brought under the domain of pictorial appreciation. Even in cases where the stylistic appearance of a film or lantern lecture might seem Victorian, classicist, or otherwise anti-modern, it could still be very deeply implicated in modernising institutional shifts. A better understanding of the link between this pictorial tradition and its modern effects within institutions of art education opens historical film studies up to re-examine the familiar narratives of genteel culture and of cultural uplift in the silent period. The movements to promote the middle-class ideals of cultural uplift were not homogeneous in the early twentieth century, and the scholarship on moral and social reform has, so far, eclipsed the importance of aesthetics within these movements. By increasing attention to the aesthetic dimension, ongoing film scholarship can counteract the potentially flattening characterisation of moralising uplift discourse in American silent film. Ideas of pictorial form proved adaptable enough to allow the didactic composition, a composition that teaches by pleasing the eye, to channel some of the morally didactic reformist energies in other directions. If the Arnoldian tradition of uplift offers one set of coordinates, the modernity of educating students to appreciate aesthetic form offers another, potentially contrasting, set. The didactic composition of picture study offers a richer field of investigation than some of the more straightforward moral reform efforts because of its aesthetic ambivalence.

It should come as no surprise that traditions of picture craft have been underexplored in early cinema and, indeed, seem counterintuitive to studies of cinema and modernity. Pictorialism and craft typically stand in paradigmatic opposition to moving pictures in the major theoretical paradigms that have shaped our current understanding of this period. For Gilles Deleuze, the modernity of the movement-image, the first truly cinematic ordering of the image, depends on a casting off of the tableau-style pictorial culture that he calls 'the order of the pose'.[36] When the Frankfurt School discussed cinema and craft together, craft usually occupied the negative opposing position. Siegfried Kracauer dismissed the 'artsy-craftsy' (by feminising it), and Walter Benjamin worried about its persistence as a refusal of the new sensorium.[37] Even Theodor Adorno, with all of his suspicion of the culture industry, still placed cinema above craft when he warned against craft's aestheticism.[38] If studies of early cinema and modernity have (thankfully) inherited these writers' interest in aesthetics as a way to theorise modern experience, they have also inevitably inherited some of their biases. Early moving pictures that do not share formal traits with modernist works of art have not benefited from the rich aesthetic-theoretical analyses of this tradition as have such rapidly edited films about technology as *Traffic in Souls* (1913). Garrett Stewart's discussion of 'modernism's photosynthesis' leaps from the Lumière brothers' 1890s play with fragmented still and moving images to the late 1920s fragmented cuts and stills of the historical avant-garde.[39] This book looks at the material left out of that historical jump. It does not dispute the theoretical traditions that have linked modernity and early cinema (it is, in fact, informed closely by those traditions). I simply intend to open up lines of enquiry into material typically seen as separate from the movement-image or the modern sensorium. At the same time that moving pictures and the work of the professional organisations like the Society of Illustrators 'tore down the stage on which contemplation moved', they collaborated with the institutions that reformed aesthetic education through a paradoxical overlap between contemplation and modernised pedagogy.[40] Tracing the radical rejection of ornamented nineteenth-century visual culture – in new works loaded with fragmentary, grotesque, or rapid serial images – forms one established historical trajectory. Another, explored in this book, is the odd modernity of picture craft: not the celebration of mechanisation, perhaps accompanied by a manifesto-driven rejection of nineteenth-century aesthetics, but something more like a modern management of the pictorial.

CHAPTER ORGANISATION

The chapter structure of *Making Movies into Art* reflects the temporal displacement that characterises so much of this material. The book begins with 1890s lantern shows and ends with early 1920s feature films, avoiding a strict chronological succession. Each chapter draws at least some of its examples from roughly the entire period of the book, even as the earlier chapters phase more towards the 1890s and the latter chapters phase towards the early 1920s. This mobility in each chapter across period boundaries – admittedly across the sea changes that occurred between early cinema and the silent feature film – may seem unusual, but the movement across these very boundaries captivated each of the figures discussed in this book. An intermedial vision of early art cinema does not just open up synchronous connections from cinema to other media. It also opens time frames, always looking forward and backward. Looking at other media means constructing future possibilities and revisiting traditions overshadowed by recent developments. Alexander Black looks forward, creating an imaginary future for the Kinetoscope in 1894, and Adolph Zukor looks back to Black's picture play as a rediscovered past for his 1919 productions. Educators look forward to the use of films in art education and producers look back to the nineteenth-century rediscovery of Rembrandt in the light of new print media. Lejaren à Hiller's early 1920s films about the painter's studio recycle 1890s bohemian student life, and 1910s film professor Victor Freeburg retools nineteenth-century empathy aesthetics with an eye towards the future of motion pictures. Finally, in the case of directors like Rex Ingram and Maurice Tourneur, the idea of the director of a new kind of art film in the

1910s looked back to the discourse about the artists in 1890s traditions like French Symbolism or British Arts and Crafts.

Making Movies into Art begins with those who first educated the public about an art of moving pictures at the end of the nineteenth century. I focus on Alexander Black in the first chapter because his projects as a lecturer, film-maker, journalist, lanternist and head of photography at the Brooklyn Institute of Arts and Sciences converge on the problems of pictorial beauty and aesthetic movement in film. I use the photographs of Black's nonfiction art lectures and 'detective lectures', from which his later fictions originated, to show how Black answered an aesthetic need and brought instantaneous photography into collaboration with the contemplative, posed picture. From these lectures Black designed a system for representing movement with the magic lantern, which he billed as an aesthetically superior class of moving picture. He shot stills of his actors moving through a *mise en scène* that remained completely fixed in relation to the camera. During the shows he performed live narration while the images unfolded through a series of dissolves, creating a sense of the actors moving through space. He called this system the 'picture play' a generation before that term would become synonymous with the feature film. Through archival reconstruction of performances believed to be lost, I show how an educational craft impulse underlies Black's attempt to create an artistically distinct answer to the cinematograph. His early moving-picture techniques derived not from the fairground, but from the art lecture and the aesthetic debates around Muybridge's motion studies. I demonstrate this in his systematic control of composition, décor, the staging of actors, the timing of dissolves and the planning of sequences frame-by-frame. These techniques erased the jerky mechanical motion of the cinematograph and fashioned a unique aesthetic of movement from varied collaborating media and pictorial traditions. Through these performances, and his articles on how to craft handmade moving pictures at home, Black presented a possible future for cinema at a time when people needed to make sense out of the rapid transformation of pictorial traditions by new technologies. Black's do-it-yourself cinema brought moving images prominently into the educational space of the lyceum, and later inspired the amateur film movement. Around the same time he was rediscovered as a founding figure for groups like the Amateur Cinema League. Producers like Adolph Zukor and early film historians like Terry Ramsaye used Black's 'art of the tableau vivant plus the science of photography' to retroactively imagine the origins of an artistically distinct film as a stable form.

Black's work and its reception mark one way in which early cinema entered the space of art education. Another way to view these art/cinema intersections is to trace how the space of artistic production enters early films. Chapter 2 isolates one tradition by which art students and the reading public learned to appreciate art and follows its intersections with the early motion picture. It argues that, in the sphere of art education and in the scenes popularised in the illustrated press by Georges DuMaurier and Charles Dana Gibson, the *workspace* of the artist helped the public appreciate how art, as work, takes place. This occurred, first, through a material interest in the studio's tools and processes and, second, through a fascination with the quasi-magical transformations in the studio between living form and picture. Cinema satisfied both of these interests by recycling studio scenes and character types popularised in the illustrated press and by creating a range of techniques in which the moving image jumps out of the frame of the composed picture. These tableau-based tricks may have contributed to a cinema of distraction and shock, but I argue that they also reflected on the process of absorption in pictures. Films about paintings come-to-life and mesmerist artists illustrated precisely those quasi-magical transformations between static pictures movement that students, eager to become absorbed in works of art, were asked by their teachers to imagine. This coincidence was not lost on many moving-image educators.

These themes converge in the chapter's discussion of Lejaren à Hiller as an art film-maker working on the periphery of the film industry. A commercial photographer for illustrated magazines by trade, Hiller came to films as a visual artist who desired to educate the public about the studio space. In his series of educational films (1919–23), supported in part by Louis C. Tiffany and the president of the Metropolitan Museum of Art, Hiller recycled artist-mesmerist types and reconstructed the historically famous studios of Rembrandt and Burne-Jones to tell a series of stories that interlaced the work in these studios with the work being done in contemporary commercial studios of New York. Hiller brought art to the masses by bringing the masses into artists' workspaces of the past, and by looking back to styles of the past. He adorned these spaces in a polished pictorialist photographers' style, and he dramatised them by recycling the frame-jumping tableaux vivants of early films set in the artist's studio.

Chapter 3 follows the migration of picture study from art schools and lecture halls to the 'Photoplay Composition' courses initiated at Columbia University by Victor Freeburg, the first film courses offered by a university in the USA. Picture study sees its most direct intellectual influence on film education in these courses; film educators and critics used this tradition as a template to study techniques like lighting, set design and staging. Drawing inspiration from the aesthetic philosophy of John Dewey, media educators advocated picture study's content-free and non-medium-specific paradigm for distinguishing certain films from the majority of productions and for discussing these films' role in American democracy. This compositional approach to film education uses Arthur Dow's adaptation of Dewey's claim that the experience of composed, beautiful form begets a desire for more, and this desire can produce proper democratic subjects more productively than more direct forms of moral uplift. The idea of composition proved adaptable, in Freeburg's work, to moving pictures and their spectators. He used these educators' formal approach, their democratic ambitions and many of their fine-arts examples to theorise film art. In addition to presenting the intellectual origins of Freeburg's writings on motion-picture composition and his resultant theory of modern art-cinema spectatorship, this chapter traces the material origins of the prints and publicity stills he used to make his aesthetic points. The film stills reproduced in his book range from Famous Players-Lasky productions like *Carmen* and *The Covered Wagon* to imports from Europe. Their circulation in Freeburg's work offers a glimpse into how an emergent tradition in art pedagogy could help to steer the afterlife of studio productions towards enduring aesthetic distinction.

Critics and educators sought a wide range of examples to discuss film art as a kind of picture craft analogous to the work conducted in the artist's studio, and two directors of the 1910s and early 20s proved perfectly suited to the project. Maurice Tourneur and Rex Ingram were not the only directors who composed beautiful pictures on screen, but they stood out in critical and commercial publicity as visual artists working in the medium of film. Chapters 4 and 5 show how they both shaped an image of the director around the image of the fine artist in the studio. Each began his career during this time as an apprentice to a well-known artist and entered the film industry through a fine-arts division of a major production company. Tourneur worked in Paris with August Rodin and Pierre Puvis de Chavannes, and Ingram studied with Art Deco sculptor Lee Lawrie at Yale University. Since each director first achieved fame as a director for a 'quality film' division of a major studio, the artist reputation stuck. No interview with Tourneur was complete without discussing his work with Puvis on the murals for the Boston Public Library. Ingram wrote about Lawrie's work as an inspiration for film art, and he commissioned Lawrie to create a special promotional sculpture for the premiere of *The Four Horsemen of the Apocalypse* (1921). These chapters read Tourneur's and Ingram's films in conjunction with the archival records of their mentorship with visual artists. But instead of arguing that Tourneur's and Ingram's films borrow techniques from their fine-arts mentors, I show how these public relationships created a critical niche for their films' experimentation. Their public personae allowed for a variety of pictorially stylised *mise en scène* techniques to be grouped together as an instance of picture craft in film directing. Not only were these techniques derived from varied sources, also they were often the work of the directors' co-workers. I discuss how Ben Carré's fantastic set designs for Tourneur and John F. Seitz's cinematography for Ingram contributed greatly to the directors' public reputations as visual artists of the screen.

The cross-media conception of feature film art had begun by the 1920s to connect very different kinds of institutions. Organisations like the National Board of Review launched campaigns to combat straight censorship in favour of a democracy-building based on aesthetic education. At the same time, film companies moved from local 'stunt' promotion to more integrated networks of publicity, and book publishers like Grossett and Dunlap promoted photo-illustrated novel tie-ins. The last chapters show how, when these diverse cross-media interests came together, they often did so around a notion of pictorial composition that explicitly mobilised discourses of turn-of-the-century aesthetic and craft traditions. The performance of the 1890s studio discussed in Chapter 2 and the pictorialist rhetoric discussed in Chapter 3 come together in the careers of these two directors, who sought to make ambitious films in early Hollywood.

Moving-picture Art before Cinema:
Alexander Black and the Lyceum

On 9 October 1894, at the Carbon Studio on 16th Street in Manhattan, the writer, photographer and lanternist Alexander Black premiered *Miss Jerry*, his first 'picture play'. The much anticipated event attracted a crowd of noted intellectuals and artists, including novelist William Dean Howells, art educator William Merritt Chase, theatre critic Brander Matthews and Brooklyn mayor Seth Low. They gathered to discuss what was essentially a feature-length moving slide show that walked in close step with the emerging cinema. This new picture play consisted of a series of still images of actors posed, photographed and projected on a screen. Black read an accompanying narrative and dissolved from one slide to the next at regular intervals in order to suggest movement. The event was meant to provoke as much as entertain. Looking forward, it raised questions about a possible artistic future for motion pictures at a time when the American public was witnessing only the first glimpses of photographed movement on rotating disks and in peephole devices. Black sought input from his circle of writers and visual artists on how best to present this provocation on the public lecture circuit. On their advice, he fine-tuned the picture play format to a programme of around 250 slides, lasting about an hour and a half. He would spend the next decade performing his picture plays at community centres, schools and museums across the eastern USA. Although largely overlooked today, these performances were continually mentioned throughout the silent era when writers posed the question, 'Who invented the cinema?'. For some critics, who had cinema of a certain artistic ambition in mind, the answer was Alexander Black.

Black toured with the picture plays extensively until 1904. Despite his large audience at the time, however, his picture plays did not develop into mainstream motion picture practice.[1] It was not until the age of the silent feature film in the following generation that he was even recognised as a kind of inventor of cinema, but not one that fitted neatly into any narrative of film's progress. Terry Ramsaye's chapter on Black in *A Million and One Nights* illustrates this. Ramsaye's pioneering 1926 motion-picture history contributed to Black's rediscovery and is still one of the most enduring accounts of Black's work. The picture play puzzled Ramsaye just as it had puzzled Black's original audiences in the 1890s. Looking back, he was struck by the odd likeness between the respected feature films of his day and Black's picture plays. Already, in the early years of the cinema of attractions, Black's picture plays told multi-act stories, and they lasted about as long as a feature film. More importantly, their unusual suggestion of movement hinted, for Ramsaye, at the suggestive subtlety he believed to underpin all art. The problem was that Black had stopped touring several years before the production of the silent feature films with which Ramsaye allied his work. It troubled Ramsaye that the picture play format did not fit neatly into a narrative of the progress of cinema. To him, the discovery of the picture play was like a paleontological botanist discovering a fossil apple in a stratum where there were believed to be no apple trees.[2] Black's work, an evolutionary anomaly, confounded Ramsaye's evolutionary model of film's progress.

While Ramsaye's evolutionary model may have long been replaced by more nuanced periodisations, what troubled Ramsaye, Black's precocious cross-media moving images, are now more relevant than ever. Instead of struggling to find a definitive invention in Black's work, I examine it as a vantage point from which to begin a history of artistically ambitious motion pictures parallel with the advent of cinema itself. Black's work fits perfectly with the ongoing moves to open cinema history to other media. It reveals how media practices converged in this period and how these moments of convergence were shaped by discursive factors as much as by technical innovations. Furthermore, for current cinema historians concerned with the intellectual and social history of those who prophesied art cinema by forging early aesthetic theories of film, the connections between critics like Ramsaye and early experimenters like Black reveal underexamined intellectual networks. Ramsaye's book is a historical artefact in its own right. He consolidated a history of the art of the silent feature film at the height of its prominence, bringing together technical and aesthetic developments under a broad arc. Black contributed to this larger intellectual tradition throughout his career. His work formed part of an entire spectrum of multi-media performances to which Ramsaye and numerous other critics compared it.[3] The picture plays were uniquely relevant for these critics because they resolved some of their recurring aesthetic questions about the recorded moving image. Even though actual motion pictures were a rare part of his repertoire, and he retired long before anyone in the film industry was interested in selling a kind of art cinema, Black nonetheless brought together a recipe of aesthetic theories of movement, pictorial appropriation and arts-institutional support that very much appealed to 1920s film industry critics like Ramsaye and producers like Adolph Zukor searching back for an early template for a cinema of distinction. This recipe will become familiar in each of the chapters of this book.

More than anything else, the picture plays' suggestion of *movement* underwrote their notoriety, for critics in the 1890s and for those a generation later. Why movement? Still photography had famously sparked anxiety in the art-loving public by removing the artist's pencil from the picture. Motion photography, another order of complexity, fanned these flames. I contend throughout this chapter that the composed movement of the picture plays addressed issues at the heart of the emerging debates about the possibility of motion-picture art. By crafting a particular type of movement in his performances, Black staged a kind of cross-media confrontation between two opposing traditions. His work navigates between nineteenth-century pictorialist traditions such as the tableau vivant, pictorial staging in theatre and illustration, on the one hand, and the new media of instantaneous photography and cinema, on the other. Pictorialist traditions generally emphasise privileged moments, repose, restraint, purposiveness, whereas cinema and instantaneous photography are frequently said to have introduced the contingency of fragmented or discontinuous instants into the visual culture. Conceiving of these two analytic categories as aesthetically distinct has proven to be foundational for recent media theorists, from Friedrich Kittler to Gilles Deleuze, who have revisited these enduring questions.[4] This does not mean, however, that multi-media historiography cannot enrich these categories by showing how they often productively overlapped. Upon close examination, it becomes hard to deny the ways that media producers exploited new creative possibilities in the period by selectively merging traditions associated with both of these aesthetic categories in their productions. In what follows I examine Black's institutional affiliations and his writings in tandem with his moving-image techniques in order to show the overlap of the composed tableau and the fragment of the film frame. His lantern lectures and his picture plays make ideal studies because they bring together instantaneous photography, pictorial culture and cinema in thematic as well as practical ways. In other words, Black engaged the widespread philosophical debates among American educators about moving-image art, and at the same time he crafted his own type of moving-picture show that illustrated and resolved these very debates.

THE AMATEUR AND THE INSTITUTE

The photographic turn in Black's writings and performances began in 1889 when he was elected president of the new department of photography at the Brooklyn Institute of Arts and Sciences.[5] One of the most prominent American lyceum venues, the Brooklyn Institute provided an institutional grounding for the intellectual history about moving pictures' relationship to art. The lyceum had served multiple constituencies throughout its long history. It was initially founded as a venue for the education of the working class, moving through several permutations until its energies filtered into the Chautauqua movement and other urban educational institutions.[6] By the 1880s, venues like the Brooklyn Institute had become major centres where aesthetic questions were addressed as part of a broader culture of education as participatory democracy. Many lyceum members had very practical motivations for attending the lectures. Membership documents from the Brooklyn Institute in the 1890s reveal a full third of their membership to consist of private and public school teachers.[7] The Brooklyn Institute also housed the meetings of other educational organisations such as the Association of Art Teachers. This professional participation in the institute suggests that these lectures satisfied a practical demand for teacher training in new developments in art pedagogy (beyond their often discussed value as morally suitable entertainment). As the teachers disseminated ideas discussed in the venue, so did educational outreach programmes like correspondence courses, which reached 180,000 subscribers by 1891.[8]

The lyceum has received less attention than it deserves given its central role as a venue for encountering moving-image technologies. Discussions of this period often bracket the significance of the lyceum with the epithet 'genteel'. To use the term in a value-neutral way, as I do here, is not necessarily to disagree with the current critiques of arts institutions as effective instruments of social hierarchy.[9] But to use the term pejoratively, as a matter of habit, can only limit the historical investigation of institutions like the Brooklyn Institute. It runs the risk of obscuring the flexible and varied member participation on which these institutes depended. There was hardly an American intellectual (or a European intellectual known in the USA) who didn't spend some time lecturing on the lyceum circuit. While a great deal of genteel rhetoric did thrive in the lyceum, it is important to understand this historically as a point of debate within lyceum culture rather than as a blanket descriptor of the kinds of discussion to be found inside. Even George Santayana, who coined the pejorative phrase 'genteel tradition', found a receptive audience for these ideas in the same lyceum that also welcomed members of the older literary generation he held in contempt.[10] It would be difficult to find some significant aspect of American public culture that was not debated, demonstrated, or contemplated in some way by lyceum participants.

As institutions of uplift go, the lyceum was remarkably open to film and instantaneous photography. When he founded the department of photography at the Brooklyn Institute in 1889, Black opened it up even more to practical demonstrations and to lectures by people such as Eadweard Muybridge on animal locomotion, Jacob Riis on the urban poor and Burton Holmes on exotic travel. Thomas Edison gave his first public demonstration of the Kinetoscope at the Brooklyn Institute, and emissaries of the Lumière company gave technical demonstrations there beginning a few years later.[11] These demonstrations using new media technologies were presented side by side with lectures on aesthetics. One evening the members could see Jules Brulatour demonstrating the new Lumière autochrome process and the next evening they could hear the avid lecturer on pictorial aesthetics, Henry Rankin Poore, give a talk on 'artistic [Pictorialist] photography'.[12] In the lecture halls at the Brooklyn Institute amateur photographers, motion picture lecturers and art educators engaged in frequent conversations, many of which grew into publications by institute members and organisers like Black.[13] Through his work at the institute, Black became a respected writer on amateur photography as well as a technician with an exacting knowledge of optical and photochemical details. He was among the educators who advocated the idea that teaching pictorial aesthetics furthered the lyceum's goals of creating a participatory democratic culture, and he worked to bring new imaging technologies into these public debates about art and education.[14]

In the 1890s Black wrote and lectured on art and presented much of his early photography work in the company of painters like William Merritt Chase, but his approach to photography did not completely follow the fine-arts uses of the medium that were emerging in Europe.[15] He kept at a distance from the Pictorialist photography promoted by British associations like the Brotherhood of the Linked Ring even as he claimed, like many early amateur photographers, that the aesthetic advancement of photography depended on the amateur. He was only tangentially associated with members of the Pictorialist movement in the USA through his organisational work at the Brooklyn Institute and his articles. Pictorialists found the sharp lines and machine-made quality of straight photographs made in professional studios to lack artistry. They countered the harsh objectivity of these photographs with a battery of softened shooting and printing techniques in an attempt to make photography more like painting. Black was clearly interested in Pictorialist art

Making Movies into Art

photography, but in a pragmatic way – as one aesthetic possibility among many.[16] He admired that Pictorialist photographers readily experimented with a variety of printing processes, yielding a range of textures and colours, but he never completely embraced the soft, painterly approach to composition as a guiding principle. Instead, he located his primary interest in the range and variety of techniques for creating line, shading and colour available for amateur experimentation.[17] His lectures sidestepped any single aesthetic vision in favour of maximum technical variety, including landscape photography, instantaneous action photography, motion pictures and three-colour projection.[18] Black saw aesthetics as his mission, but rather than promote a single aesthetic movement, he explored the variety of aesthetic possibilities for photography.

While appealing to traditions of nineteenth-century painting, Black evoked more fundamentally the fascination with optical and chemical tinkering that was a unique part of amateur photographic aesthetics. His essays celebrating amateur photography included detailed technical instructions for optical and chemical processes as well as philosophical and aesthetic discussions of photography's significance in modern culture. In 1894, he developed these shorter articles into *Photography Indoors and Out*, a book-length manual. More than purely instrumental knowledge, optical and photochemical know-how are framed in this book as indispensable components of a broader aesthetic education. Black's photo-illustrated novel, *Captain Kodak*, about two boys who form an amateur camera club, clearly conveys the value of technical fascination. Each episode in the novel focuses on a possible use for the camera. The episodes are often set in the darkroom amid thick technical description. Characters (Black's children posed as the main characters for the photo-illustrations) learn from technical mistakes and experience 'positive accidents' in their photography.[19] They introduce a novel that promotes camera-club culture by describing the pleasures of manipulating cameras and chemicals. Amateurism may be, for some of Black's readers, a genteel reaction to commercial photography, but it is important to note how his focus on (amorous) technical experimentation complicates genteel culture's promotion of the amateur as lover/artist. The love of trying out new technical processes and the love of a kind of romantic artistic expression do not completely overlap.[20]

Black spent the better part of his life promoting the possibilities of photography, film, the magic lantern and popular illustration to a public interested in the broad curiosity generated by these media. The organisations to which Black presented his illustrated lectures, concerned about new media's potential corrosive effects on traditional culture, sought to use the curiosity with these media to motivate learning and uplift taste in art and culture. He was more than an avid producer of images. He helped to establish the cultural traditions that promoted technical craft and aesthetic thought in image-making. From the late 1880s and throughout the silent era, he published extensively on photography, film and the arts, founded organisations dedicated to their promotion and edited one of the largest illustrated newspapers in the country. To trace Black's career as a lecturer and journalist within these institutions is to encounter the early intellectual history of moving-image aesthetics and the role of amateur craftsmanship in the educational uses of these technologies.[21]

THE DETECTIVE LECTURES AND THE INSTANTANEOUS TABLEAU

Black's continually revised collection of over 100 projected photographs accompanied by a lecture made its first rounds with the title 'Life Through a Detective Camera' in 1889. This lecture series and its aesthetic questions form the foundation for Black's picture plays, so they deserve to be analysed in some depth. By combining the glass slides that have survived in his family's collection with newspaper articles, publicity material and illustrations in Black's novel *Captain Kodak*, it is possible to construct an accurate account of the basic structure and themes of Black's lectures.[22] The subject and format of the lectures were developed as Black continually integrated new slides. The slides were taken by Black and, in the early years, other photographers of varying fame. The programmes divided the contributors into two categories: artists and amateurs. Black placed himself in the latter category. The different types of pictures were organised into sections. Pictures of the street life of Brooklyn and Manhattan, bathers at Coney Island, public figures, blizzards, country life and nautical scenes were among the common themes recycled and revised throughout the ten-year period during which these shows were regularly performed. The spoken accompaniment could include bits of narrative, a discussion of photography as an art and a science, and current events. Black tailored the lecture to the expectations and interests of his audiences.

As the main title of the lectures suggests, they emphasised the possibilities of the new 'detective' camera. This was the popular name given, not to the hidden camera, but to the ordinary hand camera freed from the tripod and bulky photochemical accessories of earlier camera outfits. The faddish popularity of the hand camera in the 1880s increased exponentially with the introduction of the Kodak and tapered off by the end of the next decade.[23] The advantages were ease of operation, portability and instantaneity. Black had been an advocate of this development in photography since the early 1880s.

Instantaneity was an important topic in Black's early detective lectures and, as the bookings increased, it became a main attraction. Black used an instantaneous exposure as a way to visually re-examine recognisable scenes. His lectures drew attention to the photographic medium in a way that those who trained their cameras on exotic or poor others did not. Other famous lecturers like Burton Holmes and John L. Stoddard were developing the dominant genre of the travel lecture. Their lectures were often limited to a visit to one exotic location.[24] Black, by contrast, showed pictures of widely varied genres and focused on the ability of the instantaneous photograph to reveal the local and the familiar. The show was alternatively called 'Ourselves as Others See Us'. This reference to Robert Burns's line from 'To a Louse' was a nod to Black's Scottish cultural heritage. Applied to the aesthetics of photography, it suggests identification between the subjects and the viewers. It also emphasises that the subjects are seen as they would be seen in everyday life, either unaware of or unconcerned with the presence of the camera. An early reviewer remarked that the lecture was 'copiously illustrated by photographs of people that Mr Black and others have taken unbeknownst with a "snapshot"'.[25] While Black did occasionally show some photographs of Europe, the lecture de-emphasised the draw of distant locations and the connection to modern travel.[26] The emphasis lay instead on scenes that have been 'captured in their effervescence', in which instantaneity structures a way of viewing a group of pictures.

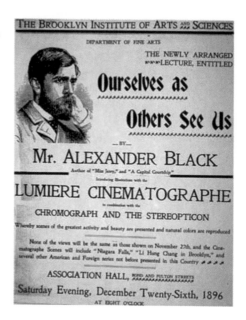

Poster for 'Ourselves as Others See Us', an alternate title for Alexander Black's nonfiction lectures (1896) (Courtesy of New York Public Library)

Instantaneity created coherence among the pictures. While unique on the lecture circuit, Black was not alone in this use of the detective camera. His innovation lay in the aesthetic application of popular tropes of instantaneous photography to the lecture format. Such popular instantaneous subjects as street scenes, marine views and the photography of bodies in motion were the main components of Black's lectures, and it is likely that his audiences came to these images with received ideas about instantaneous photography.[27] The difference here is that they were put in the service of a long-format presentation. This provided a foundation for a fictional world even if Black did not work photographs into long narratives until he made *Miss Jerry* in 1894. The candid quality of the photographs that Black reinforced in his lectures gave viewers a way to see them as part of a unified reality. We see this also in *Captain Kodak*, where the illustrations from the nonfiction lectures help to create the visual space of the characters' activities right alongside the narrative pictures of posed actors. In each case the recognisable snapshot aesthetic that these pictures share gives these fragmentary images of familiar scenes a coherent sense of space and time.[28]

Black promoted the coherent world created by the pictures with literary intertexts. The tagline used in publicity material for the early lectures was 'Pictures to Delight a Dickens', and there was clearly a Dickensian air to the portrayal of interconnected fragments of urban life.[29] Black was not particularly concerned with presenting socially critical scenes of New York's poor like those seen in Jacob Riis's 'The Other Half: How It Lives and Dies in New York' (1888). Nor did he generally take the same approach that Maren Stange identifies in Riis's lecture as 'the touristic point of view', intended to clearly demark the middle-class spectators from the subjects of his urban documentary photographs.[30] In fact, many of Black's documentary photographs were of his own family. His candid photographs of street life tended towards optimistic and humorous images of work and play. His less optimistic slides were also closer to Dickens than to Riis as they were inflected with pathos rather than paternalistic documentary distance.[31] There are many examples of these illustrations of work and play among the surviving slides and the illustrations in *Captain Kodak*. At work on the street, we see young bootblacks, organ grinders, pretzel vendors and men holding signs. The Coney Island photographs provided a counterpoint to the street scenes with their depiction of recreational activities like wading in the surf and riding the ferris wheel. In each case the quality of the candid view holds these pictures together as a part of the same urban space.

The context provided by these candid views allowed Black to quickly assess the possibilities of new imaging technologies as they became available. His slides were often hand coloured, and he experimented with natural colour processes as they became available. In autumn of 1896 he added motion pictures to the lecture. The Lumière cinematograph, with its design advantage of combining with an existing magic lantern for projection, was easily fitted to Black's existing lantern lecture. The cinematograph served as a technical addition to an existing practice, even as it received top billing in the posters.[32] The way that the Lumière brothers used motion pictures as an extension of their experiments with instantaneous photography and capturing scenes of everyday life fitted Black's purposes precisely.[33] A look at the reception of the combined film and slide lectures confirms that this was an important part of their success with audiences.

> Cinematographe [sic] pictures need a foil. Hitherto they have been commonly shown among a lot of vaudeville specialties bearing no sort of relation to the subject of life illustration. Mr Black, with a better art, has interwoven them in a lecture dealing with the picturesque features of everyday life and set off with views of his own making. It is the best tribute to Mr Black's cleverness to say that these latter did not suffer by comparison with M. Lumière's.[34]

The passage indicates how adaptable the cinematograph could be before the cinema had really defined itself as a medium.[35] The context provided by Black's lecture remedied the weakness found by genteel audiences in variety-format film projections. Included among the films shown were: the coronation of the Czar, European military parades, Niagra Falls and the Brooklyn visit of the Chinese ambassador to the USA.[36] As part of a vaudeville programme, these same films would be presented as interchangeable acts. As part of Black's lecture they became an outgrowth of instantaneous photography's ability to candidly record everyday life.

As my main interest here is the way in which this conception of the captured moment fits within an intellectual history of moving-image composition, I want to emphasise how reviewers situated Black's photographs and films as part of a larger pictorial tradition. They are 'picturesque life illustrations' dependent on a conception of the instantaneous view. Black's pictorialism does not counter his love of the snapshot. On the contrary, his references to traditions of illustration, painting and dramatic picturing depend upon an aesthetic of instantaneity.[37] This was a hallmark of Black's work from the 1880s.

Making Movies into Art

> In the open air, nothing is closed against the 'detective.' ... Fragments of street scenery, little *genre* bits in out-of-the-way corners, tableaux in rustic or town life, requiring instant capture, all impossible to the ordinary camera, are caught by the 'detective' in their very effervescence.[38]

Here Black appears to be moving in two directions at once. He advocates instantaneous capture of images, but his result is far from the views of nature's contingency that certain photography historians associate with a modern snapshot aesthetic.[39] Instead, he evokes traditions of genre painting and the tableau. These types of pictures imply composition, duration and, most importantly, a unity of dramatic or narrative event that would seem counterintuitive to link with the fragmentary snapshot. Black was committed to making pictures that emphasised the evanescent fragments of everyday life, those less accessible to other media, while still being recognisable as tableaux. It is fitting that many of the painters among those in Black's first audiences at William Merritt Chase's studio had contributed to the tradition of genre painting that Black evokes.[40] This painterly or theatrical quality does not mean, however, that Black's tableaux forego or erase the contingency of their origins. In his lectures on the relation of photography to art, Black criticises tableaux that are arranged for the camera.[41] The tableaux of the detective lectures are thus dependent on the tableaux of the canvas and the stage, but they bear a distinction in their use of the rhetoric and aesthetics of the instantaneous view.

The contingent pictured instant has been thoroughly investigated in studies of criminal photographs, chronophotography and early landscape cinematography either as completely separate from a sense of pictorial dramaturgy or as a kind of opacity that must be clarified by narration.[42] When one's enquiry shifts from landscape *études* to Black's scenes of urban life, an account of the collaboration between tableau aesthetics and instantaneous aesthetics becomes much more important. While it is indisputable that Black's spoken narration was a key factor in making his pictures legible as story scenes, the references to genre painting and tableaux establish a parallel trajectory in his relation to cinema.

FROM 'THE HORSE IN MOTION' TO 'MAN IN MOTION'

As Black developed his lectures, his interest gradually moved from the depiction of instants to the depiction of action, and from the individual composition to the composition of the sequence. For a conceptual model on which to base this sequential depiction of action, Black turned to the experiments with motion photography undertaken by Eadweard Muybridge and the painter Thomas Eakins. Black promoted his photographs of action as an extension of Muybridge's studies of animal locomotion in the brochures for his travelling lectures.

> The 'Detective' Camera has created a greater sensation than almost any other mechanical product of this inventive era. If the advance of quick photography made it possible to picture the horse in motion, the sensitive-plate in the disguised hand-camera made it easy to show *man* in motion ... The first pictures of the horse in motion astonished the artists. The 'Detective's' revelations of human life are also full of surprises.[43]

When he wrote this Black was well aware that Muybridge had completed his studies of human locomotion in Philadelphia, so in the analogy between the horse and man he is not referring to the simple graphic dissection of human movement. The analogy draws attention rather to the similar ability to reveal elements of passing time in these very different types of serial photography. Black uses the comparison with Muybridge's motion studies to distinguish his lectures from those of his contemporaries. His imaginative uses of motion studies to contextualise both his nonfiction sequences and his picture play sequences reveal him, as well as Muybridge and Eakins, to be exploring intermediary spaces between the practice of picturing dramatic situations and the newer filmic practice of stopping time and recreating an illusion of movement. Their effectiveness as lecturers on art appears to have depended on their audiences' ability to notice this ambivalent trait in their composed pictures.

Black referenced the photographic study of motion throughout his educational work in motion pictures, from his early lectures to his later picture plays. He even followed a course on anatomy by Thomas Eakins, who was known for using photographs as tools to teach anatomy and to compose many of his most famous works.[44] Black studied under Eakins a few years after he painted the Muybridge-inspired *A May Morning in the Park* (1879), which depicted a horse-drawn carriage in motion.[45] Fascinated by Muybridge's experiments photographing horses in Palo Alto with Leland Stanford, Eakins modelled the horses' legs in his painting on Muybridge's results. In Black's subsequent writing on amateur photography, he explains how Muybridge's work with Stanford caused a 'burst of merriment and wonder' among artists.[46] Eakins's course on anatomy must have conveyed some of this wonder to the young photographer. A few years later Muybridge's encyclopedic study of human and animal locomotion, completed at the University of Pennsylvania and partly supervised by Eakins, became known in Brooklyn photographic circles. The Brooklyn Library was persuaded to subscribe to the complete *Animal Locomotion* in 1888, and in 1889 Black and his colleagues welcomed Muybridge for a demonstration of his zoopraxiscope at the Oxford Club of Brooklyn.[47] Muybridge's photographs, his success at entertaining audiences in the USA and Europe with visual demonstrations and his concern (along with painters like Eakins) with the representation of movement in art guided Black's own experiments with pictorial sequencing and the illusion of motion.

Black followed Muybridge's work closely and often referenced the horse in motion as an intertext. In his early writings on photography, he discussed Muybridge in terms of the popular debate about the aesthetics of motion and scientific photography, the medium through which 'both the naturalist and the surgeon have gained a better knowledge of muscular action'.[48] He devoted a chapter of his manual *Photography Indoors and Out* to this question.

> Before the coming of instantaneous photography, people had curiously careless methods of representing the movements of a horse ... [W]hen the camera gave its report, we began to look at motion more carefully, to see more and better: and today, although artists do not yet agree to represent locomotion as it appears at any one movement, – holding that a picture should combine the impression of more than one movement, – there can be no longer the old-fashioned errors in the alternation of the feet or in the general position of the legs of the

Making Movies into Art

horse. A picture of a horse with all four legs extended widely seems like a cardboard charger, and we feel like looking for the string that holds him up.[49]

Black explains to his readers that the 'better knowledge' of movement afforded by the scientific advancements of photography has rendered certain traditions of representation outmoded. Eakins the naturalist develops this idea in *A May Morning in the Park*. While the cardboard charger model of the horse in motion may be outmoded, Black maintains that this is not the case for the informed selection and blending of multiple instants (or 'movements', as he interestingly attributes a vector to the pictured instant). He concedes that it is still aesthetically appropriate, despite the new knowledge gained by instantaneous photography, for a painter to picture motion in a way that approximates a viewer's actual experience of it. Such sentiments resurfaced in a range of writings on art, from complex diagrams in *The Century* justifying the blending of instants in a picture to Rodin's famous criticism that the photograph lies in its representation of reality, 'for in reality time does not stop'.[50]

In the reality of the lyceum circuit and the visual entertainments of the turn of the century, time did stop – often to be started again before an expectant audience as with Muybridge's zoopraxiscope demonstrations. In Black's lectures as well, audiences witnessed 'divers plunging into the sea, caught by the photograph in mid air, swimmers, runners, and jumpers in action'.[51] Black extended the idea of people caught unaware to people caught in the middle of a movement. This action photograph effect is distinct from the spontaneous picture of 'effervescent moments' discussed above. Stilled action, particularly when people are in the picture, poses a different set of aesthetic problems and possibilities. This was the source of concern for photographers like Black who had invested in aesthetic ideas derived from pictorial and performance traditions established earlier in the century.

Black's qualified enthusiasm for Muybridge's motion studies is best expressed by a situation in *Captain Kodak*.

> The detective and Allan came to the shooting-galleries where wooden deer and green lions were ceaselessly jumping ... 'Here is a chance,' said Dobbs, 'to get some of those queer things in animal locomotion. The great advantage here, though, would be that no matter when you caught the deer and lions, their legs would always look perfectly natural. That would be a big advantage. I don't like these snap pictures that show the horses standing on one foot with their hind legs twisted.'[52]

The scene of the ceaselessly jumping animals, set in motion by a rotating disk, bears a resemblance to Muybridge's zoopraxiscope demonstrations. To the photographer eager to still scenes of movement, the visual similarities between this older form of animation and the zoopraxiscope prompts a kind of wishful thinking. The detective character wants to have his privileged moment and his snapshot too. While not meant to be taken literally here, this wish illustrates an aesthetic problem around which Black shaped his demonstrations.

The cover of the detective lecture brochures highlighted this aesthetic problem when it depicted a woman diving into the sea. The diver was a popular and adaptable subject for instantaneous photographers. It appealed to photographers for whom the

Cover of a brochure for
'Life Through a Detective
Camera'. The photograph of
the diver was used
throughout the publicity
material for the lecture to
showcase instantaneity
(1890) (Courtesy of New
York Public Library)

dual interests in the frozen moment and graceful movement were not mutually
exclusive. On one hand, the irreversibility of the action heightened the instantaneous
effect. Black's diver is frozen at the moment right before an inevitable drenching that
we never see.[53] On the other hand, for all of its potentially comic contingency, the dive
is a display of (more or less) physical skill that can be performed for the camera. For
photographers engaged with the aesthetics of motion and stillness the dive's complete
arc of motion, often punctuated by one or more changing poses, made it an ideal
subject. In Black's picture the diver hovers at the top of the arc of motion and is set
against the flat horizon line.[54] A picture of the diver in the air stands in graceful
contrast to one that could have been taken after contact with the water, after her dress
became dishevelled and her posture and expression reacted to the sudden temperature
change.[55] In this picture her posture is symmetrical as is her placement within the
frame. This is not at all the awkward posture of an athlete caught, limbs and face
twisted, in a less picturesque instant of an otherwise graceful display of athleticism.
One could imagine the same posture photographed by the detective in *Captain Kodak*
from a rotating disk, though probably not in a shooting gallery. The posture is frozen
from a rapid movement, but is still plausible as pose – as a moment of rest – however
brief.

While it is the task of later chapters to discuss the development of the pictorial
aesthetics of motion and stillness in the film culture that followed the 1890s, one
example from this later period is particularly relevant here. The early film theory of
Victor Freeburg, who taught what may have been the first film studies classes in the
1910s at Columbia University, is a testament to the fact that these questions of the
aesthetics of motion in photography and cinema were foundational for this later
generation. More than his contemporary Hugo Münsterberg, whose books he taught
in his classes, Freeburg created a pictorially based theory of motion and stillness in
cinematic compositions. For Freeburg in the 1920s, as for Black in the 1890s,

Making Movies into Art

cinematic art hinges on the crises, and the possibilities, that the moving image brought to the arts of pictorial composition.

> Frequently while a director is rehearsing a photoplay scene he will sing out the command, 'Hold it!' indicating thereby that the player has struck an attitude, or the players have woven themselves into a pattern, which is so expressive and beautiful that it deserves to be held for several seconds ... But it is a peculiar psychological fact that such pictorial moments seem to occur in every movement ... Suppose we watch a diver stepping out upon a high springboard and diving into a pool. The whole feat is, of course, a movement without pause from beginning to end; yet our eyes will arrest one moment as the most interesting, the most pictorial. It may be the moment when the diver is about midway between the springboard and the water, a moment when the body seems to float strangely upon the air. We are not unaware of the other phases of the dive, yet this particular moment impresses us; to it we apply our fine appraisal of form.[56]

Beyond the similarity in posture between Freeburg's diver and Black's, I want to emphasise how Freeburg modifies the science of perceived motion by conflating it with a theatrical tradition. In reality, according to Freeburg's understanding, time seems to stop. It freezes when our perception, guided by aesthetic principles, extracts pleasing static forms from moving scenes. In this formulation Freeburg expresses an affinity between the arrested movement of a film (or stage) actor composed in a tableau and arrested movement of the free-falling diver.

A general familiarity with the pose from performance traditions was one way that people could make sense out of instantaneous photographs of motion. This context helps to explain why faster shutter speeds produced surprising images of bodies in motion even when they did not record the sprinters and galloping horses whose movements were so fast as to be imperceptible. Noted critic William Abney comments on this effect in 'the attitude of a man caught whilst walking, just touching the ground with the heel of the preceding leg'. He claims a picture like this is 'often grotesque, and conveys the idea that figures are composed in attitudes in which they are never seen, and it is their very grotesqueness that often makes them the most interesting'.[57] The movements of a man walking or a diver jumping are both slow enough to present a complete cycle of motion to an attentive observer. Freeburg admits this while he maintains that we aesthetically apprehend one still moment from the dive as a picture. The best compositions affect the viewer differently. For Abney too, the grotesqueness of stilled motion that he finds so interesting is not dependent on whether one has closely observed a man walking before. This scene is a common sight, but the instantaneous photograph presents it in a different context. The attitude is extracted from its movement and presented to a viewer or an audience for more than a brief moment. It is the off-balance, transitional body position *as a pose* that was so unfamiliar.

To develop a vocabulary that addressed these new images of physical activities writers often turned to the family of performance practices employing stopped motion and presenting bodily postures as a series of pictures. The theatrical tableau, the tableau vivant and the performance of attitudes in series were dominant modes of performance on the stage and as parlour entertainments in this period.[58] The physical foundations of these performances remained in close step with athletic developments throughout the nineteenth century. Acrobatic diving is related to these stage entertainments in many ways as part of the larger physical culture. A display of physical virtuosity on the romantic or melodramatic stage in the nineteenth century shares something with a 'fancy dive' that it does not share with a twentieth-century actor probing the depths of character psychology. The mark of a well-executed dive is that it physically articulates a set pattern of movements and postures during free-fall. The resultant spectacle emerges from a pattern of motion and posing just as it does in these other entertainments.[59] Their histories coincide as well. From the start of the sport, diving judges were encouraged to understand a continuous dive as a sequence of poses.[60] While I am not trying to claim a direct line of influence between athletic posing and pictorial acting styles or film-making traditions, their concomitant aesthetics of motion and stillness helps us to understand why we find a description of a diver's body in an early film theorist's chapter on the cinematic tableau.

It is fitting that Thomas Eakins chose diving for the subject of a painting that pointedly references instantaneous serial photography. I have argued that Black, Muybridge and Eakins should be considered together as figures whose work integrated, in different ways, the performance of attitudes and a pictorially based aesthetic with the instantaneous photography of motion. Eakins's 1885 painting *Swimming* is a vivid visual example. Given Black's admiration for Eakins, he certainly would have known this painting. The painting, which depicts a group of nude young men at a summer swimming hole, is often associated with Eakins's Arcadian works. These works, in which he painted classically themed pictures of nude figures in bucolic settings, drew from the tableau culture of the time more explicitly than other series of paintings in his oeuvre.[61] They created a tension between photographic visual knowledge of the body and the visual archive of classical poses in art. Eakins used photographic studies to give the figures' appearances and their postures a degree of detail at odds with the classicism of the paintings.[62] Eakins extends this theme to the sequential arrangement of bodies in the more explicitly modern *Swimming*. The painting bears an unmistakable resemblance to the studies in human locomotion Eakins made with a camera based on Étienne-Jules Marey's design. He was actively making these motion studies while he was working on *Swimming*. Although each figure in the painting is a different person (recognisable as his students), their combined poses mark phases of a continuous movement from reclining to standing to diving into the water. The last figure in the progression is suspended in the air with his arms in the water like an instantaneous photograph. The photographic modernity of this Arcadian grouping comes as much from the aesthetics of motion and posing as from the excess of detail.[63] Of the four figures that make up this arc of motion, the first and third are balanced in reclining and contrapposto postures. The second and fourth are transfixed in unbalanced transitional postures. Eakins stages, within a continuous arc of motion, an oscillation between the poses familiar from tableaux and those revealed by instantaneous photographs.

If Eakins integrated photographic motion study into his paintings, Muybridge's scientific motion studies had no lack of postures taken from traditional media. Unlike Marey, who carried out his chronophotography with better scientific discipline, Muybridge was unconcerned with purging the pictorialism or the dramaturgy of the represented moment from the systematic use of photography to analyse movement. In her work on 'Muybridge's fictions', Marta Braun provides the most rigorous reading of this aspect of his work.[64] She shows how Muybridge frequently rearranged, altered and combined images in his plates for aesthetic effects. Judging by Black's writing on Muybridge, there appears to have been little confusion at the turn of the century that Muybridge's classical postures and Victorian scenes were intended to be used by the painters and illustrators who subscribed to *Animal Locomotion*. This fact, which renders the scientific validity of his experiments dubious, makes these experiments all the more relevant for a pictorial history of early cinema.

Many of Muybridge's plates depict a transition from one stationary position to another. This varies from simple actions like swinging a bat or placing a jug on the floor to transitions borrowed more obviously from painterly iconography, like his sequence of one woman kneeling to drink from a jar on another's shoulder. In each case, we are not presented with an arbitrary section of movement in which each frame marks an equally arbitrary instant. Muybridge manipulated these movements to trace coherent shapes and accent privileged moments. This undermining of contingency is why theorists like Mary Ann Doane sidestep Muybridge in favour of Marey in their discussions of contingency and motion studies.[65] Scientific accuracy eluded Muybridge's experiments, but even had he attained it, his deliberate staging of transitions between distinct postures would still give the images in the plates uneven temporal weight. It is as if the tableau aesthetic and the sequential, mechanical analysis of motion were placed over each other like two transparencies combined to form a single image. Viewers are invited to read individual images in the series as poses either balanced or ungainly. They are alternately invited to read them as moments of transition in a series, but even the series has its own form of balanced closure in its articulation of a whole and distinct movement. Muybridge, like the detective in *Captain Kodak*, wanted his privileged moment and his snapshot too. This ambivalence contributed to the success of these types of images as educational tools on the public lecture circuit.

I present this notion of the overlay between tableau logic and the mechanical analysis of motion as an elaboration on what Braun refers to as the pictorialism of Muybridge's sequences. In her effort to distinguish Muybridge's pictorialism from Marey's scientific rigour, Braun hypothesises an alternative origin of Muybridge's plates. 'Indeed, in these pictures we cannot, by visual perception alone and without additional contextual information, be sure that what we see is not a narrative tableau – preconceived and choreographed gestures of what continual movement would look like in fragmentary stages portrayed by actors and actresses.'[66] The contextual information does in fact prove that this was not case. Braun's hyperbolic scenario is meant to draw attention to the aesthetic choices evident in Muybridge's compositions, but it also works as an accurate description of the direction in which Black took his stereopticon shows. The photography of actors in narrative tableaux was common practice, and photographers like Oscar Reijlander in *Juggler* (c. 1860) often faked instantaneous effects by posing actors in action tableaux and combination printing objects to make them look like they were captured mid-air. Drawn illusions of movement were made popular by the phenakistascope, a spinning-wheel device on which Muybridge based his own apparatus for animating his sequential photographs, the zoopraxiscope.

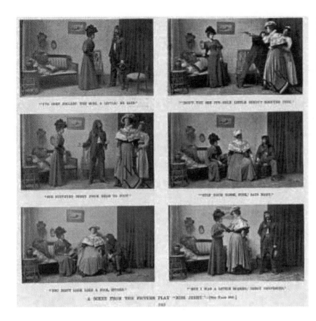

A scene from *Miss Jerry* reprinted in 'Making the First Picture Play,' *Harper's Weekly* 38 (20 October 1894), pp. 988–90

Combining these practices would allow a media educator like Black to explore a wider range of educational possibilities in this overlap between the tableau and the snapshot. The picture plays made sense as the next step.

As Black developed his lectures, he began to combine slides to create a suggestion of movement or a hint of a continuing situation, often with pictures of completely different origin. A brochure gives an intimation of this technique promising 'glimpses of character and action' in the juxtaposition of slides.[67] Black repeatedly claimed that the idea for *Miss Jerry* emerged from these experiments in composing nonfiction slide sequences.[68] Like Braun's description, the scenes were created by photographing a set of poses choreographed to suggest motion as one slide dissolved into the next every fifteen seconds. The analogy is not my own, but one that Black himself made. He says, speaking of his picture play sequences, 'the series of pictures suffer almost as much in separation as do those distressing glimpses of the horse in motion, which are true to the instant, but false to the larger fact'.[69] Black's engagement with photographic motion study grew in complexity as he moved from his detective lectures to his picture plays. He built upon the ideas developed in his nonfiction work to create projected narratives that may have been false to the instant, but were true to the larger fact.

PICTURE PLAY AESTHETICS: STILL PICTURES AS MOVING PICTURES

Black defined his picture plays as 'simply the art of the tableau vivant plus the science of photography'.[70] Only a skilled lecturer could make this formula seem so simple and straightforward. It would be inaccurate, for example, to take his description to mean that photography is an insignificant technical supplement, only an applied science

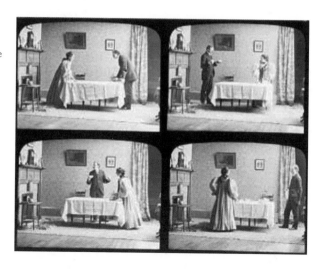

A scene from *A Capital Courtship* (1896) (Courtesy of Princeton University Library, Department of Rare Books and Special Collections)

used to record the tableaux. This narrow sense of Black's formulation would exclude the kinds of aesthetic transformations he had made a staple of his work from the beginning. Clearly, in his detective lectures Black already innovated ways to combine the tableau and the photograph, an aesthetic collaboration that outstripped simple technical assistance. These innovations only became more elaborate when Black began staging performers for serial photographs.

Black's special tableaux depart fundamentally from the tableau traditions on which they feed. One commonality among the diverse traditions of theatrical tableaux, waxwork series, tableaux vivants and shorter series of life-model lantern slides is that they share a tendency to picture moments that pop out from the flow of the story. They pictured events that were either climactic and spectacular or were staged for the clearest pictorial communication of narrative and character information. In a lantern series for *A Christmas Carol*, for example, audiences could expect iconic story scenes like Cratchit at his desk as well as the spectacular appearances, perhaps using a dissolve effect, of the supernatural characters. A relatively small number of staged pictures, between five and twenty in these traditions, calls for the economy of narration and dramatic effect of the privileged moment. Each slide must bear the weight of meaning or produce an intensity of effect. With Black's plays of 250 pictures, the task shifts from creating effective privileged moments to creating continuity through the long sequences. Reviewers remarked on this subtle but salient distinction between Black's work and other lantern narratives that used live models. A *Boston Herald* critic noted that 'Even when there is a conversation which requires the same scene for several minutes the views are constantly changing to show different expressions and postures.'[71] A scene from *A Capital Courtship* (1896) demonstrates the writer's point. Nothing happens in the scene aside from a conversation.[72] There is discussion about a broken clock on the mantle towards which the characters gesture, but the only visual progression in the scene is in setting the table. This pictured activity does not move the events of the narrative forward, nor does it typify key character relations or situations. It might be called dramatic byplay were it actually performed by the actors and not deliberately composed as a set of pictures. Rather than emphasising moments of intensified dramatic situations, the pictures form a regularly paced sequence, which integrates dramatic situations within a continuous flow of even and ordinary gestures. They are tableaux, but they are dynamic tableaux that give equal weight to the moments during which nothing particular happens.

In sequences that do require tableaux of intense action, like the only scene of violent confrontation in Black's otherwise mild-mannered story of a young female reporter, Miss Jerry, the steadily paced pictures still do not yield to the climactic moment. The climax of this particular situation is pictured as the brandishing of a gun. The actors' postures are tensed as they struggle, and a chair has been thrown to the floor. In a live performance this staged picture might have been held static for a moment. In this scene, the moment of intensity does not disrupt the steady unfolding of successive tableaux. The slide is shown for the same amount of time as the others in the sequence, so it could be read as a transitional moment like the others. The dissolve to the following slide further suggests a continuous movement rather than an interrupted series. The change happens as the narrator reads the words 'The Rose of the Rockies lowered a melodramatically huge revolver.'[73] The script directs attention to the continuous movement represented by the dissolve, connecting it to the remainder of the sequence in which the return to ordinary conversation is marked by the chair's return to its upright place in the room. Even in this climactic moment, the revolver moves to its position of rest with a deliberately composed fluidity.

The script certainly helped to cue attention to the actors' movement during the slide changes, but this only supplemented a quality inherent in the images themselves. To say that the slides followed each other 'without friction', as one reviewer put it, implies something more than evenly paced sequences of pictures. Black painstakingly constructed the slides for this frictionless effect. He carefully registered each slide and fixed the camera position so that the background and the elements of the décor remained in the same position throughout the scene. During the dissolves, the figures appeared to move through a series of poses within this stationary *mise en scène*. At the premiere, Seth Low actually believed that Black used some sort of layered animation device to make the figures move by sliding over stationary background images.[74] The picture play did not offer a complete illusion of natural movement (if such a thing even exists). It presented an alternative, a plausible representation of movement created with the dissolving view.

The dissolving magic lantern view had been used to create effects of transformation for many years. Lantern manuals from the turn of the century commonly featured anecdotes of comic and picturesque combinations of slides. They warned that the registration of slides could be accidental as well as intended: 'First of all there came a woman in peasant's dress. This was followed by a man whose lower extremities were clothed in tight-fitting white unmentionables. It so happened that one figure occupied on the screen exactly the same place as the other, so that when the lady was slowly dissolved into the gentleman, the astounding effect was produced of her clothes gradually melting from her form.'[75] Black claimed that the idea for the picture plays came from similar accidental combinations of dissolving images in his nonfiction lectures.[76] While he never used the dissolve to undress anyone, he did use it to place hats on women's heads and to make figures appear and disappear from scenes.[77] He used dissolves to make young people transform into old people and to make Victorian visual stereotypes transform into what he claimed were more accurate modern types. He developed an acute sense of the dissolve as an adaptable instrument of transformation.

Fantastical appearances and disappearances aside, something about the smooth passing time of the dissolve in itself appealed to audiences. Prefiguring cinematic uses of the dissolve, lanternists commonly used the dissolving view to depict elapsed time rather than transformations in people's dress. Transformations in landscapes, changes between day and night or between seasons utilised to great advantage the dissolve effect and the saturated hand colouring available with large glass slides. With the addition of smoke, snow, or rain effects, the lantern could rival the diorama in its ability to depict a changing landscape.[78] Black used each of these effects to create atmosphere, but he used the dissolving view mainly for its ability to depict passing time. Audiences recognised this well-known effect of suggesting time extending from one picture into another.

The dissolving view technique presented the opportunity for audiences to re-examine cinematic movement in an aesthetically deliberate way. Unlike film's mechanised movement, where one instantaneous photograph follows another in mechanical succession, the dissolving view represents change over an elapsed, indefinite time, which is under the complete control of the operator. Black's dissolves evoked transitions between the frames of a filmstrip, but his frames covered spans of time insurmountable by any physical perception of animation. His representation of movement was no illusion. It laid bare motion pictures and then aesthetically corrected them, before his viewers' eyes, according to the ameliorative, softening function of the dissolve. His dissolves cross the gaps between the frames, like those landscape slide series, with only a suggestion of passing time.

The picture play's gentle transformations would still have been ineffective, however, if they had not been partnered with an innovative approach to staging. Each slide had to be staged to depict an indefinite duration. With landscapes as with dramatic scenes, the dissolve cannot give the effect of gradual transition if it simply joins one instant to another. In a transition from a day-time landscape to a night-time landscape each slide is meant to suggest not an instant of day and an instant of night, but rather time passing in day and in night. The picture plays translated this type of temporality from painted landscapes to photographed bodies, encouraging spectators to suspend their disbelief and read each still image as a sort of living attitude.

In his picture play poses Black actively erased any suggestion of instantaneous moments. In a how-to article in *Ladies' Home Journal*, he advises those who would produce amateur picture plays to 'Avoid effects of action that will not bear the duration of twenty seconds ... Prefer moments just before or just after action.'[79] The scene of a woman slapping a would-be seducer, for example, is shown in an approaching shot and then a shocked reaction shot, but the slap is not frozen mid-contact.[80] The effect of this is a series of photographs with a strange temporality. Neither a privileged moment nor an instant of action, each slide is designed to depict *the elapsed time between the two adjacent slides in the series*. With the composition of these slides, Black revisited and elaborated the aesthetic problems he tackled in his nonfiction lectures. Instantaneous motion photography showed bodies in postures captured by a fast shutter that could not be seen by the naked eye. The picture plays inverted this effect. They suggested movement the naked eye can readily see but which cannot actually be shown in a single instantaneous photograph. They showed real people in faked time.

What the cinematograph did relatively automatically, Black did by hand. He crafted movement, and did so with a particular aesthetic purpose. The sense of passing time of the picture plays, while fluid and not altered by the magnifications of plot climaxes, is composed to appear natural. Instead of recording natural movement, they represented movement with a controlled set of manual techniques. Black revised techniques of illustration, camera positioning, dissolving views and staging, and in doing so he created a suggestion of rather ordinary movement with a complicated aesthetic pedigree. Engaged in the aesthetic debates surrounding Muybridge and Eakins, and a populariser of the art-historical traditions of picturing motion, Black's work created the picture play performance as a space for audiences to reflect upon moving-image media. He used the educational forum of the public lecture circuit to bring the traditions of representing movement in the visual arts into conversation with the cinema.

PICTURE PLAY RECEPTION: ART CINEMA WITHOUT THE CINEMATOGRAPH

The fact that the picture plays did not make use of the motion-picture devices developed by Edison or Lumière may exclude them from a linear technological history of cinema. But it makes them all the more effective for a cinema history that emphasises how institutional and discursive factors delimit the medium over time. André Gaudreault, for example, supports the definition of emergent cinema as 'a social, cultural, and artistic apparatus', as opposed cinematography: the technological precondition for the later development of the medium. In Gaudreault's formulation it is imprecise to understand early cinema as a distinct medium in the years when it was chiefly understood as a technical aid to other practices such as lantern shows, magic shows and instantaneous photography.[81] Black's productions search for an institutional framework, a 'social, cultural, and artistic apparatus', based on an imagined possibility for the cinematograph without actually using a cinematograph. In other words, Black experimented with the creation of cinema by other means in order to imagine a cinema of ambition.

Reviewers invoked cinema with nearly every attempt to define the picture plays. It was a functional analogy.

> Mr Black's picture play marks a distinct epoch in the development and use of the stereopticon. It retains a favorite means of entertainment, but it applies it in a totally new field ... Here is an absolute novelty in a favorite amusement – a good story, with continuous illustrations; dramatic situations illustrated from real life; a sort of interrupted kinetoscope; a drama before an open camera.[82]

An 1895 review in the *Boston Herald* was likewise entitled 'Sort of Big Kinetoscope'.[83] Since Edison's kinetoscope did not project images, this reviewer must have been referring to its illusion of motion. In numerous instances in his own writing, Black demonstrates current knowledge of the developments in Edison's laboratory. He was presumably in attendance when Edison staged his first public demonstration of the kinetoscope at the Brooklyn Institute.[84] In 1896, Black wrote, 'Pending the perfection of the Vitascope, the cinematograph, and kindred devices, the ordinary camera, in partnership with the rapidly dissolving stereopticon, gives freest expression to the processes of the picture play ... for a greater clearness and steadiness in pictorial result.'[85] The conceptual linkage with the cinema continued to grow with film's increasing popularity.

But the point of the reviewers' comparisons was just as much that the picture plays were not quite cinema. Their effectiveness in testing the boundaries of cinema, and hence their attraction, lay in that margin of difference. Black had little interest in imitating cinema with his picture plays. He wanted to do better than cinema. In an interview he admits, 'I have tried moving pictures, but they are too trying for the eyes, and I find dissolving views the best.'[86] He critiques cinema's technological imperfections because of a preference for a different kind of aesthetic of motion. An 1894 article in *Harper's Weekly* contains the most pithy formulation of Black's method of representing movement: 'It was not wished to produce the illusion of actual action, as the Kinetoscope of Mr Edison has since presented it, but of actual glimpses of action.'[87] The picture plays erased the 'distressing glimpses' of suspended action and the moving pictures that 'try the eyes'.[88]

Black's revised cinema invited his audiences to consider the possibility of an art of moving pictures. Like all of the experiments with early art cinema discussed in this book, the picture plays look back to nineteenth-century art for models of pictorial composition, but they also welcome the modernity of the motion picture and look ahead to its artistic future. To enact cinema's pictorial retrofit, Black carefully avoids the visual discontinuity of instantaneous photography and mechanically reproduced motion that was essential to early cinema's popularity and would later become essential to modernist film-makers. Exhibited in a period spanning from the invention of motion picture technology to the beginning of the nickelodeon era, the picture plays challenge the raw contingency of cinema with a new kind of movement assembled from traditions of nineteenth-century tableau culture, painting and related pictorial arts. The picture plays soften the distressing glimpses of the horse in motion and the kinds of mischievous grimaces noticed in the Lumière brothers' still photographs with a handmade, deliberate aesthetic of motion that bears a mark of propriety from earlier in the nineteenth century.[89] This move makes sense in terms of Black's audiences. His first audiences in New York were 1890s painters suspicious of photography and its implications for the arts. His audiences during his national tours were lyceum patrons suspicious in their own way of these new visual entertainments from the fairgrounds and vaudeville houses.

But this explanation by itself would be incomplete. Even if the picture play was a form without a future, it did not simply reanimate artefacts of the past. Black was hardly a traditionalist refusing to acknowledge the possibilities of the changes happening in his media environment. He was a pictorial innovator in journalism, a populariser of instantaneous photography and a modern showman. The success (albeit with rapid turnover) of hybrid forms like the picture plays raises the question, as Christine Gledhill puts it in relation to cinema's adoption of fragments from the

Victorian stage, 'when did the nineteenth century end? … How far into the future are these fragments carried and how long does their significance remain the same?'[90] The picture plays carried on fragments from pictorialist traditions while challenging the limits of what cinema was and what it could become. The erasure of jerky movements and disjointed instantaneous poses may have appealed to the aesthetically conservative tastes of lyceum audiences, but the very experiment in creating a series of frictionless tableaux as an answer to cinematography's frictions just as importantly prompted these audiences to confront modern ideas about the representation of movement in painting, sculpture and cinema.

The aesthetic of softened motion made the picture plays contemporary. It presented a viable collaboration among varied media and pictorial traditions at a time when people needed to make sense out of the wholesale appropriation of these traditions by new technologies. The fluidity of movement, the constructed duration of the postures and the persistent comparison with cinematography ran against received notions about the illustrating and emphatic functions of the tableau. This prompted reviewers to make written and graphic comparisons to the evenly paced photograms of a filmstrip.[91] But this was a filmstrip that could never be resolved into the ungainly transitional postures found on an individual film frame. It bore no traces of the nondeliberate movements that the cinematograph could not help but record. It was an aesthetic alternative. Far from being simply nostalgic in style, the picture plays staged precisely the kind of negotiation of media traditions that helped audiences consider the future of their media environment.

The picture play format was not created to solidify into any kind of self-contained medium. It was not an underdeveloped form waiting for another technology or medium to complete it. Its draw for audiences depended not on novelty of its stories, but on the novelty of its form. It was most importantly for its audiences, a media experiment, not quite one known medium and yet not quite another. Partly for this reason, *Miss Jerry* remained by far the most popular of the four picture plays Black listed in his ledger.[92] He continued to set up performances of *Miss Jerry* long after he had developed the increasingly complex *A Capital Courtship* and *The Girl and The Guardsman*. Neither did he seek to expand the picture play format outside of the lyceum circuit. Black could conceivably have adapted the plays to more commercial theatrical venues, but he, and the audiences at the time, understood the picture plays' closest relatives to be educational lectures and not dramatic entertainment. The picture plays were tools for aesthetic education. The lyceum audience prized the didactic value of the picture craft animating *Miss Jerry*.

CONCLUSION: A HISTORY WITHOUT AN INVENTION

Black wrote in the 1890s about the picture play as a kind of imagined future for motion pictures, but after his touring shows tapered off and the coming of the nickelodeon this imagined future was largely forgotten. Only when the terms 'picture play' and 'photoplay' had become names for the feature film did Black's work emerge as important to cinema history. The picture plays were once again relevant, this time for imagining the multi-media roots of a certain kind of cinema. Beginning in the

Alexander Black greets
Barbara La Marr and George
Fitzmaurice on the set of
The Eternal City (1923)
(Courtesy of New York
Public Library)

mid-1910s, writers understood Black's first screening of *Miss Jerry* within the same artistic horizon as the films made a generation later. In answer to the question 'Who invented cinema?' many 1910s writers nominated Black, suggesting that *Miss Jerry* 'was the very first picture ever shown!'[93] If Black's novel synthesis of pictorial arts allowed spectators in 1896 to imagine possible futures for the kinetoscope and the cinematograph, it also allowed filmgoers twenty years later to imagine an early incarnation of the recent films of artistic distinction. Critics revived his work, and leaders of the film industry invited him to Hollywood to meet current stars and directors.

A 1915 article in the *Picture Play Weekly* uses, for the first time according to my research, a nickname that would stick with Black's picture plays throughout the years of renewed interest in them. The writer claims that, 'The photo-play era began with Alexander Black … but it was a *slow movie* … The real impetus to photo-play production did not come until 1910.'[94] Adolph Zukor was among those who seized on this term 'slow movie'. Zukor uses the term in a Paramount film acknowledging Black's achievements and in his personal letter to Black, which was partly reprinted in *Moving Picture World*:

> Before you presented 'Miss Jerry' the screen had only still pictures. Then came your 'slow movie', in which you gave the effect of movement – long before the motion picture mechanism was perfected – making your audiences think the characters in your drama actually moved.[95]

The term 'slow movie' gets at the heart of the significance of the picture plays in their afterlife. With a certain casual precision, it identifies the ambivalent relation to cinema in the picture play's aesthetic of motion. The picture play represents motion, like a movie, but with a slow progression of frames. It is not slow motion, a well-known effect, because it suggests a kind of natural pace. There is still a motion 'effect', however, because it is markedly distinct from attempts to record natural movement. While the picture play represents the ordinary passing of time, it possesses an elongated sense of transformation between scenes that is reminiscent of slow motion. This effect of motion, the picture play's most conspicuous characteristic in the 1890s, drew more interest in the 1910s than the more obvious connections to the feature film such as scene construction, feature length and narration.

Even in the age of the feature film, the 'slow movie' still had something to teach motion pictures about art. Among the critics who noted the picture play's continued relevance, Terry Ramsaye indicates most clearly what was at stake in this assessment.

> The Black picture play made the audience work, even if unconsciously, to fill the gaps in the motion record. The distinction is as sharp as between wit and slapstick ... The slow movie ... was in fact a motion picture in which the eye received a minimum of cues to keep the mind on the desired emotion path. Imagination had to fill the long gaps in the visual record. The film drama of to-day presents four times as many images a second as Black gave in a minute ... The modern screen thereby supplies ready-made imagination, and requires relatively almost no imaginative or intellectual abilities for its observation.[96]

In trying here to explain why the picture plays could never have succeeded with 'the lowbrow audiences of the variety houses', Ramsaye promotes a truism of aesthetic philosophy popularised on the lecture circuit. Beautiful compositions should use form to trigger aesthetic satisfaction rather than simply illustrate. His hyperbole notwithstanding, Ramsaye laments that if only photographic movement could be composed like suggestive pictures, then the inherent contradictions in the phrase 'motion-picture art' could be resolved. For him, the 'slow movie' explored this possibility.

The picture plays' distinct form granted them an ambivalent character, not just a hybrid character. Given this recurring tendency to see the picture plays as a kind of cinema but also as something else, a current historian might replace Ramsaye's metaphor of evolutionary anomaly with a nonlinear metaphor. The picture plays, more than simply conglomerates of practices, staged a kind of frame-jumping effect where the properties of one medium stepped out of another in order to provoke critical reflection. The picture plays generated continuing curiosity because they oscillated between the tableau and the film frame, between living pictures and motion pictures, or between an allegiance to pictorial culture and an advocacy of the 'new' rhetoric of mechanically recorded bodies in motion. This ambivalence, fundamental to visual culture of the period, unfolds from Black's seemingly simple claim that he wanted to combine the art of the tableau vivant with the science of photography.

This staged oscillation between media, or between assumptions about what different media do, sparked a reception of picture plays that could not be separated from a visual analysis of the performances, especially considering how this cultural reception, in the form of newspaper reportage and various rediscoveries, often reached a wider audience than the shows themselves. The picture plays were something to be considered as much as seen, and this consideration engaged broader aesthetic topics about motion, stasis and pictorial composition with a surprising sophistication. Black himself was very engaged in these discussions, both in his writings and during his lectures. The fact that Black performed the picture plays on the lyceum circuit, which accommodated public lectures more frequently than audiovisual fictions, indicates that the interest in his shows was not entirely different from the interest in public lectures or articles about Black in *Harper's*. Black's audiences approached new media technologies as educational, not fairground or vaudeville, wonders.

Black's work marks a gap in the knowledge of American media history, but the reasons for his misfit in this history makes an excavation of his work more than an act of filling in a gap. The parallels between his prescient 'false start' and the well-known developments in instantaneous photography, motion study, early cinema and the feature film lends critical perspective to this nexus of media practices. Black's work is not just a missing piece in cinema history; it helps to define a vantage point from which to view early cinema history.

Experimental forms like these staged cinema's encounter with the pictorial arts. The discussion surrounding this encounter amounted to a scattered, but functioning, form of media criticism. In the 1910s and 20s they were joined by the first American aesthetic film theories by figures like Vachel Lindsay and Victor Freeburg, which relied heavily on notions of pictorial beauty and cross-media connections to establish a set of criteria by which films could distinguish themselves. The picture play may never have become a mainstream practice, but the questions posed by this experimental form were not shelved alongside the slides for *Miss Jerry*. Instead of looking for the offspring of the picture plays, one might do better to ask how and why these questions resurface in other experiments in art-educational cinema and moving-image aesthetic thought over the next two decades.

2

Moving Pictures Imagine the Artist's Studio

It seems natural to look to the lyceum circuit for early moving pictures that were aesthetically deliberate, that sought to link cinema with the other arts and that taught audiences to do the same. But what about those links that lie beyond this more directly educational sphere? Outside the lecture hall, early motion pictures did not have the most direct relationship with aesthetic education. Yet is no secret that early films are filled with art. Artist's models posed for the camera in allegorical tableaux. Visual artists made their livings by demonstrating their artistic labour in action. On-screen painters and sculptors dreamed, had fun and encountered dilemmas in their studios. The question here is not whether these types of films were prevalent, but rather how to contextualise them to determine if and how they may have helped to make movies into art. The benefit to looking at early art cinema not as a movement, but as a convergence of art institutions, intellectual history and the moving image is that these intersections happened even before people started properly talking about specific films as works of art and specific directors as painters and sculptors of the screen. If we begin our early histories of contemplative cinema only once critics began seriously to reflect on these issues in the later silent period, then we miss the ways in which many films, made long before critics started talking about the possibility of an art cinema, already reflected on the motion picture as an art of absorption. Because they relied so heavily on other artistic and performance traditions for material, early artist's studio films engaged many of these judgments and concerns. They traded in notions of contemplation and picture craft and accommodated an educational impulse that continued into the art films that would follow.

As in each section of this book, this chapter is about looking forward and looking back. It seeks out the contemplative in early cinema, and early cinema's afterlife in a group of later contemplative films by the advertising photographer and part-time film-maker Lejaren à Hiller. Under examination here are the fantasies of artist's workspace, particularly the moments when the desire to know about the work of artists intersects with the dreams of art come-to-life. Most of the examples come from material surrounding the publication of *Trilby* (1894), the famous illustrated novel in which the mesmerist Svengali kidnaps a Latin Quarter artist's model who, under his trance, becomes a famous singer. For years after the publication of this modern best-seller by Georges DuMaurier, one of the first of its kind, the American public exhibited a mania for related material referencing the novel and its illustrations. It makes sense that in the publicly circulated moving images of what was quickly termed 'Trilbymania', early cinema found ideal situations for staging fantasies about the artist's studio. The contemplative or reflective aspects of such sensational material might be less immediately apparent, but these fantasies of the studio space do overlap with simultaneous efforts to consider and appreciate the work of visual artists. And they persist for much longer in the form of adaptations, including Hiller's educational films.

Consider one brief exhibition scene, of a Hiller film discussed at length later, as an example that raises the kinds of questions best addressed with a cultural history that moves back and forth across periods. An audience in upstate New York is watching *The Sleep of Cyma Roget* (1920), a debut film by a curious magazine photographer from Manhattan. The film is essentially a Trilby story about a mesmerist exerting influence over an artist's model. As the projectionist changes reels, a group of performers come on stage and perform a series of poses set in an artist's studio. Several of the poses recall famous paintings on display in American museums, and the models in this entr'acte transform still paintings into live performance. This scene was familiar enough around the turn of the century. It would have recalled several examples from variety shows, possibly fairground entertainments, or, in a more upscale venue, a society tableau vivant performance. But Hiller's film was no short about an artist's model designed for a typical variety-show audience in the 1890s. It was a seven-reel feature, conceived as a quasi-educational film in 1919 and exploited commercially as high-class entertainment. The film not only recycles early cinema tropes into a feature-length art film, it also fuses variety entertainments and art education. To innovate in the field of aesthetic education, it turns back to 1890s performance practices and to the representation of an 1890s studio. The themes and tricks of the earliest films about art and artists prove difficult to leave behind. Tracing an earlier cultural history of these themes, before discussing the work of Hiller, will provide a better sense of their affinities. The movement across periods here does not span early cinema and the film industry. It moves from the absorbing art-studio scenes of early cinema into the peripheral productions that inhabit the eclectic scene of early American art cinema.

THE *MISE EN SCÈNE* OF THE STUDIO

Learning to contemplate a painting or a sculpture in late nineteenth-century America certainly involved understanding formal principles and their psychological effects. The emerging picture study tradition made sure of this. But those aspiring to knowledge of the arts also benefited from imagining how art, as work, takes place. Illustrated magazines, lantern lecturers and film-makers each deployed the *mise en scène* of the art studio, with its tools and its workers, as an edifying space.[1] These scenes provided something in addition to interchangeable content for sensational theatrics. They brought to the display of art an element of the how-to that many scholars have located in the broader visual culture of the era.[2] Scenes of the artist's studio could reveal, within the compelling romantic setting, the act of creating aesthetic form. In other words, one effective way to teach the public to truly see pictures was to show pictures in process. Using well-known images of the studio, sometimes modified to increase this effect, educators could avoid recycling traditional hierarchies of artistic genius and focus, instead, on the artist's tools and the support of models, students and other craftspeople in the workshop.[3]

The studio space had a particular relevance in the rapidly professionalising American culture of design and illustration around 1900. Every aspect of the modern artist's teaching studio was professionalising. Models earned standardised wages posing now for illustrators, for photographers and for life model classes with an expanding student base.[4] Educators supported tools for a new kind of life class in their campaign for an image of artist and model that would fit an environment of emerging professional societies, celebrity artist-educators and booming business in the fields of illustration and design. In the contemporary American studio, they alleged, industry and transparency were on the rise. Models posed, artists created form from life and students learned to do the same. Buyers and critics, too, conducted much of their work in the studio at this time. As such a hub of activity the studio space provided a fertile setting for creating the mythology of the Gilded Age art world at large as well as the mythology of particular schools and artists of the more distant past. The public desire for images of the inner workings of the studio, particularly for images that fused historical fact and fantastic mythology, seemed insatiable around the turn of the century. As the public interest in seeing artists, models and students at work increased, so did the professional management of image. By the 1890s in New York, this management had become commonplace. It continually appealed to a material curiosity about the *mise en scène* of the studio space itself, about its equipment, its props, its eccentric décor.

The illustrated press in the 1890s played a significant role in shaping public perceptions of studio life. Many of the artist types can be traced to a handful of illustrators. From the USA, Charles Dana Gibson's illustrations for *Life* magazine repeatedly explored and satirised New York artists, critics and collectors. From England, the most influential of art satirisers, George DuMaurier, became a household name. No history of the public perception of the artist in the 1890s, even in the educational realm, is complete without considering DuMaurier's *Trilby*. DuMaurier illustrated for *Punch* in London, but the success of *Trilby*, which essentially compiled and narrativised the artist stereotypes he had been developing for years, was unstoppable. It curculated around the world, but it achieved the largest share of its success in the USA. For those among the magazine-reading public who claimed a sense of the *mise en scène* of the artist's studio, this sense was in some way traceable back to Gibson or to DuMaurier's *Trilby* types.

When illustrators depicted the artist's workspace, they aimed to distinguish real work from mere fun in the artist's studio. In the representation of the modern studio, commerce-savvy artists and art educators had to navigate around a series of types that art historian Sarah Burns has termed 'clowns'.[5] The clown artists included the absinthe-drinking mess like Marie Corelli's Gaston Beauvais, the coarse unwashed foreigner like DuMaurier's Svengali and the Wildean dandy. Artist's models, too, were subject to a similar set of distinctions. Caricatures of the *lorette* and the dilletante society woman emerged in comedic contrast with the *modèle professionnelle* as satirical illustrators and vaudeville comedians ran these types through every manner of physical humiliation.[6] Emerging media and growing institutions of design, illustration and professional modelling actively participated in the defining and coding of these types.

The tactics of comparison are essential here. Absurd caricatures of artists and models, in themselves, do not necessarily reveal much about changing institutions of art until they function alongside the informative aspects of studio spaces. This is where DuMaurier and Gibson are most illustrative. They paid just as much attention to their depictions of the ateliers, to the positioning of the easels, the working of a life model class, the impromptu fencing matches and the daily trips to the Louvre as they paid to their clowns. DuMaurier and Gibson knew the *mise en scène* of the Paris studio quite well, having both made pilgrimages there as young art students. They exploited the studio's imaginary aspects while also making their concrete knowledge of the studio an object of intense focus in their work. Their readers wanted to see inside the studio, and they viewed these depictions as real. Even in scholarly histories of nineteenth-century art institutions, written decades later, these illustrated depictions are often used as historical evidence. *Trilby* is treated more as a memoir than as popular fantasy.[7] That DuMaurier and Gibson both became commercial illustrators who chronicled and satirised an art world very different from their profession is in fact less arbitrary than it may initially seem. They helped to usher in what is commonly referred to as a golden age of illustration, and the growing market for commercial work like theirs was a major factor in the professionalisation of art schools. At the same time, they functioned as chroniclers and mythologisers of aging salon exhibitions, of the French atelier and the lifestyles of bohemians and aesthetes. Put simply, they showcased an aging studio mode in the very medium (illustration) that helped to bring about this mode's obsolescence.

These tactics of comparison worked inside contemporary teaching studios too, as educators crafted their own studios as places of performance to the public. Some, like William Merritt Chase, confronted the challenges of public scrutiny by presenting himself in his studio with such precision that other art educators sometimes left aside the subject of Chase's painting and lectured instead on the style of his studio and his dress. Among his notable students was the young poet, aspiring painter and not-yet film theorist Vachel Lindsay. In what were likely Lindsay's first lectures on the visual arts, which are preserved in a student notebook from 1905 (with original underlining), Lindsay describes Chase as 'A great artist, a great teacher, and a great stylist (personally).' Lindsay placed Chase in sharp contrast with the velvet-jacket decadents and related aesthetic clowns. He instructed students to study Chase's mannerisms in John Singer Sargent's 1902 portrait of him holding his palette and brushes, dressed impeccably in a three-piece suit, ornamented with spectacles and a tie clip. Sargent's portrait stages Chase frontally with his arms open, depicting him, Lindsay notes, as someone who has spent 'many years before the public'.[8] Chase strongly believed, and Lindsay affirmed, that this presentability of the studio space was essential to the development of American art education. He painted a series of pictures of his studio, staged class photographs in the space and used this publicised venue to host cultural events like Alexander Black's premiere of *Miss Jerry*. This new image of the studio, which accompanied a turning away from long apprenticeships and a hierarchy of genre, founded enduring institutions in this period. Although Chase's tenure at the Chase School was brief due to personal differences, the school he founded, at which Vachel Lindsay delivered his first lectures, renamed Parsons, remains one of the country's most respected schools of design.

John Singer Sargent, *William Merritt Chase*, 1902. Oil on canvas, 158.8 × 105.1cm (© The Metropolitan Museum of Art, courtesy of Art Resource, NY)

I will return to Lindsay in the next section and offer instead two preliminary connections between this studio space as workspace and educational space and early cinema. The first thing that Burns's discussion of aesthetic clowns is likely to bring to mind, for a scholar of early cinema, is the abundant clowning in films set in artists' studios. In some early films set in studios, such as *The Artist's Dilemma* (1901), the clowning is literal; an actual costumed clown does the painting. More often, the films mobilise the caricatures Burns discusses in her work. Artist-clowns dream in early cinema much in the same way that those who fiend for opium, hops, or rarebit dream. Their fantasy studio spaces serve as pretexts for the tricks, apparitions and physical humiliations that audiences wanted to see the medium deal out to its clowning performers. In these films, artists often fall asleep and dream of their work as more erotically available, and the films are quick to parody these fantasies. In *The Artist and the Mannequin* (1900), for example, a model impersonates a mannequin only to get close enough to knock down, with a broom, the Svengali-look-alike aesthetic clown. These artist's studio films demonstrate cinema's interconnectedness with the commercial and graphic arts in the public reception of the artist's studio.

The popular performances of the lightning sketch and the express sculpture offer a promising second tradition to examine for these connections. Bracketing for a moment the special effect of seeing a drawing created before our eyes, these performances demonstrated the undeniably skilful production of likenesses in chalk, pen and clay. The motion picture aided this demonstration with its ability to fix point-of-view and document moving process. If the educational merit of lightning sketches may not

Making Movies into Art

spring immediately to mind when considering their popularity on vaudeville stages, it is important to note that they were celebrated in the lyceum and at the Chautauqua as well.[9] In these spheres, artists such as James Stewart Blackton, cinema's most successful lightning sketcher, worked across genres. Displaying seascapes along with facial caricatures, working live in chalk while also drawing for the *New York World*, Blackton occupied a similar position as Gibson and DuMaurier relative to changing hierarchies of pictorial genres and mediums. Chalk drawing was a kindred medium to popular illustration, having strong ties to caricature and having emerged roughly around the same time as the engraving processes favoured during the golden age of illustration. In this sense, the institutions set on identifying aesthetic clowns and staging artistic work in illustration could function as a revealing context for the lightning sketch, casting Blackton's sketches as a demonstration of skill in a new, anti-hierarchical, commercial medium. This was not their only effect to be sure, but it is one that makes sense particularly when considering the fact that the clean-cut Gibson's criticism of the decadence of painters goes hand in hand with his professional work as founding president of the Society of Illustrators. Blackton and Gibson were both professional illustrators who experimented with new media and forms of distribution. While they worked in different spheres, they each sought to break down hierarchies of fine arts through a combination of satire and professionalisation. They engaged, parodied and thus comically demystified the process of composition using a medium that, like illustration, stood to benefit from the dismantling of the hierarchies of types of studio work.

THE MOVING IMAGE JUMPS THE FRAME

The image of the artist's workspace, functioning as an instructive space in the age of picture appreciation, runs into distinct challenges when it is adopted by cinema. While searching for links to aesthetic education, how does one account for the shocks, surprises and sudden transformations that characterise not only the broader landscape of early cinema, but specifically early films in which the other arts make an appearance? The notion of a cinema of attractions, not necessarily in the ways that Tom Gunning's field-defining essays theorised it but in the way the phrase often serves as a shorthand to describe most moving pictures before 1907, has de-emphasised those elements of early films that might highlight restraint and encourage the viewer to contemplate and reflect on the image. Lest these shorthand appropriations of the concept of attractions relegate decorous compositions and thoughtful viewing to irrelevant status, a polite and insignificant crosscurrent of an impolite fairground medium, an early history of art cinema must point out at that films produced in the first decade of moving pictures could also extend, not explode, aesthetic traditions rooted in the other arts and thus could, in some cases, even cooperate with the interests of professional arts societies and reformers in arts education.

Early motion pictures that borrow from the other visual arts certainly could work in a contemplative mode, even outside of the lyceum. Charles Musser, for example, has identified a 'cinema of contemplation' in opposition to the 'visual eruptions' of the cinema of attractions. He argues that films operating in this mode 'encouraged spectators to experience a mesmerizing absorption'. Landscape films like *Niagra Falls* (Lumière, 1897) evoked the tradition of Cole and Church, and tableau vivant films invited contemplative comparisons to original artworks. This mode depends on exhibition format (i.e., looped films allowing sustained viewing) as much as a particular film's mode of address, but when these conditions are met they encourage the same kind of gaze that art-appreciation groups sought to cultivate at the turn of the century. Musser notes how often the gilt frame surrounds moving pictures in advertisements in order to encourage contemplative modes of viewing borrowed from painting. By putting the image in a frame they work to 'mesmerise', not shock, the viewer.[10] To the extent that moving pictures set in artists' studios help to frame pictures and reveal the labour of artists they, too, belong in the category of an early cinema of contemplation.

And yet art-studio films never seem to behave. The framings in studio films would seldom be as interesting were they not also ambivalent about the function of the frame. They commonly encourage a contemplative mode, but they do so while presenting a kind of boundary that asks to be crossed. They dare the moving image to jump out of the frame, usually through a process of magical transformation. Early films that recall painting and sculpture, particularly the ones that place the viewer in the studios of these other arts, were more often than not frame-jumping films. They dramatised the moment of transformation from still to moving image, from painting to life and from life to sculptural form. What happened so often inside of studio scenes, increasingly when these scenes were presented in moving pictures, was precisely not a methodical illustration of the artist's process. More often than not in these scenes of creation in an artist's workspace bodies, objects and apparitions jumped from one medium to another, from pictorial space to diegetic space, or from still to moving images. Artist's-dream films readily staged tricks and superimpositions whose magical transformations depended on the creation of a picture. Lightning sketch artists employed them too. They choreographed their performances not as a step-by-step progression, but as a kind of sudden transformation. By waiting until the last moment to draw the crucial part that makes the image recognisable – the eyes of a face, for example – the lightning sketch performance could follow the dynamic of the magic show more closely than the how-to manual.[11] Accounting for films about the artist's studio as scenes of reflection on art means also considering these scenic metalepses, these magical effects around the act of composition.[12]

It is not a coincidence that these frame-jumping effects are omnipresent in early films that reflect on the pictorial arts. Dissolving magic lantern views, tableaux vivants and comedic sketches had all played with the boundaries between static compositions and moving scenes, but early motion picture technology provided new possibilities for augmenting these frame-jumping effects of other pictorial traditions. The first Lumière exhibitors staged the transition from still to moving picture, which offered a spectacle of moving from one medium (the magic lantern) to another (motion pictures) just as much as it presented movement as a spectacle in itself. The motion picture could augment the tableau vivant, too, with its relative lack of depth perception. When a body, filmed in a frame, is posing completely still, it is much easier to read as a two-dimensional figure in a painting or on a poster. The frame-jumping effect amplifies when this body suddenly joins the artist or the poster admirer in motion.

In order to address the question of how these startling cross-media effects relate to the contemplative mode of art appreciation, I take a different tack than other studies of the picture come-to-life. Lynda Nead's expansive study of moving pictures in nineteenth-century visual culture focuses on the uncanny dimension of this Pygmalion effect.[13] She explores the rupturing of the frame of the static composition as a kind of haunting, interpreting themes of sudden animation in terms of cultural anxieties about the boundaries between living reality and dead images. What remain to be explored in greater detail are the intermedial reflections that these haunting animations have in common with the comedic and the instructional transformations performed inside the studio. Metaphors of death, rupture and haunting all imply irreversibility, and in cases when these entertainments reflect on their mediums, reversibility is precisely the attraction. The forming of a picture commands as much attention as the bursting of a picture's frame, and often both happened in the same performance. This is why, despite its less catchy resonance, I prefer the term 'frame-jumping' to 'frame-bursting'.[14] The metaphor of bursting the pictorial frame, whether by surprising movement or integrated live performances, could potentially mislead if it only implied a one-way destruction of the static composition. Frame-jumping effects do not dramatise a final casting off of the confining frame with movement. The effects of mechanical movement or moving models shift back and forth across this boundary, highlighting a change in perception essential to the appreciation of pictures.

One reason frame-jumping attractions might appear antithetical to absorbed film viewing is because absorption has typically been cast in editing-based terms. Other aesthetic traditions point to alternative models of cinematic absorption. The staple texts used by American art educators at the turn of the century repeatedly ask their audience to imagine these frame-jumping effects as they learn to appreciate a work. Vasari's ever-reprinted volumes encourage readers to see the 'living' flesh in Raphael's paintings and to look closely at the Mona Lisa's neck to 'behold the very beating of her pulses'.[15] Conversely, the creation of static form from life was an equally compelling transformation. Art educators invited students to imagine the transformation of a landscape or a face into a picture. Using texts from a patchwork of canonical authors including Vasari, Lessing and Ruskin, American art educators mobilised the fantasy of sudden animation and the fantasy of a sudden fixing of a recognisable composition in order to teach a broader public how to be engaged with, and thus to appreciate, pictures. These same fantasies flourished in early films about art.

Frame-jumping is at once an astonishing effect and an effective tool. What could justifiably be seen as the antithesis of absorption or contemplation can become its instrument. Frame-jumping can foster appreciation of aesthetics by promoting absorption and contemplation. The films of the artist's studio feed on the popular interest in the studio space and reflect on aesthetic absorption in a way that borders, at times, on the didactic. In these settings for transforming life into composition (and often, magically, compositions back into life), the art in early cinema overlapped with early art cinema. These scenes helped address questions fundamental to thinking about cinema in aesthetic terms, to conceiving of the handmade in a mechanical medium, and to considering aesthetic contemplation at a time when shifts in the media landscape seemed to signal its rapid decline.

TRILBYANA: TRANSFORMATION AND ABSORPTION

Since DuMaurier's illustrations of studio life were some of the best known, it should not come as a surprise that the phenomenon of 'Trilbyana', as an 1890s publication dubbed the frequently recycled situations and characters from *Trilby*, provides a wealth of examples of the films and performances that employed frame-jumping effects.[16] One could say that the reception of *Trilby*, especially in North America, was a pictorial reception as much as a discursive one. First, DuMaurier's experience as an illustrator for *Punch* far outstripped his abilities as a novelist. These illustrations took precedence above the text as the story gained popularity. *Trilby*'s public presence took the form of a network of interrelated pictures. The illustrated journals printed stills from the plays as well as cartoons spoofing them. Within a few years of the initial publication, several films were made from the story.[17] As its images and plot situations became part of the vernacular, the number of amateur and professional burlesques and adaptations increased exponentially. Gestures, poses and styles of dress became famous through continual translation across visual media. Numerous copyright battles were fought over cartoons, photographs and unofficial adaptations. Legal rights became increasingly difficult to defend in proportion to the unprecedented volume and variety of pictorial references.[18] The styles of movement and dress of Trilbymania spanned from burlesque houses to highbrow parlours, as evidenced by the newspaper accounts of drawing room tableau vivant performances based on the illustrations.[19] And these performances occasionally made it out of the drawing rooms, as was the case with art educator Eric Pape's production of *Scenes and Songs from 'Trilby'*, on 9 February 1895. The same translatability that lent itself so well to mass distribution of the novel rendered these ubiquitous images difficult to control. As these runaway adaptations took off, they began to encircle similar themes.

The most striking consistency among the burlesques, brief citations and full adaptations is the way that they combine mesmeric absorption and influence with the production of a picture or the translation from one medium to another. These entertainments undeniably prefigure the effects seen in films like *The Artist's Dilemma*. In many of these burlesques Trilby and other characters freeze into pictures under mesmeric influence, and pictures come to life under this influence. In a burlesque of the story called *Thrilby*, performed at the Garrick Theatre in New York in 1895, the mesmerist 'Spaghetti' uses his influence to freeze the characters into a series of tableaux.[20] In the 1897 vaudeville sketch 'Fun in an Artist's Studio', a disguised Svengali uses his power to transform the artworks in the studio. He points at a canvas to make it change into different paintings and then mesmerises a statue of Trilby. The statue then emerges from the pose and does the Trilby dance popularised by *A Model Trilby*.[21] A visual record of this barefoot dance can still be seen in the film, *Ella Lola a la Trilby* (Edison, 1898). The most visually concise example from the period of Trilbymania is *The Poster Girls and the Hypnotist* (Biograph, 1899). A mesmerist makes passes over a couple of posters, causing the women posing as billboard images to step off the wall and walk away with him.[22] Mesmerists since the 1850s had demonstrated their craft by freezing subjects before an audience.[23] The *Trilby* phenomenon exploited this cultural trope of the frozen mesmeric subject to present transformation into and out of pictorial form.

Making Movies into Art

This fantasy of mediated mesmerism spanned lowbrow and highbrow entertainments and ventured into the territory of aesthetic education. The burlesques and adaptations repurposed DuMaurier's ponderous comedy of manners as a vehicle to reflect on the relationship between the moving image and pictorial media. These versions repeatedly use the tableau vivant and trick cinematography like that seen in *The Artist's Dilemma* because the liminal character of these techniques makes them especially suited to staging the jump from one medium to another. If the adaptations are reflexive, then the theme of mesmerism becomes reflexive as well. Mesmeric absorption becomes a useful fantasy for thinking through the questions of attraction and absorption in pictures – the very same questions that art educators sorted out for their students of composition. Considering the *Trilby* adaptations together gives a better sense of how frame-jumping and the rapt absorption of the mesmerised infuse turn-of-the-century media culture that spanned the vaudeville house, the school, the lyceum and the salon.

Trilbyana's frame-bursting effects – in which mesmerism catalyses transitions between action and static pictures – explore, in the domain of vernacular performance, the same types of media metaphors explored by aesthetic educators and early film theorists. They illustrate the need to account for alternative models for conceiving of absorption in early cinema. The classical account of absorption has as its foundation editing and the unfolding of the narrative, but the focus on this tradition in film studies has overshadowed the pictorial theories of absorption that bore more direct relevance to early art cinema. The intellectual history of art education can nuance a stark opposition between frame-jumping and absorption without denying the startling discontinuities of frame-jumping effects. This other tradition of absorption, pictorial contemplation, comes to cinema from the visual arts.[24] It accompanies early cinema into the feature film, and remains a central preoccupation of art educators who ventured into discussion of moving pictures. Pictorial contemplation in film, even during its media-reflexive interruptions of the story's action, does not necessarily distance the spectator from the film. It exists as a countercurrent to narrative absorption, offering its own type of absorption.

I do not want to claim that one would be mistaken in pointing out the abundance of editing- and story-based approaches to cinematic absorption in this period. Hugo Münsterberg's film theory (although even Münsterberg's book contains elements of a theory of pictorial beauty – a byproduct of his classicism) is an illustrative contrast to the tradition I am exploring, especially because it links an editing-based approach to hypnotism.[25] Münsterberg invokes hypnotism repeatedly throughout *The Photoplay*, usually in order to argue that film's freedom from the limitations of space, time and causality (in contrast to theatre) are the basis for its power of suggestion and hence its aesthetic force.[26] 'The whole technique of the rapid changes of scenes, which we have recognized as so characteristic of the photoplay, involves at every end point elements of suggestion which, to a certain degree, link the separate scenes as the afterimages link the separate pictures.'[27] Münsterberg establishes here and throughout his book a direct chain from the movement between frames to the movement between shots and scenes. He maintains that linking frames into motion and linking shots into scenes requires an activity of the mind.[28] From the first movements of the shutter on, the film departs from the requirements of the physical world and directly engages the spectator. This engagement heightens film's power of suggestion over theatre, of which the 'extreme case is, of course, that of the hypnotizer whose word awakens in the mind of the hypnotized person ideas which he cannot resist'.[29]

Pictorial aesthetics and the film industry are the subject of the next chapters, but I want to return to Vachel Lindsay to conclude this section because his writings on film art, written around the same time and in epistolary correspondence with Münsterberg, speak directly to the possibility of absorbing frame-jumping effects. When Lindsay, as much a showman as a poet, seeks to define moving-image art, he uses a frame-jumping imaginary to do so. In *The Art of the Moving Picture* he sets painting, sculpture and architecture into motion, structuring the book around a metaphor of artworks animated. But, like the traditions of using animation to teach art, these fantasies of art come-to-life do not provoke anxiety. They illustrate what the attentive eye already saw in great works of painting and sculpture, and they reveal the sculptural form that the attentive eye will eventually learn to see in cinema. He imagines the body of a Kwakwaka'wakw actor from *In the Land of the Head Hunters* (1914) as a moving bronze sculpture like *The Sun Vow* (1899), and he sees the stills from a moving picture as pictures in a gallery collection.[30] Among his favourite actors, he frequently mentions the sculptural quality of Douglas Fairbanks's body. In *The Progress and Poetry of the Movies* he compares Fairbanks's modern athleticism to the tradition of the Diaghilev ballet, as movement that forces one to imagine a static composition.[31] 'Michael Mordkin, leaping from one end of the stage to the other, seemed to pause in midair, seemed for a curious instant to be half-suspended there. ... It was indeed a curious illusion, a conquest of the eye. This same slow motion leap, which was later developed by the slow motion camera, is carried on now by Douglas Fairbanks.'[32] Lindsay's move from the perceived suspension of a *Ballets russes* dancer through slow- motion cinematography to the brawny balletic leaps of Fairbanks invites comparison to Alexander Black's move from the painterly composed instant of his diver to the sculpted motion of his 'slow movies'.

The interest in Lindsay's theories of a universal language have made it easy for film historians to forget that for Lindsay, as for his art-education mentors from 1905, absorption is a pictorial affair. Moreover, following traditions of education in the visual arts, not in syntax or narration, he mobilises the fantasy of animation – of a suddenly or subtly living picture – to teach his audience how to be absorbed in a composition. Moving images realised this fantasy. In *The Art of the Moving Picture*, Lindsay notes how he wants to film the famous murals at the Boston Public Library. He imagined motion to spring from static works, and also to be inscribed in them. We miss a salient aspect of early film theory if we do not understand ideas like these to be linked to his early art education. Before he began to write about cinema, Lindsay tried his hand at the art lecture. These lectures took place in 1905, not far from the performances of frame-jumping Trilbyana, when he was still a student at the New York School of Art founded by William Merritt Chase, Robert Henri and Frank Alvah Parsons. The student notebook at the Parsons archive reveals that Lindsay lectured on a number of topics (besides Chase's sartorial cunning). Those familiar with Lindsay's fervent, mystical Americanism will not be surprised to learn that his favourite subject was American art. Even when he lectured on Buddhist art (another of his eclectic interests), he managed to interpret Buddhist work as Rooseveltian.[33] His lecture on the painter, lecturer and author of art-education textbooks John LaFarge betrays a young Lindsay interested in imagining fluidity between still pictures and moving shadows. He instructs the students to examine LaFarge's *The Ascension of Our Lord* at the Church of the Ascension on Tenth Street not far from Chase's studio. Like a good museum copyist, the student sketched LaFarge's painting in his notebook and annotated it with Lindsay's instructions to notice how, while LaFarge 'cribbed from the old masters', in his painting 'the shadows were not so dead'. They gave 'rather the sensation of a passing shadow touching the surface'.[34] From the sensation of motion in painting to a theory of painting in motion, Lindsay revelled in these intermedial metaphors. These brief passages place Lindsay in the lecture hall, surrounded by the students of Henri and Parsons. This scene, taking place in one of the most influential and enduring spaces of art education in the country, offers a compelling link between the fantasies of living work in art-education discourse and one of the first books that attempted to theorise the moving picture as jumping from, and into, the frame of art.

LEJAREN À HILLER'S *NEVER-TOLD TALES OF A STUDIO*

Trilbyana persisted, after DuMaurier's death, in films and performances of the 1910s. Many of these adaptations, not the least of which was Maurice Tourneur's production for Equitable/World in 1915, continued to combine haunting tableaux and a stylised setting with sudden shifts in address. But if the aim here (Tourneur returns in a later chapter) is to establish Trilbyana's connection to the networks of illustrators and institutions of art education, then the creation and aftereffects of another *Trilby* story deserve attention. The largely forgotten film series created by Lejaren à Hiller, beginning with *The Sleep of Cyma Roget* in 1919–20 and continuing through the Triart films of the early 20s that brought famous paintings to life, demonstrates the kinds of elaborate (if brief) alliances that could form during attempts to make movies into art.

In order to make sense of Hiller's rich and esoteric films it is imperative to first understand the context of his studio portraits and his staging of the portrait studio. Hiller was not a film-maker by profession. He was a commercial photographer, with an artistic reputation, who made his living staging tableaux for illustrated magazines. A member of the Society of Illustrators, he is best known as a pioneer in the shift to photographic illustration. He was indebted Gibson and DuMaurier, and like them he was obsessed with the studio space as a fantastic historical setting filled with the types and activities of the turn-of-the-century artist. He only embarked on his first film project after he had established himself, like William Merrit Chase before him, by marketing the trappings and workings of his studio space. But whereas Chase categorically rejected aesthete clowning, Hiller staged his studio practice in playful quotation of studio types. Hiller amplified the bohemian lifestyle mocked by DuMaurier and Gibson, but he also tempered these visions by continually showcasing his craft as a photographer and his ability to manage a productive commercial studio. A critic for the *New York Tribune* summed up the sentiment about Hiller's studio around the time he began making films when he described the photographer's 'mysterious, yet mechanically perfect darkroom', as a place that combined 'business, craftsmanship, human interest, and art – a truly entertaining spot'.[35]

Hiller posing as a painter with models in his photography studio (Courtesy of Visual Studies Workshop)

Hiller tried to live *Trilby* from his student years well into the 1920s. His sketchbooks and diaries as a young art student in Paris read like an uncensored version of DuMaurier's novel, with drawings of can-can dancers, cats in garret apartments and his artist's-model companion smoking in bed or exiting the apartment in an ill-fitting Trilby-like topcoat on a mission, the caption notes, to find cocaine.[36] His performance of this lifestyle in 1910s Greenwich Village gained attention for him and his studio, and one of his real skills was his ability to recast his 1890s Latin Quarter-style excesses as fashionable eccentricities of the emerging white-collar creative class. When Hiller was not making tableaux for magazines, he photographed hundreds of models and showcased his studio for an interested public. Models debriefed the press with 'true stories' of the professionalism of his studio.[37] Wealthy women posed for him seeking both social notoriety and possible commercial success in advertising or the cinema.[38] Hiller actively participated in these activities. He was known to don costumes and jump into the frame with his models. When an illustrator's trade journal or newspaper decided to run articles about his studio space, he often staged his own self-portrait. He shot himself with full studio lighting and sometimes with props. If alone, he would stand in a jaunty posture with a smirk, with his gaze to the side and sleeves rolled up, ready for work. If in long shot, he would stage himself in a tableau of the artist at work

Making Movies into Art

with the model in the studio. After spending several days browsing the photographs and newspaper illustrations in Hiller's archive, one realises the difficulty in drawing a clear line between the types of self-presentation in the newspaper articles about Hiller and the photographs in which he posed with his models.

With his first film, which he produced largely with his own money and the help of a borrowed group of Vitagraph actors, Hiller expanded the public reputation of his studio space into the educational sphere. He says in his proposal for the films 'the whole plot is laid around an artist's life and the majority of the scenes are to be laid in the studio that I lived in at 151 w 23rd St for eight years. To incorporate into this scheme whatever experiences or incidents of any interest that might seem fit that occurred to me directly or indirectly as an art student for the last 25 years.' He lists his own experiences in the 23rd Street studio as raw material for the films: 'The Hindu slight of hand performer who used to come around. Committee meetings of the Society of Illustrators. Fencing, and a real duel. As many well-known artists as possible should be introduced.'[39] The scenes he describes alternate between the sensational and the practical, between bohemian melodrama and meetings of well-known artists and professional arts committee members. Sometimes it is difficult to distinguish which came first. Fencing matches, duels and magicians could be found just as easily in the fictions of the studio as in Hiller's memoirs.

The result of this experiment, which survives only in fragments, was released under a few different names that reflect this combination of mesmerist fantasy and studio document. It was first called *The Sleep of Cyma Roget*, then *The Devil's Angel*. Critics for the *New York Times*, *Moving Picture World* and *Wid's Daily* preferred the series title: *Never-told Tales of a Studio*.[40] Far from being a never-told tale, the film must have seemed quite familiar to many viewers. It clearly recycled *Trilby*, returning to the stereotypes and plot lines generated by DuMaurier and Gibson. A young artist's model, Cyma, moves into a studio space occupied by three art students. As in *Trilby*, these young men try to help her escape the influence of a Svengali-like 'Hindoo scientist', a mesmerist who comes out of the mysterious East, whose influence plagues her even after his death. Many of the tableaux, in this film structured as a series of tableaux, so resembled *Trilby* that they could have been used as illustrations for DuMaurier's book. The playful homosocial scenes in which the artist's model poses for the three young artists (one of whom was played by Hiller himself), and in which they make her a bed on the floor next to their triple-decker bunk bed strongly evoke the playful scenes between Trilby and the trio of young art students illustrated together in the novel as 'the three musketeers of the brush'. The climactic tableaux mirrors Trilby's death scene. With influence that continues beyond the grave, the orientalised mesmerist, like Svengali, renders Cyma unconscious. Only Hiller reversed *Trilby*'s tragic ending, having the artists effectively resurrect the model and save her from a premature grave.

If titling the film *The Sleep of Cyma Roget* emphasises the haunting influence of the mesmerist, referring to it as the first in a series of *Never-told Tales of a Studio* indicates what Hiller understood, as with *Trilby*, to be its more unique value. He distinguished himself as an outsider to cinema, claiming in an interview that having spent more time in painter's studios than in film studios made him particularly suited to bring this world into motion pictures. 'Never before has the real "atmosphere" of the painter's studio been revealed in the pictureplay. The absence of experience and first-hand

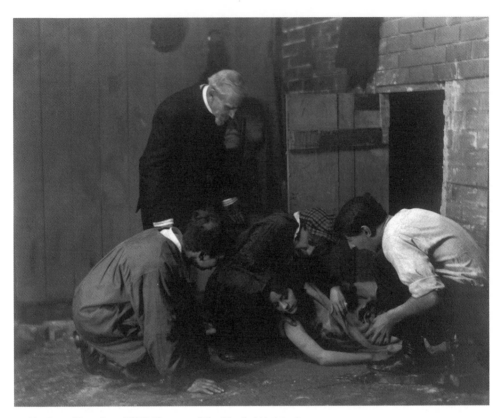

The Sleep of Cyma Roget (1920) (Courtesy of Visual Studies Workshop)

information on the part of directors who have heretofore essayed to depict studio life has made it impossible for them to accomplish this object with truth and sincerity.'[41] It is no exaggeration to say that he intended the film as a kind of diorama of a studio. Not only did he integrate the same props used in his old working studio, he also integrated the space itself. He had recently moved uptown, to a much larger studio, after finally deciding to take a position with Underwood and Underwood.[42] Declaring his new corporate space to have an unsuitable *mise en scène* for the project, Hiller built inside it a detailed replica of his former studio to be used as the main setting for his series.

As meticulous as Hiller was in his pursuit of accurate detail, the final film looked unlike any purely informational diagram. Like other *Trilby* adaptations, including Tourneur's well-received production, Hiller's film betrays an interest in décor worthy of a set designer for Symbolist theatre and a mastery of lighting and exposure in league with Pictorialist photographers. As an illustrator, he was known for bringing art photography, with its pictorial *mise en scène* and 'Rembrandt lighting', to advertisements in *Cosmopolitan* and *Ladies' Home Journal*.[43] In his film, overexposed windows, chiaroscuro and heavy asymmetrical blinds create a *mise en scène* that avidly displays its plasticity, and thus its connection to the other arts. It is precisely these qualities that make Hiller such a revealing synthesiser of the traditions and cultural

Making Movies into Art

tropes outlined above. In Hiller's film, as in his life, the chronicles of the art studio and pictorial composition work together. The setting and themes of the story seemed to authorise an ornamental pictorial style that draws attention to itself as a composition. Critics saw this composition as another guarantor of skill.[44] It complemented his claims, not unlike Gibson's and DuMaurier's, to have knowledge of the inner workings of the spaces where artists learn and practise their craft.

If *Cyma Roget's* pictorial style and connection to the mesmerising pictures of Trilbyana is not enough to confirm how much Hiller flaunted its creative anachronisms, its exhibition history surely is. Hiller contracted the road-show distributor Clark-Cornelius to release the film, and several live performers travelled with it. Helen Gardner, whose role as Cyma came at the end of a strong career with the Vitagraph Company, appeared on stage to introduce the film in Pottsville, PA. She was introduced by a prominent local publisher, who also arranged a society event to complement the screening, at which one of her gowns from the film was on display. It was perhaps her involvement in the road show that prompted *Exhibitor's Trade Review* to deem the exhibition of the film to be 'along high class lines'.[45] The other main actor in the film, Peggy O'Neil, went a step further than Gardner and performed an entr'acte in which she depicted 'a number of famous artworks' as tableaux vivants. The road show also featured a separate group of artist's models who performed 'popular poses' in a 'studio scene'. If anyone in the audience did not get that the film intended to revitalise intermedial performance traditions from the days of early cinema in order help them appreciate something about the other arts, the live prologues and entr'actes would have corrected this confusion. As he diverted his attention from photography to film, the tropes of the mythologised studio, the tableau vivant, the attraction of the artwork come to life, all seem to acquire a new vitality in Hiller's work. Compared with typical feature film exhibition, even with the more elaborate road shows, the exhibition strategy for this film framed it as a kind of return to the those performers of artist's-studio scenes who simultaneously populated the variety stage and the public lecture circuit in the early years of moving pictures.

If such thematic obsessions and exhibition strategies seem out of place in silent film history, it is this misfit that offers a rare perspective on the cultural terrain of art cinema at the time. Hiller's foray into art film-making did not constitute a career shift, but a conscious effort of someone who framed himself, productively, as an outsider to the film industry. He employed a similar battery of pictorial techniques as prestige film-makers, but his professional affiliations overlapped little with career film-makers of the time. And each of these affiliations were necessary to pull off the specific kind of ambitious cross-media convergence he had in mind for the series. Hiller the photographer created commercial photographs using Rembrandt lighting and aesthetic costumes and props. Hiller the creative-class spokesman effectively crafted a persona that merged bohemian typology with the trappings of the professional. Hiller the film-maker combined fashionable pictorial stylisation with a document of the workspace. His still portraits were finished compositions in which the studio space was transformed by chiaroscuro into a commercially polished pictorialism. His film revelled in stylised images while at the same time revealing the craft behind the polish. It illuminated the backstage of the studio as a pictorialist space of fantasy, but also as workspace and educational space, placing his studio into contact with studios of different times and traditions. This strategy served as a template for his series of educational films.

TRIART PICTURE COMPANY: FROM TRILBYANA TO ART HISTORY

The *Sleep of Cyma Roget* was made under the auspices of organisations only obliquely connected to the film industry, and so it should not have surprised everyone involved that it created its stir primarily among those organisations. DuMaurier did not live long enough to see Hiller's take on his story, but Gibson did and was thrilled with the result. In a letter to Hiller after the premiere of the film, Gibson commends Hiller's 'knowledge of composition, light and shadow' and his 'attention to accessories and details', thanking him on behalf of the Society of Illustrators.[46] In Gibson's letter, later mentioned as one of the film's laurels in the *New York Times* review, he indicates that pictorial aesthetics, combined with a detailed *mise en scène* of the artist's workspace, can further the interests of the professional organisation of which both he and Hiller were members. As president of the Society of Illustrators, Gibson volunteered to serve on a committee that would offer the institutional support and guidance needed to realise Hiller's film series. The Society of Illustrators was not the only organisation that looked favourably on the possibility of an art-film series by Hiller. Gibson was joined by the presidents of the National Sculpture Society, the National Academy of Design and the Metropolitan Museum of Art. Representing the business of the applied arts, Louis C. Tiffany agreed to round out the committee. The composition of the committee perfectly characterises the professional streamlining of art discussed in the introduction to this book and in early sections of this chapter. This cultural authority would vote on a series of paintings, and Hiller would design tableaux that would capture the spirit and some of the history of the original works.[47]

With the support of these institutional leaders, Hiller brokered a deal with producer Issac Wolper to find the best audience for the series. The financial backing would come largely from Long Island art patron, Vera Royer. The only real modification to Hiller's initial vision was that the series would be more directly educational and historical than *Never-told Tales*. Wolper knew that these films would do best to inhabit peripheral markets. He founded Triart Picture Company to cater to those specific production and marketing needs. As educational shorts, they could supplement a programme with a feature that had artistic ambitions, or they could play on their own in alternative venues. Wolper saw the possibility of a long afterlife for the films in these spaces. 'It is a fact that there are twice the number of projecting machines in the non-theatrical fields (schools, churches, clubs) than the theater. We are confident that there is a demand for such pictures wherever there is a projecting machine.'[48] Not intended to reach a mass audience at once, the films could circulate widely over time and could provide occasions for professional societies to open channels of engagement with a wider public.[49] The production and exhibition of these films could be also publicised as society intellectual events. Hiller himself supported this move in the direction of educational uplift. 'I should help familiarize people with famous paintings; create a taste for better things; in short, bring Art with a capital A to the masses.'[50]

To ensure that the format of the series was not pulled in too many directions by the various interests involved, each project would need to be consistent with the others in style and length and would try where possible to employ a common creative team (among them Herbert Blaché and Mary Astor). Each would be two reels long and would follow the same format; the *mise en scène* of the artist's studio space would frame and/or form the centre for each film. The Triart films would bring masterpieces to the masses by bringing the masses into the workspace. The films would read, thanks to Hiller's pictorially stylised staging and lighting, as equal parts art lecture and art film. As Royer explained to her hometown paper, 'Why not use the wonderful lighting effects that have been developed in movies to get people to appreciate the lighting and the coloring that artists use'?[51] Each film in the Triart series enacted this combination of art-historical content and pedagogical stylisation. They each began with a shot of the painting and explanatory intertitle that functioned like a museum caption label and then explored a pictorialist fantasy space as the living story emerged from the painting. As the painting-inspired story came to a close, each film ended in a final tableau that turned attention back to the original painting. They provided frame-jumping artist's studio films for another generation of viewers. The films looked back to the absorbing fantasies of life emerging from a picture as well as to the educational dimension of these fantasies. The first and last films in the series are the most remarkable in this regard.

The Triart advisory committee would likely not have selected Edward Burne-Jones's *King Cophetua and the Beggar Maid* for Hiller's first film if the goal were to bring five of the most important paintings, from the entire history of art, before film viewers. The choice reflects a more complex negotiation among supporters and a careful attention to the kinds of paintings best suited to an art film designed to bring them to life. The committee chose works they believed would lend themselves to the mission of aesthetic education through moving pictures, and towards this goal it seems that a work's canonical status was less important than its teachability. What *King Cophetua and the Beggar Maid* may have lacked in cultural capital in an era adjusting to modern art, it made up for in its suitability for art-educational cinema. Burne-Jones and his circle fused art and life in a compelling way. The rich biographical details of this circle, the Pre-Raphaelite Brotherhood, made for an exceptional intermedial story, as did the fact that Tennyson and Shakespeare had each written versions of the story. The pictorialism of the Pre-Raphaelites had possibly fallen from fashion in the art world, but films that aspired to art at this time were still largely pictorialist. And if some Pre-Raphaelites were partly unfashionable because of the sloppiness of their craft, Burne-Jones was an important exception. Compared with Dante Gabriel Rosetti, Burne-Jones could at least boast an attention to technique and a studio discipline perfect for a film designed to teach aesthetics by showing the inside of the studio space. Unlike others in his circle he incorporated craft techniques from the decorative arts, such as the raised sculptural bodies and gold gesso in *Cupid's Hunting Fields* (1882). He was the most art-historically minded of the Pre-Raphaelites, with an attention to the techniques of early Renaissance art that art lecturers emphasised. The selection of Pre-Raphaelite art for its accessibility and its stories and Burne-Jones for his studio craft made sense for the inaugural film of the series. It could work as an art film for critical viewers, as an educational film for a wider public and as a work suitable within the social world of backers of the series. It is telling that all of these factors came together in the film's premiere. Royer, along with fellow art patron William Brooks, hosted the film's premiere as a meeting of prominent artists and educators.[52]

The film that premiered at this society event established the structure of the films in the series – in which living characters emerge from and return to a famous painting, as a tableau vivant set in motion. The effects of early cinema merge with absorbing pictorial style and the display of a famous studio space from the first scene. Following an image of the painting and explanatory title, the scene opens in Burne-Jones's often sketched, painted and photographed parlour.[53] A large carved oak table occupies the centre of the room and an outside light casts shadows of branches and the leaded glass on the rear wall. Here Burne-Jones reads Tennyson's 'The Beggar Maid' and envisions his painting in the manner of so many projected, stereoscopic, or staged artists' dreams. An overlap dissolve transitions from a contemplative Burne-Jones to a living picture of the painting. Burne-Jones was known for figuring aesthetic absorption as trance or as sleep, an interest that fitted well with Hiller's interest in Trilbyana. Hiller begins his series with a tableau of Burne-Jones himself in a state of trance-like absorption that eventually produces a picture. All of this precedes the introduction of the characters. Before the story begins, the film presents the painting itself, then an image of the artist absorbed in his work, then the painting come to life. It returns to the frame-jumping tricks of early cinema as a way to teach the public how to appreciate art.

The film's narrative follows a cross-class romance between the two models who sit for the beggar maid painting. Burne-Jones's studio thus serves as the primary setting for the story, while his work serves as the main plot catalyst. Hiller staged the climactic scene in the studio where the two young lovers from different social worlds are brought together to pose. The final tableau, announced by the intertitle 'the work of the master', arranges artist, models, painting and beholder in a dynamic composition. The poor model's guardian lays his worries about her relationship to rest when he sees the couple, posed as King Cophetua and the beggar maid, being painted by Burne-Jones. This is the first time the guardian, and the viewer, see the painting. The staging makes it uncertain whether he is looking at the model or at the painting of her. Hiller stages the tableau precisely to make it appear that he sees her through the work of the painter. In this climactic scene, the educational and dramatic components of the film converge on the production of the work. The same brush strokes that complete the historical work also complete the formation of the romantic couple.

The Triart series seemed to grow in ambition and scope with each new film. They began to move back and forth from the past to the present, and from the old world to the new. The last selection was by far the richest in this regard. With its own significant history in the USA, and its reflexive themes of artist and subject, *Portrait of a Young Artist,* thought at the time to be painted by Rembrandt van Rijn, played directly to the Triart committee's interests and to Hiller's strengths. Like many paintings sold as Rembrandts in the nineteenth century, *Portrait of a Young Artist* has since been attributed to a follower of Rembrandt. In the early twentieth century, however, this painting was still a Rembrandt, and one of considerable reputation. Other Rembrandt paintings received more critical praise, but this work had its own claim to celebrity because of the circumstances of its acquisition. Henry Clay Frick had

Making Movies into Art

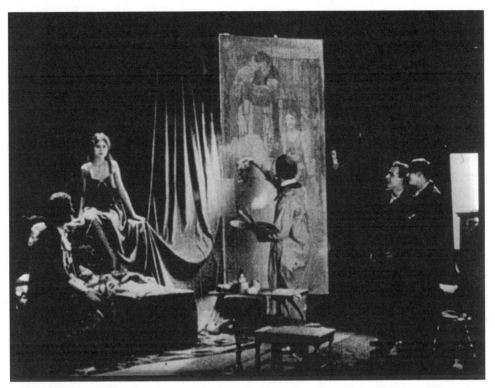

Final tableau from *The Beggar Maid* (1921) (Courtesy of George Eastman House, International Museum of Photography and Film)

purchased the painting for $38,000, moving it from its previous home in the castle of a Yorkshire earl to his home in Pittsburg. Frick was eager to translate his vast wealth, gained from his deployment of violent union-busting muscle in his steel mills, into an ambitious art collection, and Rembrandt's name recognition and cultural capital for collectors was unparallelled in the late nineteenth century. The high-profile acquisition marked the beginning of one of the most prominent private collections of old masters, particularly of seventeenth-century Dutch art, in the country. During his lifetime, Frick was notoriously protective of this collection and the private space in which he housed it. He turned down repeated offers from magazines like *Arts and Decoration* to run stories on his collection or to photograph objects in it.[54] He made only a few exceptions for institutions like the neighbouring Metropolitan Museum, where he was a board member and where president Robert De Forest was a trusted friend.[55] Upon his death in 1919, shortly before the Triart committee selected the work to be filmed, Frick left his collection to the public. The works were not to leave his house, but after the death of his widow (in 1935) the public would be granted access to the collection. Selecting *Portrait of a Young Artist* for Hiller's most ambitious film makes sense in the context of the painting's American afterlife; it was a major purchase with broad appeal, it was housed nearby and it embodied the negotiations around the public accessibility of art.

The Triart committee (probably headed by De Forest on this decision) clearly understood that this privately held work had strong potential for public motion-picture art education. It was a painting, by an old master, of a student of painting, set in a workshop. Scholarship since Triart's time has greatly expanded the knowledge of Rembrandt's workshop, repositioning him as a point in a vast network of students, assistants and imitators, including the unknown artist who actually painted *Portrait of a Young Artist*.[56] But his reputation as an educator and a workshop manager was established even in the early twentieth century. Rembrandt's studio was the most pictured in Europe at the time, and historians of his work took note of the details about this space. As a portrait, the painting does not include a vast array of tools, props and pigments, but it nevertheless shows something of the art student's process. He holds a stack of drawings or etchings of classical poses in one hand. The brush in his right hand and the pile of brushes on the table indicate that he is using the sketches as a reference, for a painting that exists outside the frame.[57] The tools, canvases and life models outside the frame are suggested even as the formal dress, lighting and frontal gaze adhere to the conventions of the portrait.

Hiller and Blaché set out to make a film that put these reflexive aspects of the painting at the forefront, and to do so they constructed what has to be among the most elaborate configurations of artists' workspaces in the history of cinema. The film frames a modern story with a scene of seventeenth-century Amsterdam in order to generate explicit discussion of the aesthetic and social relevance of Rembrandt in New York in the early twentieth century. This is a common enough pedagogical strategy, but the central tableaux of the film make clear that Hiller was interested not simply in Rembrandt the man (and his works), but in Rembrandt the workshop leader. Hiller's *The Young Painter* (1922) can be read as specifically concerned with the way an old master's workspace could inform modern depictions of the studio workspace.

While all of the surviving material from Hiller's films indicates his fascination with the artist's workspace, Hiller exploited this choice of original work with a *mise en abyme* of reflections on the studio. *The Young Painter* rests on an armature of three, linked studio spaces, each of which bears a relation to studio types that were significant in the world of art education. The film begins in Rembrandt's workshop, and the first major tableau of the film visually diagrams a kind of circular reflection on the work of the artist. The tableau forms around a scene of instruction, after a life model session, during which the viewer witnesses the creation of the *Portrait of a Young Artist*. Rembrandt becomes absorbed by the exercises of a young art student in his workshop, who refuses to end his workday and dutifully copies a piece of educational sculpture. To show Rembrandt composing his picture of the young artist, composing his picture of the sculpture, Hiller positions Rembrandt's canvas directly behind the sculpture. He creates a closed triangle or circle in which the sculpture as pedagogical tool lines up with the master painting the student, who copies its form. Hiller continues this relay across three centuries with his next cut. Roland, a young artist and World War veteran contemplates Rembrandt's portrait in his rural Long Island studio. We learn this is not the original painting but yet another educational copy the painter made as an art student while the painting was hanging at an unnamed gallery. Fusing fiction and

Rembrandt and student in his studio. *The Young Painter* (1922) (Courtesy of George Eastman House, International Museum of Photography and Film)

historical fact as these films do, perhaps De Forest, Blaché and Hiller imagined it to be the Metropolitan Museum's exhibition of the painting in 1909. In any case, the modern young painter has an old master. First created in the seventeenth century, the film's *Portrait of a Young Artist* moved from an English castle to an American museum exhibit, where it was copied by the young art student.[58] His copy hangs in the centre of his rural studio, where it inspires his own masterpiece: another portrait of a young artist named Helen (Mary Astor), whom he teaches how to paint. The work that forms the centrepiece of this film is a copy of a painting about a student learning to paint, and it serves as inspiration for a portrait of a model, love interest and student.

If Rembrandt's studio frames the film, the characters are introduced in the second studio on Long Island and conclude their stories in the third in Manhattan. The local referents for each of these modern studio types, including those referring to famous art teachers, abounded in the illustrated press. At the beginning of his career, after his return from his studies in France, Arthur Wesley Dow converted an old store into his famous atelier in Ipswich, MA. He continued to summer with students there whenever school was not in session at Pratt or Columbia. An artist, like Dow, with ties to the Arts and Crafts movement was likely to be found in spaces like Hiller's fantasy Long Island studio. Hiller reinforced this connection by showing his young painter hewing his own firewood, sitting on handmade furniture and carefully attending to his brushes and other tools. William Merritt Chase, too, had a country studio and summer school on Long Island not far from where Hiller shot the exteriors for *The Young Painter*, at which he staged his popular tableaux vivant performances in the early 1910s. But Chase was, of course, best known for his Greenwich Village studio, which could have been one of the points of reference for the Hiller's set for studio number three, where the story ends. Because he believes social barriers to have made his love impossible, Roland moves to an urban studio in Greenwich Village where he finishes Helen's portrait – his homage to Rembrandt's portrait – from idealised memory while slowly dying of consumption. The young artist of Hiller's film moves wildly across a range of workspaces. Inspired by an old master's studio, he establishes himself in a rustic cottage studio and ends his days in a larger and well-appointed (a fact continually noted by the homeless boy he takes in) urban workspace. While Hiller's film does not directly reference Dow and Chase, it accesses the familiar lexicon of studio types that Dow and Chase used in halftones for their course advertisements in illustrated magazines.

As in the *Beggar Maid* film, the artwork and the studio space do not serve as mere background to the fiction, they drive the climactic situations. They overlap absorption in the story and contemplation of the painting. The final tableau in the Greenwich Village studio offers just such simultaneous closure to the love story and to the pedagogical themes of art appreciation. Since Hiller the commercial photographer loved careful composition as much as he hated subtlety, this web of reflexive associations among artists, their props, paintings and students is instantly legible. Viewers of his films needed not wait for intertitles or character actions to provide clarity and closure. Hiller delivers the appropriate 'too late' bedside tableau called for by this melodrama, but he also stages the painter's deathbed in the open studio space. The portrait of Helen occupies the centre of the frame as a record of his final living efforts, and the Rembrandt copy haunts the frame in the background. Hiller maintains the link between this space, the modern narrative and the old master, by ending the film in a workspace filled, not only with characters, but also with their works. The spirit of Rembrandt that Hiller and Blaché superimpose on the image to guide the painter's spirit seems redundant, but what it lacks in subtlety it gains in richness of association with the common uses of these superimposed spirits in nineteenth-century visual culture from the Pepper's Ghost illusion on stage, to the superimposed imaged of ghosts in magic lantern shows, print photographs and early cinema projections. Hiller and Blaché use a technique more at home in early cinema to make Rembrandt's spirit jump the frame into the contemporary Manhattan studio. In this climactic moment cluttered with reflexive references to the other arts and other times, the trick cinematography functions as part haunting, part artist's fever dream and part allegory of the artistic satisfaction of having completed a new masterwork.

The Young Painter was Triart's most reflexive film. And given that Hiller's flair for presenting his own studio space inspired his venture into motion pictures, it would seem incomplete to conclude this section without returning to this original studio space, the one not depicted in any of the Triart films, but still present in their larger mission. *The Young Painter* in particular provided an important intermedial link between historical studios with easels and modern studios with cameras. The business of the commercial artist and the name of Rembrandt were deeply intertwined by the

Final tableau from *The Young Painter* (1922) (Courtesy of George Eastman House, International Museum of Photography and Film)

late nineteenth century. Nineteenth-century Rembrandt portraits, the Rembrandt process in etching, Rembrandt colour paints 'made in Holland' and Rembrandt lighting in 1880s photography are just a few of the examples how the professions of commercial illustration, design, art supply, photography and (soon after) film avidly traded in the cultural currency of Rembrandt's name. Hiller, a commercial photographer known for his pictorial compositions, knew that the subject matter of *The Young Painter* alone would remind viewers of chiaroscuro, rich colours and virtuoso depictions of the human face and hands.[59] But Hiller's particular interest in Rembrandt's studio serves as a reminder that commercial photography and cinema relied on Rembrandt for something more. Svetlana Alpers has shown how Rembrandt's shadowy late-period portraits mark a reflexive moment when 'the relation between the painter and his model(s) in an interior space was made a subject of art'. She claims that reflection on the studio space as performative space was mimicked in nineteenth-century studios where photographers, more than simply dropping Rembrandt's name to denote an artful portrait, 'orchestrated the staging of life [in their studios] that was implicit in the Rembrandt studios'.[60] Hiller's work continued precisely this tradition in which professional photography sought to model its own studio practice on traditions in painting that mythologise the relationship between the artist and sitter, and that reflect on the studio space as a space of performance.

CONCLUSION: PATCHWORK METHODS, COMMON GOAL

Triart may not have been the most typical, enduring, or profitable film enterprise, but its brief series vividly captures a particular constellation of art, education and early cinema. Where a broad cultural history of the art studio and moving pictures can point out thematic currents that run between the illustrations of Charles Dana Gibson and early films set in the artist's studio, between frame-jumping tableaux vivants and art education, or between early cinema's multi-media history and the idea of art cinema in the late 1910s, the Triart archive demonstrates how all of these connections could work together in a single project. It is one thing to argue – as in the first part of this chapter – that the intellectual history of aesthetic education and the rise of commercial illustration overlap in the vernacular afterlife of *Trilby*; it is another thing entirely to have a record of Gibson himself, so pleased by a *Trilby* film created by one of his colleagues in the Society of Illustrators, that he agrees to co-sponsor, with the Metropolitan president, a series of elaborate tableaux vivants designed to teach people how to appreciate pictures. The kinds of associations among professional arts societies, aesthete ateliers, art collectors and motion pictures that have to be painted with broad cultural-historical strokes in the first section of the chapter, course explicitly through the archived details of Triart's never-told tales. Triart was not itself an enduring institution. It was a tactical alignment of enduring institutions. The series brought cinema into direct contact with a diverse group of arts professionals, each of whom had his or her own stake in redefining art education.

Modern art educators of many stripes had to reckon with tradition in order to promote a vision of art pedagogy that suited both professionalising commercial artists and an expanding public interest in art appreciation. In both spheres it became useful to teach picture study, or composition, more as a process in a workspace than as a kind of inspiration passed down along a rigid hierarchy of great works. This growing movement was compatible with those seeking to appreciate art, with people who wanted to teach picture study in high schools and with aspiring design professionals. The Triart series points out one way this intellectual history could merge with ideas of motion-picture aesthetics. Everyone involved in the Triart series sought to reflect on the possibilities of cinema and to strengthen the connections between film art and painting. Their efforts addressed a set of questions not far from emergent theories of moving-image aesthetics. They bring to the surface a minor current in the intermedial films of early cinema and a major, but underexplored, current in the first theories film art: that spectators can be absorbed, not only in the moving picture's literary qualities, but also in its pictures.

But this approach is not without its contradictions, which I should address in a final point before the next chapter's detailed discussion of early cinematic theories of pictorial composition and absorption. The challenge of linking cinema, photography and popular illustration to this movement in art appreciation, one that runs through many of the examples in this book, is that whenever those working in commercial media express pictorial ambitions, they draw from the other arts so wildly. The film-makers, photographers and critics discussed in each of these chapters are nothing if not difficult to pin down within a single pictorial tradition or art movement. Hiller's appropriations from three centuries of art history offer a case in point. In returning once more to the art educators with whom I began the chapter I want to suggest that the abundance of citations of the other arts, even the citation of styles that fundamentally contradict one another, do not necessarily contradict a more stable notion of pictorial composition.

American art education faced this particular artist's dilemma long before its exchanges with cinema. The fact that educators like Dow and Chase worked to build efficient, composition-focused courses and studios never required of them a rigid or homogeneous curriculum. On the contrary, one of the distinguishing characteristics of American schools is how they felt entitled to appropriate and combine educational practices from different times and different countries. More than a single tradition, the American art academies formed piecemeal, as a patchwork assemblage of educational practices: from the Kensington school, from the Parisian atelier system (before Impressionism), from the Arts and Crafts movement, or from Japanese watercolour training. Even as the management of the working and teaching studios professionalised and fed the growing design industries, the methods across and within schools were allowed to be quite eclectic. The advertisements for the Art Student's League of New York, where Chase taught painting for many years, sometimes seem willfully out of place. Photographs used in the League advertisements between 1900 and 1915 showcased the life class while other branches of the applied- and fine-arts curriculum, which boasted fine career prospects, never made the cut as promotional images. The life class was one of the strongest gestures to the nineteenth-century French and British schools that still captured the American public imagination and still inspired pilgrimages by aspiring American artists.[61] Many schools, while they taught courses in modern applied arts, sought to simulate the nostalgic systems already outstripped by the influence of modernist traditions and of more practical curriculum developments. Far from erasing their origins as out of date, the publicity material for dozens of schools around the country traded in scenes of the studio that proudly displayed their appropriations. The patchwork of studio practices created spaces of performance that pointed to the places and times valorised by books and lectures on the arts in history.

This patchwork nature of American art education is one of the realities that made theories of composition so effective. Because composition is an abstract and non-genre-specific approach to aesthetics, one that tries not to distinguish between the fine and decorative arts, it could unite a broad range of activities in the teaching studio. Theorists of art education aimed to put diverse practices – such as the life class, copying from classical sculpture, or print-making – onto the same field, and thus to open up art education not only to a small group of apprentices but also to a wider public for appreciation. For the casual student of art, there is a move towards recognising artistic production in any medium as the work of composition. One versatile way of presenting that work to the public was to bring the public into the workspaces. Using examples from Rembrandt's workshop to the original Parsons classes in Chase's 10th Street studio, art educators could break down outmoded structures of cultural authority and stage art as composition, as a much more accessible form of work. Posing for pictures, dressed up and engaged with students in their studios, educators like Chase helped to show the public where twentieth-century art education was headed, even as their curricula seemed like a mottled pastiche of the past. Picture study could bring each of these instances of looking backward onto the same plane as interchangeable performances. Studio spaces and the work that transpired inside could be linked, and they are in Hiller's films across centuries and across oceans. In this sense there is something of the *Portrait of a Young Artist* in Sargent's *William Merritt Chase*. Each portrait incorporates work in process, but also acknowledges the viewer. The artist meets the eye with his gaze, but also with his sartorial precision. He conducts the work of the studio, holding the tools of the trade, but he emerges from the oily background into the warm portrait light in full acknowledgment of the formality of this act of performance.

3

Cinema Composition: The University and the Industry

By the mid-1910s, certain films' status as art, as something worthy of study, re-exhibition and preservation, had emerged as a regular topic of debate among critics. An old and prestigious university would naturally believe itself to be in a position to move these debates forward and find the art within the new medium, even if a practical college film curriculum was still a long way off. In the autumn of 1915, Columbia University took this step and added the first in a series of courses on 'Photoplay Composition' to its successful university extension programme. Taught by recent drama PhD Victor O. Freeburg and soon after by film critic and screenwriter Frances Taylor Patterson, these film courses were in many ways the first of their kind. Freeburg and Patterson projected films and stills in class for close analysis; they organised demonstrations by film-industry writers and directors to help teach the craft of screenwriting; and they taught many of the new works of film criticism in an effort to foster appreciation of film art. The courses synthesised practical and critical exercises in order to promote better film-making through a greater appreciation of film as an aesthetic medium.

The courses were nothing if not innovative. Not only did they offer a broad theory of the aesthetics of composition in motion pictures, incorporating work by other early film theorists like Vachel Lindsay and Hugo Münsterburg, they also attempted a new level of analytical detail in their methods of visual instruction. Freeburg's courses were complemented by a student club that ensured careful viewing and reviewing of films, and practical visual examples abounded in his classroom. Not content simply to discuss cinema composition in the abstract, Freeburg regularly called on his class to compare a photograph of a work of art (by Rembrandt, Millet, or Myron) with a still from a film. He showed some film stills as examples of good composition and others as bad. He took a hands-on approach to teaching film aesthetics, often asking his students to manually cover part of a film still or to flip an image upside down in order to envision a different, better composition. In an environment where film's tendency to distract threatened its legitimacy, Freeburg and Patterson took great pains to position cinema as a medium of contemplation, not of distraction.

Columbia's early film courses may not have set contemporary academic film study in motion, but their rich archive reveals a moment of traction in the broader history of art cinema. It marks the first juncture in which Hollywood feature films made contact with a rapidly modernising and diversifying higher education system. And this point of contact, this conception of film art, occurs under the sign of picture craft. I have been arguing throughout this book that defining early art cinema usually involved creative borrowing from other media, and that the visual arts provided abundant intellectual resources for these appropriations. The next three chapters look at creative borrowings between educational pictorial theory and early Hollywood films with highly publicised pictorial style. The cinema composition courses at Columbia make it possible to trace these borrowings with the pedagogue's perspective in mind.

The Columbia courses' status as an initial, if not a foundational, moment in American film study has garnered occasional recognition in film history. In the past thirty years a handful of scholars have cited their work or recognised the anomaly of their programme.[1] However, an increased interest in Patterson's and some of Freeburg's work has emerged in a few more recent projects. These studies have shed light on the Columbia programme as a largely forgotten prologue to later institutional developments. Dana Polan has shown how the Columbia courses mark a first attempt at a coherent film pedagogy, which would find a lasting home in neighbouring institutions like the New School and New York University.[2] Peter Decherney has focused on the Columbia courses' relation to the culture of the film archive preceding more influential efforts such as Iris Barry's work at the Museum of Modern Art.[3] In detailing Patterson's pedagogy and institutional associations, Polan's and Decherney's recent discoveries inform my intellectual history of the specific aesthetic traditions that began to cohere in these settings.[4]

My history of the Columbia curriculum situates Freeburg's and Patterson's work within the pictorial tradition. Thus my periodisation forms a sort of prequel to Polan's and Decherney's. Rather than conceiving of Columbia's film offerings as a false start in the development of institutions of film education and archiving, I am interested in how aspects of Columbia's courses owed debts to earlier developments in art pedagogy. They derive from ideas developed in the American lyceum of the 1890s and from discourses of pictorialist photography championed by 1910s arts lecturers and by commercial photographers like Hiller. Early film educators may seem anomalous when viewed through later developments in film studies, but their lectures fit squarely within this pictorial tradition. They built on the lyceum educators' approaches to visual art, and (most importantly, although perhaps by necessity more than by explicit intent) they modernised the pictorial idealism that dominated the lecture halls.

By emphasising composition Freeburg effectively de-emphasised narration and the literary aspirations of feature films of the time. Pictorial form overshadows other art discourses. Whereas for film producers any kind of artistic legitimacy was good publicity and any form of uplift a boon, the pictorial tradition exemplified by Freeburg and continued by Patterson holds to a more specific aesthetic path. The fact that picture craft could serve a social assimilation of cinema does not mean it should be reduced to these effects and lumped together with the more robust strategies of legitimation founded on historical theatre, Broadway celebrity and literary merit. Picture craft had its own intellectual history. Freeburg's and Patterson's claims hinged on the possibility of relating cinema to the discussions about the form of canonical paintings and sculptures, which were thought to educate viewers in the fundamental principles of compositional beauty. The task was theoretical before it was practical. The effort to guide theatrical, university and museum policy went hand in hand with the effort to map traditions of studying the visual arts onto film aesthetics.

Freeburg's and Patterson's work, while not as philosophically systematic as Münsterberg's *The Photoplay*, still engages theoretical questions in motion-picture aesthetics. They consolidate ideas from the critical discourse, and they resonate with current questions in film and media theory. While they need to be understood as part of larger social histories, they also deserve to be engaged as aesthetic theory with direct application to film analysis. This is why I take care in what follows to reconstruct this work as a film theory indebted to several key figures in early twentieth-century aesthetic and pedagogical thought before discussing Freeburg's two most frequently cited Paramount films, Cecil B. DeMille's *Carmen* (1915) and James Cruze's *The Covered Wagon* (1923). Freeburg and Patterson theorised art cinema, but they also looked closely at films. Their aesthetic theory of the pictorial moving image engages enduring questions of the role of film technology in creating art, and their love of examples helps to position these theories in context with films produced, advertised and critically dissected during these years.

PICTURE STUDY: FROM THE ART LECTURE TO THE FILM LECTURE

Institutionally, the Columbia extension programme was built on the model, and by some of the same people, as the most prominent art-education venues in New York.[5] Intellectually, Freeburg's and Patterson's notion of 'photoplay composition' followed the picture study tradition developed in these institutions. Freeburg cites several art educators as essential influences on his approach to film, particularly Arthur Dow and the popular lecturer Henry Rankin Poore (to whom I will return later).[6] Dow's formative influence on picture study has come up several times in this book, and it is important to note Freeburg's debt to him. Freeburg valued the way that Dow opposed the academic method of art education based on rote copying, proposing instead a synthetic method wherein all media and genres of spatial arts (representational or not) are subsumed under the concept of composition – its three main elements being line, shade and colour. Under this revised model of art education, all practical education in painting, sculpture, textile design and photography should emerge from a basic model of appreciation. Confronted with picture study's prominence, Freeburg found ways to make use of its broad influence and adaptability as he sought models from which to build his aesthetics of moving pictures.

Dow taught at the Pratt Institute in Brooklyn and was active in the Brooklyn Institute and the Association of Art Teachers in the second half of the 1890s. He compiled his method of instruction in his 1899 book *Composition*, and it became a standard textbook in the field. After this time it seems that few lyceum lecture schedules were complete without a lecture by an art teacher or museum curator who bore his influence. The methods of picture study featured prominently alongside the various scientific and historical lectures that toured the lecture circuit. In essence, Dow wanted picture study to do away with what he called the traditional academic method of art instruction, which separates representation and design. In this older method, design and the decorative arts take a secondary place in relation to accurate depiction. Dow struggled against the way that learning how to paint and draw according to this model puts utilitarian skill in copying nature over the development of what he and

THE THREE
ELEMENTS
I.—EXAM-
PLES OF
LINE AND
NOTAN HAR
MONY

Examples of the three basic elements of Arthur Wesley Dow's *Composition* (1899)

other progressive educators referred to as 'creative power'. It puts rote mechanistic learning ahead of the fostering of a desire for better form.[7] In opposition to the academic method, Dow proposed a synthetic method wherein all media and genres of spatial arts (representational or not) are subsumed under the concept of composition – its three main elements being line, notan (light and dark) and colour. The composer of pictures assembles these elements to create, like the musical composer, an overall sense of harmony. In this broad sense of composition design supercedes representation. In Dow's textbook on *Compositon*, which went through several editions, he makes a point of juxtaposing Botticelli with Gothic architecture and Japanese nature prints with Persian rugs to demonstrate that the same principles of design in art transcend the specifics of genre, tradition and medium.[8]

Dow's (and later Poore's) method fitted well with the mission of progressive education. It marked a turning point in aesthetic education in its emphasis on consumption over production, all the while linking the consumption of art with innovations in educational philosophy. Dow emphasised pictorial composition because he believed it went hand in hand with the formation of efficient democratic subjects. More than technical skill, he wanted to teach appreciation as a form of creative power. In Dow's words, 'appreciation [of pictorial form] leads a certain number of people to produce actual works of art ... but it leads the majority to *desire* finer form and more harmony of tone and color in surroundings'.[9] This directed desire, or 'interest' to use a term from John Dewey's writings on education, dominated the progressive educational philosophy used to shape late nineteenth-century programmes from the lyceum to the university.[10]

This pictorially based theory of art appreciation influenced a wide range of artists and movements. In the coming years, the Brooklyn Institute became an influential site

Making Movies into Art

for discussion of pictorialist photography, with nearly monthly lectures on the subject by people such as Sadakichi Hartmann and Clarence White.[11] It also served as an important exhibition space for Pictorialist photographers: notably Arthur Dow's student Gertrude Käsebier and Clarence White's student Karl Struss.[12] The Institute encouraged photographers, film exhibitors and critics to reflexively relate new media to questions of pictorial composition. It is precisely this reflexivity that makes the Brooklyn Institute and institutions like it significant in the formation of cinema's identity as a medium. While the discussions in the institute never achieved the coherence and rigour of the 1910s and 20s books on film art, they anticipate these later writings more directly than one might imagine.

By the early 1900s the Brooklyn Institute's lecture series and extension courses stood as models for effective public education. The Institute could have taken the opportunity to expand these offerings, as alternative educational institutions were needed to accommodate the growing immigrant communities in New York that were largely excluded from traditional university programmes.[13] But the focus of the Institute's attention was moving increasingly towards expanding the new Brooklyn Museum and its collections. Part of the reason for this shift is that universities had by this time taken some of the responsibility for establishing adult education programmes.[14] Columbia University's extension programme is a prime example, and during its formative years it maintained an intimate relationship with the Brooklyn Institute. Columbia administrators continually looked across the East River for precedents, guidance and even personnel. Columbia president Seth Low, a longtime friend of Alexander Black and the Brooklyn Institute since his time as mayor of Brooklyn, set up immediate connections with the Institute in his efforts to begin developing extension teaching at Columbia. In 1903, Arthur Wesley Dow was invited to leave his post in Brooklyn to head the art department at the Teachers College of Columbia. Columbia's full-fledged extension programme began the following year, and it was run by the Teachers College for the next decade.[15] In 1913, Columbia further expanded its extension programme by recruiting Milton Davies from Brooklyn, where he had served as supervisor of lectures at the Brooklyn Institute.[16] Davies became the assistant director of the extension education programme and started the Columbia Institute of Arts and Sciences on the Brooklyn model. In Davies' correspondence with Columbia administrators, he repeatedly defers to the successes of the Brooklyn Institute, from broad educational philosophy to minute questions about the day-to-day operations of the Institute.[17]

It is important to see the intellectual energy behind Columbia's cinema courses in 1915 as a part of this institutional framework. Freeburg was a graduate student at Columbia during the establishment of its adult education programme. He was hired to teach film in an extension teaching programme modelled largely on the success of the Brooklyn Institute. While Freeburg was trained as a theatre historian, he founded a 'Cinema Composer's Club' and taught 'Photoplay Composition' in an extension programme where the art curriculum was set up by Arthur Dow himself. It is clear that Freeburg and the administration saw his course in Photoplay Composition and his Cinema Composer's Club as extensions of Dow's picture-study approach to art education. Dow's pedagogy was essential in shaping Freeburg's approach to 'composition', a broad term not originally restricted to pictures. The term began, in fact, as a musical analogy adapted to pictures. Interested in the term's multi-media reach, Freeburg borrowed it from Dow, who earlier had borrowed it from aesthetic philosopher and Asian art collector Ernest Fenollosa (a mentor he shared with Ezra Pound).[18] Freeburg encouraged his students and the members of the Cinema Composer's Club to understand film art, as form, in the same way this circle of art educators encouraged their students to understand any other spatial art – as an expression of the basic principles of pictorial composition.

Some of the current scholarship on Freeburg has interpreted him as a functionary of classical Hollywood narrative.[19] Of course, no practical course on screenwriting would get very far without addressing the basic components of story, but it is just as important to note how the courses' ostensible practical aims (creating stories for the screen) never quite fell into synch with their intellectual origins (defining pictorial beauty). Freeburg consistently maintained that dramaturgy must be integrated with effective composition, so that composition, at least in theory, could take priority. It may seem counterintuitive that he taught feature-length narrative screenwriting using a method that valued pictorial form over story, but this only indicates his level of commitment to Dow's method. As he explains, 'The appeal of the photoplay is pictorial, as well as dramatic. ... But the dramatic appeal of the photoplay, that is, the appeal to the heart and the brain, is also through the pictorial.'[20] Freeburg, the scholar of dramaturgy and student of famous theatre critic Brander Matthews, had turned his attention to pictorial composition as the principle that unites cinema's many appropriations from the other arts.

Freeburg gives priority to composition over narration even in his approach to editing, which is usually characterised as the most narrative-bound aspect of mainstream film form. 'On the screen the edges of pictorial values cannot well be separated; they must touch as closely as the negatives in the film. This makes it all the more important to be careful of the joining. If pictures are not properly joined they will break in the aesthetic test just as surely as in the projecting machine.'[21] Freeburg equates the progression of frames and the cut. This move is comparable to other editing-based film theories, but his version of this analogy reveals his paradigmatic focus on pictorial composition. Continuity of motion is not simply a mechanical illusion. Continuity in editing is not simply achieved when narration renders the cut invisible. They are both governed by how one composition flows into another pictorially – that is, how the lines, shapes and shadows of one scene relate to those of the next scene. Editing, like the progression of frames, must follow the rules of pictorial composition. Filmic beauty, a species of pictorial beauty, could then be taught the way art educators taught pictorial beauty in other media.

Conceiving of cinema as an art of composed pictures was not necessarily a new idea. Several film critics had made claims like this, particularly Vachel Lindsay, noted in the last chapter as having encouraged his readers to cut out and arrange pictures from film fan magazines in order to highlight the main schools of motion-picture art.[22] Freeburg taught Lindsay's book in his class, and when his own book on the subject was published, it even included an advertisement for Lindsay's book that strongly emphasised (in more explicit terms than Lindsay ever did) its pictorial approach. 'The main thesis of [Lindsay's] book is that the moving picture is essentially graphic rather than dramatic; the tendency of the art of the moving picture is away from its ostensible dramatic interest, towards the mood of the art exhibition.'[23] Freeburg's *The Art of Photoplay Making* supports this general idea, but, in borrowing from Dow and other educators in the picture-study tradition, it took these claims a step further. The composition of the book, which he adapted from lecture notes, largely follows a didactic art workbook model used by Dow and his colleagues. Freeburg found precedents in this practice, and experimented with extending its methods to film. Dow used reproductions of sculpture, painting and graphic design to produce comparative arguments about composition. Freeburg added film still reproductions to these comparisons in a way that had not been done systematically by Lindsay, Münsterberg, or any previous writer on the cinema. He was experimenting with a method that has today become a standard practice in the scholarly analysis of film.

In order to illustrate his lectures and his books Freeburg collected a visual archive that set him apart from other art educators. He appropriated publicity stills from their more commercial uses. In his two books on pictorial beauty in film, Freeburg illustrates the text with eleven reproductions of paintings and sculpture, and twenty stills from films. I have located archival files of publicity stills for over half of the films mentioned by Freeburg, and in each of these cases I have found his exact illustration among the stills. In addition to the stills used for illustrations he mentions dozens of other scenes in the text of his chapters. Whenever these non-illustrated examples include some detail in their visual description, they usually matched a publicity still for the film. Visual publicity material from the film companies clearly enabled a significant part of his study, pedagogy and writing. The use of stills for analysis has been taken for granted for so long in film study that it is important to note Freeburg's innovation in appropriating material produced for the purposes of another institution. In some cases these purposes overlapped; after all, Freeburg did use publicity stills to publicise films. But, more often, his negative examples and his discussion of films no longer commercially relevant seem oblivious or even contrary to the organisations that produced these images.

The stills allowed him the luxury of reviewing and manipulating film compositions in a manner akin to what he saw in art-education textbooks. He used a photograph of the *Venus de Milo* for the frontispiece to his first book, instructing his reader to dissect it (as a picture) with three lines in order to diagram out the compositional balance and rhythm of lines of the sculpture. He then translated this exercise, illustrating the effectiveness of line and balance in film scenes by instructing his readers to view the compositions next to other famous works or from different perspectives. With Paramount's *Audrey* (1916), for example, using an exterior scene of a woman crossing a river on a fallen tree, Freeburg tells the reader to 'crop' the scene by manually covering the left and lower halves of the picture in order to see a more dynamic composition. In another section he tells the reader to turn the same picture upside down to correct the top-heavy imbalance in the composition. While this didactic use of pictures was common on the pages of Dow's workbooks, using a film still for this purpose was a different matter. Freeburg appropriated film publicity, repurposed it for the classroom setting and for an extended reading public.

In 1917 Frances Taylor Patterson joined Freeburg as an instructor, continuing to run the small programme for several years after he left. She took the practical task of getting students to produce scripts more seriously; it would not be wrong to set

Compositional exercise, using a still from *Audrey* (1916), in Victor Freeburg's *Pictorial Beauty on the Screen* (1923)

From *Audrey*. Cover up the left half of this picture and the lower half of the remaining part, and the quarter which then remains will contain a more pleasing and dramatic composition than that of the view taken as a whole. See pages 53 and 71.

Freeburg and Patterson against each other, with Freeburg as the aesthete proponent of graphic composition and Patterson as the proponent of commercial narrative clarity. But this separation becomes more complicated when considering Patterson's teachings and her work outside of the university. Since Freeburg left Columbia after only a few years, his books could largely ignore the realities of teaching film production. Patterson taught Photoplay Composition at Columbia for about fifteen years, and her goal was to teach people how to write professional-looking screenplays. She wrote her first book, *Cinema Craftsmanship*, as a textbook for precisely this purpose.[24] Naturally in such a work, the mechanics of plot and character construction would take priority. But despite her interests in screenwriting instruction, some of the preoccupations of the picture-study tradition influenced her as well. She taught pictorial composition in her intermediate course, using some of Freeburg's models and Vachel Lindsay's writings as texts.[25]

More significant than their attempts to train screenwriters, Freeburg and Patterson worked throughout their careers to cultivate a medium identity for cinema that would align it with reformist traditions like Dow's synthetic method of fine-arts pedagogy. They hoped an appreciation of composition in film would guide the tastes of the public, which they contrast with 'the mass', in desiring better films.[26] The handful of students who did succeed in selling scripts to film companies were like Dow's 'certain few' who went on to create art objects. They were ancillary to the goal of training 'the majority', in Dow's words again, 'to desire finer form and more harmony of tone and color in surroundings'.[27] Despite the ostensible focus of teaching narrative screenwriting, the cinema composition courses found themselves deeply intertwined with the evolving field of art education.

Patterson far exceeded Freeburg in her involvement with institutions of film reception outside of her courses, and she conveys a sustained interest in picture craft in these efforts. From 1920 on she worked for the National Board of Review and contributed regularly to its journal, *Exceptional Photoplays*. For this journal she wrote articles praising directors such as Victor Sjöström for his slow, contemplative compositions.[28] Her thoughts about other directors of pictorially composed films

Making Movies into Art

followed a similar tack. She promoted, just as actively as Freeburg, directors like Sjöström, Rex Ingram, (*Broken Blossoms* era) Griffith and Maurice Tourneur so that American film screens could become an 'International Motion Picture Gallery'.[29]

Freeburg and Patterson staked their claims about cinema's cultural value in large part on this idea of the 'motion picture gallery', which helps to explain why she made so much of Ingram's background in sculpture and Tourneur's in painting. It also explains why Freeburg includes lengthy illustrated analyses of the movement in paintings and sculptures, and why he began *The Art of Photoplay Making* with the *Venus de Milo*. A book of this title required a household-name masterpiece as its frontispiece. Patterson and Freeburg were claiming a place for film, not in some new and marginal department of the museum, but rather right next to the museum's canonical artefacts from the history of western art. At this time halls of casts of classical sculpture were seen as important components of the museum's pedagogical mission. Curators frequently gave priority to these exhibits with perceived pedagogical value over those that contain less canonical one-of-a-kind works.[30] Sculpture galleries showcased works that could teach, and what they taught was deeply interrelated with Freeburg and Patterson's hopes for cinema's value as art.

MOVEMENT, CONTEMPLATION AND THE 'TABLEAU'

Like many of the early critics and lecturers who attempted to conceptualise moving pictures in relation to the fine arts, Freeburg and Patterson continually returned to the issue of movement. For them, movement presented an overarching theoretical problem that had not yet been adequately and directly addressed. Because it ratchets inexorably forward, cinematic movement disrupts the quiet second glance of the contemplative viewer. Because the movement is mechanical, it does not privilege beautiful moments over ugly ones. And even if a film includes many beautiful static pictures, it nonetheless moves. Movement must be accounted for. Patterson expresses some of these problems eloquently in her second book, *Scenario and Screen*, when she recounts an argument with a museum director who stubbornly denied film a place in his museum. She responds:

> Perhaps it is the quality of motion which seemed to the museum director to be at variance with the quiet contemplation which pervades a museum of art. Yet, after all, the motion picture does no more than take up the thread of action woven by the imagination around a painting or a piece of sculpture. There is violence in the *Laocoön*; there is action in the *Winged Victory of Samothrace*. ... The photoplay goes only a step beyond the captured moment of canvas and marble and bronze and gives continuity to the suggested action.[31]

She does not refer to the director or institution by name, but her disagreement was directed at places like the Brooklyn Museum. William Henry Goodyear, tyre heir, scholar of classical sculpture and fine arts curator at the Brooklyn Museum, showcased replicas of the *Laocoön* and the *Winged Victory of Samothrace* at the head of the room looking out over the rows of other famous works in the museum's hall of classical sculpture.[32] Given the continued institutional connections between the Brooklyn

Institute (the parent organisation for the Brooklyn Museum) and Columbia's extension programme, Patterson may have been responding directly to Goodyear and to the arrangement of sculpture in this room.[33] Although he loved the magic lantern, Goodyear was suspicious of motion pictures. He used his lantern slides almost as surveying tools. Yes, photographic slides were there to educate the public, but Goodyear also used them to measure architecture. He ran plumb lines through cathedrals before photographing them and pen lines across his photographic slides to identify and illustrate the subtle refinements that he believed, following John Ruskin, characterised craft labour before the Renaissance. Goodyear had no imagination for cinema's potential as a similar type of surveying tool, and no patience for its disruption of the contemplative tone favoured by Ruskinians like himself.

Both of Patterson's 'moving' sculptures stood out among those mentioned in discussions about whether and how artists should represent movement in static media. The *Laocoön* was the better known of the two because of the continuing interest in Gotthold Ephraim Lessing's 1766 thesis on the limits of painting and poetry.[34] Lessing's book, a staple in most nineteenth-century discussions of aesthetics, is directed precisely against this suggestion of action in painting and sculpture lauded by Patterson. She seems to be picking up on revisions to Lessing's ideas about action and repose articulated in the nineteenth century and gaining momentum among American art educators in the first part of the twentieth, even by Goodyear himself.[35]

But even if these sculptures suggested movement, they still evoked 'quiet contemplation', a phrase with a specific reference in the history of aesthetic education. Lessing's work became famous for its imperative of stasis and repose in painting and sculpture. The spatial arts should not suggest action and they should value repose over ecstatic bursts. In Lessing's legacy, of which Goodyear, Freeburg and Patterson form a part, scholars expanded their interest in the dynamics of sculpture and painting, even as most of them still hoped to retain some of the aesthetically conservative prescriptions of Lessing's thought. An early theorist of cinema like Freeburg could certainly count among those who sought to embrace dynamic art. But he also held onto strict prescriptions about avoiding dissonant compositions in static and moving forms. He referred to frenetic movement or sharp contrasts, which do not yield some larger compositional unity, as 'pictorial hysterics'. He had no concerns about dynamism in art *per se*. When dynamism degenerated into pictorial hysterics, however, it became the enemy of contemplation.

Freeburg lays out the exact philosophical pedigree of the term 'contemplation' in his books, and it is worth taking some space to discuss what this term means to him. He derives the term from a model of spectatorship rooted in psychological aesthetics and German theories of empathy. Freeburg himself did not study in Germany, but he was influenced by many of the German émigrés, such as Hugo Münsterberg, who brought these theories to the USA.[36] Freeburg knew Münsterberg's wide-ranging work, but his primary interest in pictorial composition made it impossible to follow Münsterberg's approach to film form and spectatorship. In *The Photoplay*, Münsterberg based his analyses of film form almost exclusively on editing and narration. For him, the basic processes of human attention and memory manifest themselves most clearly in the progression of frames and cuts. Freeburg was interested less in the functions of story (guiding attention and memory) than in film's plastic form, so his theory takes the tradition of psychological aesthetics in a radically different direction.

The two Anglophone writers on psychological aesthetics whom Freeburg acknowledges most frequently are British aesthete Vernon Lee (Violet Paget) and Münsterberg's colleague Ethel Puffer. Lee was perhaps best known for revising the tradition of British aestheticism represented by her friend Walter Pater and continuing it into the 1910 and 20s. She contributed significantly to making German psychological aesthetics available and accessible to the English-speaking world. She explored empathy aesthetics in her books *Beauty and Ugliness* and *The Beautiful*, supporting a visceral notion of empathy in which spectatorship implies bodily activity.[37] A picture, or a pictorial aspect of a thing, activates a neuromuscular mimicking of form, a process that Puffer refers to as innervation.[38] To the extent that these bodily movements are conducive to the healthy functioning of the organism, the form that activates them can be considered beautiful. She develops this notion in *The Beautiful* and argues that bodily mimicry is an effect of a more primary psychological process whereby the mind reiterates form in the process of perception. Beauty produces a sense of contemplative satisfaction through this reiterated perception. Freeburg adopts Lee's definition, citing *The Beautiful*, and bases his analysis of film art 'on the understanding that a cinema picture is beautiful when the subject and composition together put the spectator in a state of contemplative satisfaction'.[39]

But contemplation takes time, precisely the kind of deliberate extension of time eliminated by the projector's spinning shutter. This time for contemplation may be taken for granted with painting and sculpture, but cinema has always intruded on the spectator's time with a mechanised movement out of the viewer's control. Mary Ann Doane describes this intrusion on the time of the spectator as a basic characteristic of film aesthetics:

> Unlike previous forms of visual representation, in which comprehension took time (writing, sculpture, painting), the cinema, because it was mechanical, subjected its spectator to the time of its own inexorable and unvarying movement. Previously, the time of viewing had been in the control of the subject, allowing for contemplation at leisure. The technological basis of the cinema incarnated the regimentation of time in modernity, its irreversibility.[40]

Doane's characterisation of the modern spectator's time re-examines a discourse as old as the first discussions of motion-picture art. In an understandably less developed form, this basic idea circulated even in the 1910s. Freeburg's work confronted a persistent problem among critics who acknowledged the regimented modernity of cinema's movement and yet refused to give up the spectator's time for contemplation. He needed to account for moments of contemplation in a medium that, according to a competing discourse that even he occasionally embraces, epitomises the standardisation and inevitability of mechanised movement. Like many other proponents of aesthetic cinema, he addressed this persistent problem by turning towards the performance tradition of the tableau.

Freeburg appropriated the tableau differently than Black or Hiller. His aesthetic theory marks a point when film critics transformed this tradition as they borrowed from it. On the stage, playwrights, performers and directors worked together to put actual pauses, or tableaux, into the performance. Why not replicate this directly on film? The film director could create film sequences that give the viewer time for pictorial contemplation by building tableaux into the flow of the action by commanding the actors to hold their position during significant moments. Freeburg certainly welcomes the tableau in cinema because it is part of a tradition that routed the notion of the composed picture through performance traditions and modern media practices. He does not, however, depend on the tableau as the practical standard in film art. Here his film theory diverges from the formal tradition of pictorialism as explored in Vardac's *Stage to Screen* and updated in Brewster and Jacobs's *Theatre to Cinema*.[41] The use of actual tableaux is only one practical solution and was perceived by many, when Freeburg wrote his film books in 1918 and 1923, as increasingly old fashioned. Tableau vivant films like those made by Lejaren à Hiller were an exception to the rule at this time. Freeburg's conception of pictorial beauty in film involves more than just praise of films that use this technique adapted from live performance. Techniques that involve shooting relatively static scenes and having the actors pose only reinforce what he believed to already be happening in the mind of the film viewer.

With his tableau-like model of the perception of moving forms, Freeburg locates the spectator's time for contemplation within the very medium that seemed to ensure contemplation's demise. He illustrates this most clearly when he associates the cinematic tableau with the perception of the movements of a diver. He claims that in viewing a well-executed dive viewers automatically perceive it as a series of pictorially harmonious static positions rather than as movements in their entirety. The viewer appraises beauty at the moment when the diver appears to hover for a moment in a balanced mid-air posture. This mode of perception occurs in every movement, whether the bodies in motion have actually paused or not. Freeburg builds his pictorial taxonomies in both of his film books from this basic assertion:

> In many real or cinematographed actions it is a moment rather than a movement, which impresses the eye and remains in the memory; that is, that in such actions the mind always retains a static instant, or tableau, rather than the movements which lead up to, or away from, that tableau.[42]

The mind and the eye retain static instants, but not in the way that photography retains static instants. He is using the tableau here as a figure for the way privileged moments impress the mind *as if* they were briefly held static. He compares this abstract conception of the tableau with the instantaneous photograph in the same passage.

> Take the simple case of a man running. The part of the step which we see most vividly and recall most easily is the moment when his legs are farthest apart. ... When an instantaneous photograph is made of the runner it often happens that an unfamiliar moment is recorded by the camera and we express surprise that a man could ever get his legs twisted in such a strange position. The testimony of the photograph is proof that in the case of the runner our eyes grasp and our minds retain certain selected moments rather than transitions, which consist of all of the moments in consecutive order.[43]

Instantaneous photography represents 'all of the moments in consecutive order'. Freeburg believes these contingent instants to be true, but they do not necessarily elicit the experience of beauty. The contingent instants, made visible in a convincing way by film and photography, no longer signal a one-way shift in the experience of moving images. While the modern world may be composed of any-instants-whatever in rapid succession, the aesthetic experience of this world escapes such rigid restrictions. It returns to human experience precisely what the apparatus threatens to take from it.[44]

Freeburg is clearly building on the older discourse that began with the advent of instantaneous photography. But his suspicion of the instantaneous photograph bears a salient distinction from the earlier suspicions about the camera being faster than the eye. He does not simply reiterate the well-worn claim that artists should create composite pictures of bodies in motion in order to replicate the human eye's inability to register rapid movement. This earlier notion that painting should replicate only what the eye can see finds its justification in a bodily deficiency. It asserts that the sluggish, imperfect design of the human eye, plagued by fatigue and clouded by afterimages, can only passively register movements below a certain threshold. Freeburg's static impressions are active where the afterimage model is passive. It is not a bodily deficiency that loses some of the 'transitional instants'. Instead, the viewer's desire for formally perfect compositions actively extracts these 'tableaux' from the arbitrary instants that surround them. Dow's cultivation of active aesthetic desire operates here. The task of the cinema composer is to offer images that stoke this desire for satisfying compositions, and the critic must promote the kinds of films that encourage tableau-like contemplation.

Here is where the promotional efforts of the companies like Paramount converge with Freeburg's aesthetic theory.[45] The overwhelming majority of the forty films Freeburg discusses in his books and lecture notes were Lasky/Paramount films. The company's productions of the mid-1910s, while not the only examples, did promote several techniques of lighting, staging and art direction that dovetailed with a picture-study approach to film education. Always the advocate of purposive craft, Freeburg lauded the craft of artificial lighting and the greater range of effects it could provide over natural light. He doesn't mention 'Lasky lighting' or 'Rembrandt lighting' by name, but he praises low-key effects lighting in several Lasky films, like *Sweet Kitty Bellairs* (1930), created by the people who adapted these 'Rembrandt lighting' effects from their days working for David Belasco's theatre productions.[46] In place of Rembrandt, Freeburg uses Jean-François Millet, whose *Angelus* had experienced a robust afterlife in American art classes, the sale of inexpensive lithographs and visual quotations like D. W. Griffith's *A Corner in Wheat* (1909).[47] Freeburg reprints and analyses *Angelus* in *The Art of Photoplay Making*. More than its historical importance, he praises its compositional balance in the play of light and shade on the nearly silhouetted figures. He felt that the light in the painting supported his call for effects lighting in films. Film-makers were keenly, if at times cynically, aware of the advantages of this lighting style, the most famous example being the exchange between Cecil B. DeMille and Samuel Goldwyn: 'for Rembrandt lighting the exhibitors would pay double!'[48] Freeburg's analyses of lighting in painting and film basically allied with these motives. They corresponded with industry efforts to legitimise their products, but they also attempted to give these cross-media associations more analytical rigour than they had in the company publicity kits and short reviews. This pulled his aesthetic prescriptions away from producers' publicity interests almost as often as it reinforced them.

Freeburg's examples of pictorial beauty in films allied with other film legitimisers of the time, but selectively so. He chose not to follow the path of praising a film based on the legitimacy of its performers. The famous players of Zukor's productions held less interest for Freeburg than the work of the art directors and cinematographers. Where Vachel Lindsay focused on actors' bodies (like Mary Pickford and Douglas Fairbanks) for his discussions of pictorial beauty, Freeburg preferred long shots in which the performer's body formed one small part of a larger composition. His focus on composition occasionally runs counter to the strategies of performer-focused industry uplift strategies, as evidenced in his exclusion of Geraldine Farrar from his repeated discussions of DeMille's *Carmen*. Securing the opera star Farrar for the part of Carmen was a major undertaking for Lasky and DeMille. Farrar was among the best-known legitimate performers in the country. The lion's share of publicity about the film's status as an art film surrounded her role in it. Medium shots of Farrar in dramatic tableaux comprised the majority of the film's visual publicity material. But Freeburg left these images out of his lectures and left Farrar out of his discussion of the film. In fact, he seems to dislike the way tighter framing privileges her performance in the climactic scenes when Don José leaves for Seville and when he kills Carmen and himself. He contrasts this star-focused framing with long-shot compositions from the film. 'Pictorially these tableaux are less interesting than the bull fight. ... and less beautiful than the marine view at the opening of the play.'[49]

Freeburg consistently preferred long-shot composition over closer framing. This in itself set him apart from contemporaries like Münsterburg, but the specific types of long-shot compositions he preferred help to delimit his picture-craft aesthetic in more concrete terms. Sorting through his exemplary scenes reveals a pattern for preferring *mise en scène* that is layered in depth over a *mise en scène* in which the frame is divided into side-by-side spaces like graphic panels. He distinguishes these two tendencies when he criticises Ben Carré's famous set for Maurice Tourneur's *Hand of Peril* (1916). Freeburg was unimpressed with Carré's multistorey building, built without a front wall to show action in multiple rooms simultaneously. 'The nine-room cross section did not, of course, look like a picture at all, but rather like a plumber's advertisement.'[50] To contrast this misguided composition, he offers an illustration from the tavern scene built by Wilfred Buckland for DeMille's *Carmen*. This scene includes a nested sequence of foreground, archway, background and exterior. 'The director has recognized his opportunity of composing in depth, or distance, and his four locales being separated by nothing but air, fall together into a single composition.'[51]

The *Hand of Peril* set illustrates, in an extreme form, a common technique of dividing the film frame to depict simultaneous related actions. Freeburg argues against this technique even in its milder versions, like in *The Scarlet Woman* (1916) when a wall separates a private conversation from the woman secretly overhearing it.[52] Using the still from Lasky's *Audrey*, mentioned earlier, Freeburg instructs his students to cover the left portion of the frame for better compositional balance despite the fact that this would crop out the other 'hidden' actor and reduce his clear presence in the story to a

Cross section from *The Hand of Peril* (1916); tavern scene from *Carmen* (1915)

murky suggestion. In his rejection of these divided spaces, Freeburg may have been averse to techniques that seemed too obviously inherited from the stage, but this is unlikely given that he was trained as a theatre scholar and that he welcomes other theatrical inheritances in film. A more likely explanation might return to the principle of suggestion that art educators used to teach pictorial composition.[53] Divided spaces, illustrated in extreme form in *The Hand of Peril*, show character relations the way a mechanic's exploded diagram illustrates the parts of a machine. It risks sacrificing aesthetic suggestion for instrumental clarity connecting the picture and the narrative. Freeburg is interested in expanding the pictorial suggestion in a work even, occasionally, at the expense of narrative clarity. His analysis of the tavern scene in *Carmen* highlights the distinction between Freeburg's suggestive 'tableaux' and the tableaux techniques deployed on stage and screen. To the extent that a tableau could be thought to diagram the relations between characters in a dramatically significant situation, it runs the risk of undermining effective, suggestive, cinema composition. He finds most compelling the way *Carmen* builds line, light and shade into compositions that exhibit unity, rhythm and/or repose.

I want to make clear here that as I discuss how Freeburg promoted the compositional unity of *Carmen* over its narration, I do not mean to suggest that DeMille, Buckland and Wyckoff had a similar disregard for narration even in their most showy interior compositions. The tavern scene, in fact, exemplifies how their staging and lighting can deftly shift attention to the significant narrative moments in a long take. It begins with the rear door closed, and the lighting highlights the officer in the foreground. When the doors open, the light from outside draws attention to Carmen's entrance at the rear of the building. As she approaches the officer the action again shifts to the foreground, and the two soldiers block the doorway in the background to neutralise its distracting glow. Freeburg ignores these instrumental narrative cues and selects for his illustration the moment when *Carmen* pauses in the doorway, the point of greatest visual variety within each layer of the deep space. Despite motivations behind the scene's careful staging in depth, Freeburg treats his production still like a painting and values its unified balance of lines, shapes and planes. Here, the tavern scene exhibits tableaux in the traditional sense as well as Freeburg's modified sense. Following Brewster and Jacobs's definition of the stage picture, it contains a series of mini-narrative situations, each given its own pictorial emphasis. Following Freeburg's compositional definition of 'tableau', the scene invites aesthetic contemplation as a static picture, one not entirely defined by storytelling and therefore separate from those moments before and after.

MANAGING TABLEAUX: THE ECONOMICS OF FILM SPECTATORSHIP

By now it should be clear that Freeburg's search for continuities between cinema and the pictorial arts meant retooling theories of what art does to its viewer. It is these meditations on film spectatorship that reveal, in another aspect, the odd modernity of a motion-picture theory rooted in the picture-study tradition. By creating his analogy with the prolonged stasis of the tableau, Freeburg emphasises how the film spectator actively takes time for pictorial contemplation, time upon which film's succession of instantaneous images continually intrudes. This time for contemplation rejects Münsterberg's editing-to-narrative-based approach. The picture takes priority over narration and requires a temporality of the spectator that is neither fused to the time of the apparatus nor its extension in the forward movement of narrative.[54] But in de-emphasising the cut as the foundation of film aesthetics Freeburg still had to account for its function. He needed to develop a model for perceiving pictorial composition in multiplicity and in sequence, which could overcome the discontinuity of the cut. In other words, if Freeburg downplayed the progression of frames and cuts for the film spectator, he needed to develop an alternative system that accounted for the aggregate pictorial experience of a feature film.

He addresses this problem in *Pictorial Beauty on the Screen,* drawing from Puffer's and Lee's notions of the neuromuscular mimicry of form. Beautiful forms stimulate healthy innervations. The progression of frames and cuts in a typical feature multiplied this experience exponentially and so required a rationalisation of the process of perceiving the stream of pictures. To satisfy this requirement, Freeburg develops a film-specific economics of aesthetic expenditure – a model of managed innervation.[55] He begins *Pictorial Beauty on the Screen* by explicating this higher order of organisation. He describes pictorial beauty in film as a kind of amplified 'pictorial efficiency'.[56] Innervation takes energy, and pictorial movements have a practical, potentially calculable, economic value with regard to the expenditure of this energy. Certain forms such as jagged angles, jump cuts and sharp contrasts require a greater psychological expenditure. If these forms are placed at the points where emotional expenditure is not necessary, then they are wasteful.[57] This efficiency or waste is compounded by every shot. The cinema composition of a great film-maker, by contrast, 'economizes the work of the eye and the brain'.[58] It tunes the spectator's physiological response to an otherwise overwhelming flood of images.[59]

In practice, this economy of aesthetic response led Freeburg to some fascinating, if largely unrealisable, prescriptions. Most of his examples of ways to economise a progression of images are limited to single transitions, but he does make some suggestions for plans of composition that follow the arc of entire films. For *Carmen,*

Making Movies into Art

after praising the pictorial composition in several of the scenes, he complains that these compositions do not build towards the end of the film. He dislikes the way the medium-long shots of Farrar's performances, pedestrian from the standpoint of pictorial composition, lose energy. They dissipate the pictorial charge of the bullfight or the seaside smuggling scene. While emotional involvement with Carmen and Don José's climactic scene may trigger a sensational response dramatically, Freeburg counters that the composition requires less aesthetic expenditure by the viewer when the scene should be requiring more. It is a curious prescription, considering that to reshape the film in this way would result in an oddly abstract final reel. The melodrama would be keyed to an ever-heightening progression of pictorial compositions. '[T]he crises or climax of the drama [w]ould coincide with ... the most artistic stage composition in static or fluent forms', not necessarily around tableaux composed for their dramatic clarity as is the case with DeMille's film.[60] Freeburg is not talking about speeding up editing to heighten suspense, nor does he suggest simply ending films with a final spectacular scene. His method of economising aesthetic expenditure to coincide with films' climactic moments would likely yield abstracted story films resembling forced experiments in aesthetic synthesis rather than works that build from industry standards and practices.

BEYOND THE TABLEAU: INSCRIBING MOVEMENT

Picture-study educators often embraced photography, but they largely left motion pictures out of their discussion of pictorial composition.[61] They had created a vocabulary flexible enough to apply to Persian rugs or Renaissance marble, but the uncertain relationship between plastic form and recorded movement remained outside of their scope. Freeburg, in the most original and inventive sections of his writings, worked to negotiate this uncertain relationship. Far from collapsing cinematic movement into an appreciation simply of static composition, Freeburg worked to develop a vocabulary that interrelated cinema's static compositions with its moving compositions. In other words, he moved beyond the tableau and sought to understand cinematic movement itself as a kind of graphic inscription.

Let me illustrate Freeburg's application of graphic inscription to cinematic movement by juxtaposing it with a passage from Paul Souriau's *Aesthetics of Movement*, first published in 1889.

> We admire a line traced on a piece of paper by the hand of the artist, but can there be not only as much grace, but as much true beauty in the curve described in the sky by the flying bird? Why can't we say that this curve too is a work of art because, because it leaves no concrete trace? That, after all, may be the only reason.[62]

Cinema technology, with its origins in the motion studies of Souriau's notable contemporary Étienne-Jules Marey, offers a solution to his lament. If motion picture technology challenged Freeburg's love of careful pictorial composition with its mechanised contingent recordings, it also provided an opportunity.[63] It converted movement into tangible marks on celluloid and thus opened up new ways of considering movement's aesthetic effects on the viewer's body. Even though film's recreation of movement did not produce for viewers the Marey-ist lines that Souriau imagined, considering these marks as repeatable aesthetic phenomena made it possible to discuss the aesthetics of movement in terms of viewer-based theories of composition. Freeburg was clearly working in this vein when, in *Pictorial Beauty on the Screen*, he broke 'pictorial motions' down into different categories of expenditure: work, play and rest. This aesthetic taxonomy of pictorial motions presumed that cinema's trace of movement had cleared the way for movement's discussion in graphic terms. Movements, like graphic compositions, could then be categorised using the same economic model of bodily expenditure in the perception of art.

Freeburg was not the first critic to attend to the inscriptions on celluloid as part of film's unique properties as a medium, but he did move this discussion into the domain of art. Other accounts of these inscriptions much more commonly discussed their evidentiary properties, not their aesthetic patterns. As a tool for observation and scientific analysis, the inscription of movement opened up new fields for exploration of events. Controlled experimental events, everyday events and events which escape ordinary perception became available for a range of analytic and synthetic operations. For Freeburg, cinema's ability to analyse motion, scientific uses notwithstanding, enhance rather than detract from its pictorial dimension. Beyond the possibility of recording movement as events, the graphic trace on the celluloid connects ideas about the form of movement and the form of sculpture and painting. Understanding cinema as a moving record made certain aesthetic ideas possible. It revealed the medium's ability to render movement itself plastic and to render film a graphic medium. Even Lumière's *Arrival of a Train at the Station* (1895) was primarily, to Freeburg, a dance of line and perspective.

For his examples, Freeburg identified fundamental principles of beauty in art education, particularly William Hogarth's line of beauty, and imagined how these principles could relate to traces of movement left on the filmstrip.[64] Suspicious of camera movement, Freeburg tended to find his examples of inscribed movement in exterior vistas. In the second book he contrasts the unaesthetic sight of a man riding a horse in a straight line down a hillside with the beautiful rhythm created by the same rider winding his way through the brush. This was something of a refrain in his work. His preference for western landscapes and their lines of beauty was already evident in 1918, when he used the horseback scene from *Carmen*. Illustrating his text with an often-reproduced still from the scene, he admired its balance and rhythm. The road on which Carmen is riding cuts Hogarth's line of beauty into the landscape. The figures in the landscape 'take up the thread of action woven' around the static composition. They encourage the viewer to imagine movement as a type of graphic inscription.

But none of Freeburg's examples traced a moving line of beauty through a picture more evocatively than Paramount's 1923 adaptation of *The Covered Wagon*. If one or two figures riding horses through a scene could suggest an answer to Souriau's problem, long, moving processions of covered wagons in the western landscape directly inscribe the very pattern that Souriau wished the bird's flight could inscribe in the sky. The wagon train goes a step further than the lone rider and creates a massive moving line. The movement draws a pattern on the film and single-file repetition of the wagons renders this movement palpable against the background of the western

From *The Covered Wagon* (1923). Frontispiece for *Pictorial Beauty on the Screen*

landscape. In his repeated adulation of *The Covered Wagon*, Freeburg waxes poetic about the film's massive 'white line winding in slow rhythm'.

> Again and again, the wagon train becomes a striking pictorial motif, and, whether it has been seen creeping across the prairie, following the bank of a river, climbing toward a pass in the mountains, stretching out, a thin black chain of silhouettes on the horizon, curving itself along the palisade-like walls of an arroyo, or halted in snow against a background of Oregon pines, it always adds emphasis to the intense drama of the pioneers.[65]

His stretched attempt to equate compositional beauty with dramatic emphasis notwithstanding, Freeburg reads the compositions in this film as something approaching Walter Ruttmann or Viking Eggeling. The undulating movements of the wagon train made design fluid.

The Covered Wagon did not just illustrate principles of composition, it took on emblematic status in *Pictorial Beauty on the Screen*. And this status was not entirely unplanned by its producers. In a letter to Adolph Zukor before the film began production, Jesse Lasky expresses his excitement for the pictorial possibilities of the film if made on a large scale.[66] A year later, after its first wave of critical success, Lasky explained to Zukor the importance of exploiting the film, not through their ordinary distribution channels, but rather as a road-show feature coordinated by D. W. Griffith's road-show manager J. J. McCarthy. He notes how critics have recommended the film to be taught in schools but, 'at the same time, the picture has a tremendous appeal to the masses'.[67] Lasky wanted the mass exhibition of the film to grow out of its promotion as an art film, and it worked. Screenings of the film were set up as social events. Paramount staged the New York premiere at the Plaza as a philanthropic fund-raiser ushered by Girl Scouts and 'members of the younger social set of New York'.[68] An early review in *The Morning Telegraph* quoted a college history professor, who saw a 'Brilliant Future for the Educational Values of the Motion Picture', promoting the film as visual education.[69] The Paramount publicity booklet for the film was filled with illustrations connecting its scenes to esteemed paintings of the American west as it claimed that the film may be the best ever made. The film had its road-show release combined with engagements at places like the Criterion theatre on Broadway, where it would break *The Birth of A Nation*'s (1915) continuous-run record by the end of 1923.

Freeburg likely saw *The Covered Wagon* that summer at the Criterion as he was working on his book at the nearby National Arts Club, and he was evidently pleased by the film's snowballing reputation. Lasky's films from 1915 had set into motion a provisional partnership of art education and industry picture craft. The public sentiment surrounding Lasky's 1923 production aligned it effortlessly with the aims of pictorial education. An emblematic statue of Venus was no longer needed to guarantee *Pictorial Beauty*'s aesthetic rigour. For the 1924 frontispiece, Freeburg set ancient Greek sculpture aside in favour of a still of Lasky's wagon train, and 'the simple strength of its moving pattern'. Freeburg even dedicated his book to the film's director: 'To James Cruze. Because the various types of pictorial beauty described in this book may be seen richly blended with epic narrative and stirring drama in "The Covered Wagon" a cinema composition That Will Live.' The dedication brands the film as a future classic and as an emblem for an early theory of an American art cinema. It contends that film technique, industry publicity and intellectual traditions in art pedagogy could form strong alliances, as they did in this film, around the notion of picture craft.

CONCLUSION: MOVING PICTURES AND NEW TENDENCIES

Whether through static contemplation or moving inscription, film's relation to the aesthetics of movement has underpinned attempts to define art cinema in the classroom. Freeburg and Patterson described cinematic movement as an extension of the kinds of movement suggested in painting and sculpture, and in doing so they took on the task of validating cinema as a medium capable of producing works like these other arts. But what makes this early educational experiment so compelling is not simply that film could imitate the works sanctioned by museums and Chautauquas. To describe this project as a one-way strategy of imitation would conceal a more important point about the modernity of the relation between film and the other arts. By re-examining cinematic movement in relation to canonical sculptures they were also re-examining these sculptures by way of cinema. Accordingly, while validating cinema in relation to the pictorial arts, they helped to forge a winding route back to those same qualities of motion-picture technology that had made it such an object of fascination for modern artists working in other media.

Of all the picture-study educators that influenced the Columbia film courses, Henry Poore best illustrates this final point. His ambivalent fascination with modern art, which grew after his visit to the 1913 Armory Show, sheds light on Freeburg's assessment of pictorial motions in cinema. As ideas about movement and repose in pictorial composition filtered into American institutions of art education, they helped to foster a distinct aesthetic. They enabled some critics, by looking back at movement in sculpture, to embrace some of the more radical gestures of modern art while still holding onto a kind of pictorial idealism. Dow, Goodyear and, especially, Poore epitomise this aesthetic.[70] They approach developments in modern art and new media with cautious optimism as a process of negotiation, which hinged on the aesthetics movement and composition. In *The New Tendency in Art* Poore admonishes what he calls the 'Bergsonism' of Post-Impressionism with some conservative points from Lessing's *Laocoön*.[71] Post-Impressionism's primitivism, vitalism and attempts towards synesthesia remind Poore of Lessing's caution that painting should remain quiet in order to offer itself up to proper contemplation. But then later in the book, when he addresses specifically the aesthetics of movement, his confidence in this conservative position fails him. He admires Futurist painting for upsetting Lessing's mandate and opening painting to successive impressions as well as 'fertile moments'.[72] In *The Conception of Art*, he elaborates on his interest in the expression of movement in static media by re-evaluating a series of sculptures, from classical works through Carpeaux and Rodin to the contemporary dynamic sculptures of Loredo Taft and Bela Pratt. Poore's conditional praise for these works reveals that while a new relationship with movement underpins his idea of art's future much in the same way as the modernists he praises, he does not follow the Futurists in what he describes as their outright rejection of contemplative 'pensive immobility'.[73] Poore, like Freeburg, proposes a compromise.

At the same time that Freeburg and Patterson were searching for continuities between cinematic motion and well-known poses of sculpture and painting, a parallel pictorial tradition in art education was re-evaluating the movements in these sculptures in order to address questions prompted at least in part by the development of moving-image technology. A taut expression or some dishevelled locks of hair in a sculpture occupy the same liminal space between movement and repose as cinema compositions.[74] The suggested movement in the *Winged Victory* and in Carpeaux's *The Dance* showed a way, for some art lecturers, towards an alliance between new manifestoes about movement in art and the principles of composition and repose that helped to establish American institutions of art education a decade earlier. The emerging field of American film criticism in the late 1910s and early 20s offered new opportunities for addressing the same set of concerns.

Freeburg and early twentieth-century art educators share parallel aesthetic positions on new developments in art.[75] While the new art is nourished by a rethinking of movement, its determining conditions should not cast off the pose. Rather, these critics hoped to find aspects of acceleration and repose in productive collaboration. Freeburg's pictorial aesthetic isolates two aspects of film: mechanical movement and the physical trace of this movement. Recognising these attributes as part of cinema's medium identity marks the first step in recognising the determining conditions of cinema to be contingency, velocity and mechanisation. But by conceiving of the inscription of movement in plastic terms, Freeburg managed to hold onto elements of a notion of repose so important to certain principles of composition without disavowing the seemingly antithetical aspects of film's medium identity.

Repose and contemplation still have a place in a medium he admits is characterised by contingency and distraction. To see these multi-media art educators as parallel thinkers in this respect is to revise the critical histories that would cast their tradition as either a retrograde anti-modernism or as representing a transition from one order to another. Picture craft was always a hybrid notion. The pictorial analysis of mechanically recorded movement made film technology relevant to that combination of modernism and pictorial idealism that motivated Poore's and Dow's generation of art critics.

This tradition marks one of the primary attempts to bring into focus a coherent theory of film art in the years when the pictorial still held sway as a unifying aesthetic paradigm. It foreshadows some aspects of the imminent discussions of montage films or visual composers, like Viking Eggeling or Walter Ruttmann, while remaining distinct. For these educators, cinema's managed procession of static compositions and moving inscriptions were to be found not in abstract films, but in mainstream features – even if theorists such as Freeburg pushed for greater compositional abstraction in these films. It was a blockbuster like *Carmen*, with its staging and lighting derived from legitimate theatre, that forged a new path in its flow of sequenced compositions. It was *The Covered Wagon*, successful for its familiar nationalist myths and decorous landscape, that also exposed a tangle of undulating lines. This anomalous theory of film art promotes a film medium that, while possessing a certain reflexivity, is nonetheless absorptive. It warned against what Freeburg called 'pictorial hysterics' in instantaneous photographs; it did not appreciate their convulsive beauty. In valuing decorum, proportion and formal harmony while conceptualising film viewing as a rationalised economy of the senses, its distinctly modern spectator encounters an aesthetic world in which distraction and contemplation realign but do not necessarily exclude one another. The reasons why this would seem counterintuitive are the same reasons why the pictorial tradition that Freeburg represents has been neglected in film history. To rediscover this work is to overturn assumptions that have led to this neglect.

4

Painting with Human Beings:
Maurice Tourneur as Art-film Director

The film director has made frequent, but always oblique, appearances throughout this book's discussion of intellectual history, lecture halls, museums, art periodicals and universities. The next two chapters move these appearances to the centre. They show how the aesthetic traditions discussed in the previous chapters intersect in the careers of two studio directors in the 1910s and early 20s. Maurice Tourneur and Rex Ingram made challenging films, but they did not typically claim to be heroic inventors of film techniques. They made prestige features that rarely, if ever, verged into blockbuster territory. Their work was compositional and museum friendly. They achieved notoriety not by blazing a trail for the medium, but by looking back at their backgrounds in the other arts. Affinities like theirs, in which a director not only borrows from the other arts but also takes on a public role as a painter or sculptor of the screen, form a vital part of art cinema as a tentative mode of early Hollywood film-making.

Maurice Tourneur stood out as one of the great early mediators between the fine arts and studio film-making because, as anyone who read his press knew, he 'began life – the important part of life, that is – studying Art and spelling it with a capital "A," in the Latin Quarter of Paris'. [1] He could claim years of experience in the studios of famous painters and sculptors. He knew the inside of an 1890s Parisian atelier better than Georges DuMaurier and could recreate the studio scenes in his adaptation of *Trilby* (1915) from memory. By revisiting his own artistic past in the famous studios of the 1890s he created a space for his films in the American film industry. He advertised closer ties to painting and sculpture than other film-makers, and he carried on aestheticist and avant-garde traditions through these ties. I trace these relationships, in their actuality and in their promotional excesses, in order to show how they created a productive ˢpace for a certain kind of work. There were certainly other pictorial directors. But most of them established their careers later, or were marginal to the major productions of their time. Tourneur entered the early film industry making prestige films; he was not marginal in the 1910s. His films provoked American film critics and viewers to consider a different type of film, an uncommon film perhaps, but not a type of film that could only thrive outside of the mainstream. These were high-profile appropriations of workspaces and traditions in the visual arts. Among his contemporaries during this crucial period in the history of American art film, Tourneur was particularly adept at integrating the concerns of producers like Nicholas Schenck and Adolph Zukor with those of critics like Freeburg and Patterson. It was a precarious position to occupy, and it was successful in this way only for a time.

Tourneur's position as a public figure informs my analysis of his work. While considering technique and his recognisable style, I also pay close attention to the way his publicity helped to mediate these styles and techniques. This approach to film authorship in the silent era has been invigorated by recent historiographical work by people like Jane Gaines, Shelly Stamp and Mark Cooper.[2] I would emphasise the nuanced definitions of film authorship that were being formed by critics at the time. Consider, for example, Frances Patterson's definition in *Scenario and Screen*:

> [the director] is the potential audience. ... [H]e furnishes the contact between the actors and that vast and unknown group of people beyond the celluloid. Their fire and enthusiasms come too late to enter into the production; so the director of the picture must needs anticipate them. ... [H]e not only directs the action, but furnishes the audience reaction to it.[3]

She goes on in this chapter to describe Tourneur and Rex Ingram as the exemplary visual artists among directors, but her definition of director here suggests how complicated that association is for her. Style is only one component of the director's expanded role. Writing and performance constitute the production, and she imagines the director somewhere in between this production and the audience. Positioned more as a mediator than a creator, the director helps to guide reception. Following Patterson's lead, I situate my visual analysis among other factors that contributed to this mediator function of the director. I look at style, promotion of the director and reception of the films as interlocked components of their roles as fine-arts directors at this time.

Tourneur's art films show how every translation of a technique or theme from one medium to another can also function as a cultural reference. They reference works and traditions of painting and sculpture with a healthy eclecticism – a microcosm of the eclectic circulation of these traditions in the broader American public sphere. The ways that Tourneur and his collaborators developed their stylised techniques comprise only one part of their contribution the American art film in the late 1910s and early 20s. They also actively shaped their films' cultural references through their own efforts and through cooperation with film companies, critics and educational programmes. This is where Tourneur and Ingram, the focus of the following chapter, stand out. While they did have a few peers producing notable pictorial films, no directors positioned themselves so effectively as painters or sculptors of the screen. Their position within the film industry affected the way their films could look, the way discussions about them circulated and the way they were seen. The sections of this chapter trace Tourneur's provocations within the film industry, his production context as well as his public reputation, and offer examples showing how Tourneur helped to link his intermedial, pictorial films to organisations with varied motivations. The focus here is not exactly on the development of his practice, but rather on how his films provided a public platform for engaging pictorial art traditions like Symbolism and decadence.

Making Movies into Art

IN THE ATELIER OF PUVIS

Tourneur's reputation as a director who 'Paints with Human Beings' grew beyond simple analogy throughout the mid- to late 1910s as the trade and fan press mythologised his mentorships with the sculptor August Rodin and, more extensively, the muralist Pierre Puvis de Chavannes.[4] No American interview with Tourneur was complete, it seems, without mentioning either his apprenticeship with Rodin or that he helped Puvis sketch the murals for the Boston Public Library. These artists' specific reputations helped to contextualise Tourneur's work beyond casting it as 'painterly'.[5] The American public knew Rodin and Puvis well, as two of the most internationally influential artists affiliated with French Symbolism. During this time, American museums readily acquired Rodin's casts, and Puvis's installation at the Boston Public Library caused a stir in the art world. Rodin himself ranked Puvis among the greatest living artists. He presided over banquets in Puvis's honour in 1895 and began sculpting a monument to him in 1899, which included three figures – a bust of the artist, an apple tree and a figure of 'eternal repose' – in an arrangement that evokes the allegory and simplicity of Puvis's murals. Rodin's conversations on his deathbed dramatically confirm this link. Records of these conversations from 1917 have preserved his dying words on the greatness of Puvis's work and the privilege of having known him.[6] This publicity cast Tourneur as more than a pictorial stylist. His stylised films participated in a larger exchange with the work of these famous artists. Associating himself with these artists, Tourneur took on a role of emissary from their studios.

It is revealing that the press gave priority to Tourneur's work in Puvis's atelier. It reflects a particularly American cultural appropriation of Symbolist aesthetics. The same qualities that had made Puvis so influential to European Symbolist artists of the 1890s appealed to modern American art educators, although for different reasons.[7] The Symbolists of the 1890s admired his flatness, his break from realism and chiaroscuro as part of the triumph of the aesthetic over positivism. In other words, they liked the way his canvases diverged from the empirically visible world. American art educators and curators saw these same flat, muted canvases as examples of efficient modern composition. Arthur Dow defended the merits of his Boston mural against its detractors, and reproduced Puvis's work in the multiple editions of his art-education textbooks.[8] Noted critic and poet Sadakichi Hartmann informed his readers that without Puvis, Monet and Whistler would not exist.[9] And the curator and painter Arthur Davies considered Puvis an indispensible part of the 1913 Armory Show.

Puvis also appealed to more conservative American tastes. In early twentieth-century American art criticism and public lectures, the previous two decades of French art both fascinated and provoked suspicion. Puvis aroused this fascination while still allowing a traditionalist like journalist Henry Adams to cite his Boston mural as the 'greatest painting ever made'.[10] Puvis's style and his methods proved adaptable in American museums and other educational institutions, where the more decadent Symbolist traditions were less appropriate. His interest in mural painting led him towards allegorical figures rendered in muted colours and attitudes of Apollonian calm. These qualities in his work gestured towards pre-Renaissance frescoes he studied in Italy, even though he worked almost exclusively in oils. Puvis employed none of the potentially unsettling detail of William Holman Hunt or the lurid colours (and themes)

Inside the studio of Pierre Puvis de Chavannes at Neuilly. On the wall is a section of the Boston Public Library mural entitled *The Inspiring Muses* before it was shipped in 1895

of Gustave Moreau, and this made him more successful than these fellow early Symbolists in serving mainstream American aesthetic interests. Further separating him from other Symbolist precursors' methods, Puvis employed a craftsman-like approach to creating work.[11] Again, unlike the notoriously private Moreau, Puvis ran his atelier with the discipline of a guild, which appealed to those Arts and Crafts-influenced art educators discussed at length in previous chapters.

It is no coincidence that Tourneur associated himself directly with Puvis's Boston work. Puvis's compositions were a common fixture in American art-education textbooks, but his notoriety always faced a challenge because his murals could not be transported across the ocean for regular exhibits. The Boston Public Library murals, shipped in pieces from France and installed on site, offered American audiences their only opportunity to see his work on a scale that bore physical witness to his studio practices in Paris. In the emerging American film industry Tourneur occupied a position as an aesthete: a Symbolist and a cinema craftsman. By placing himself in the atelier of Pierre Puvis de Chavannes twenty years prior, working on what would become Puvis's only installed work in North America, he could convincingly assume both of these roles. He could act as a conduit between the film industry and the popular subject of the 1890s French studio life while maintaining the importance of

Making Movies into Art

craft in art-making. The quality of work in Tourneur's studio could reflect the quality of work in Puvis's studio.

QUALITY FILMS, IMPORTED FILM-MAKERS

Tourneur's association with quality films began in Paris, in collaboration with several influential figures in French theatre and cinema. In 1909, the French Éclair company decided to expand beyond its popular serial adaptations with its new ACAD subsidiary (Association cinématographique des auteurs dramatiques). Headed by the respected stage actor Émile Chautard, ACAD would follow the model of Pathé-distributed *film d'art* and SCAGL (Société cinématographique des auteurs et gens de lettres) and adapt dramatic work in a variety of genres with more direct claims to legitimate culture. Chautard proved an exceptional mentor (even though he made only a limited number of films as a director). He took Tourneur, who had built a stage career touring with Gabrielle Réjane's productions, under his wing.[12] Chautard brought Tourneur to ACAD and supervised his stylised adaptations of such stories as Gyp's *Le Friquet* and André de Lorde's *Figures de Cire*. When Éclair decided to expand its production business to the USA with a new studio in Fort Lee, New Jersey, Chautard and Tourneur ranked among the promising talents sent from France to the new location.

Their time at American Éclair was short lived, however. After a severe studio fire in 1914 and the financial pressure felt by most French firms at this time, Éclair liquidated its American operation, leaving its employees to find work in neighbouring Fort Lee companies like Lewis Selznick's World Film Corporation. Chautard and Tourneur easily made the transition, as their ACAD experience fitted well with World's mission to film famous plays. Former theatre producers William Brady and Lee Shubert hired Tourneur to direct a series of adaptations for World including *Trilby* and *The Wishing Ring* (1914). These films drew from his French stage experience, and occasionally even quoted French stage productions. In Tourneur's famous adaptation of *Alias Jimmy Valentine* (1915), which on the French stage had starred Émile Chautard as *Le Mysterieux Jimmy* not long before they both emigrated to the USA, the climactic film tableau recreates the tableau from Chautard's play.[13] After making modified *films d'art* for ACAD and World, Tourneur moved to the upscale Artcraft label for Paramount and then to his own production company backed by his colleague Jules Brulatour.

Each of his French collaborators bolstered Tourneur's reputation as an early art film director in the USA, but none was as important as Ben Carré. The fact that he worked on thirty-four of Tourneur's films means that Tourneur's trademark pictorial style was truly a collaborative creation with Carré. In their work together, we can see a familiar constellation of techniques – often adapted from their previous work in theatre – around the idea of pictorial composition. Like Tourneur, Carré adapted his fine-arts training for work in the theatre, designing sets for Paris productions before moving to Gaumont and then to Éclair studios. He brandished his early training in painting, describing himself as a painter first and an art director second, and he continued to exhibit his paintings and drawings at galleries in Los Angeles throughout his life.[14] In their films together, the pictorial framing of scenes with strong foregrounds, as well as the open-wall sets, scrims and layered backdrops can be traced back to their work on the stage. But while these techniques may have been adapted from the stage, in Tourneur's films they realign themselves with pictorial screen art. After all, the scrims and layered backdrops, especially when combined with careful camera placement and lighting, could reference works in paint. And the foreground frame could gesture towards Pre-Raphaelite paintings, popular fantasy illustrations, or lantern slides as vividly as the proscenium arch.

Carré included foregrounded silhouettes in Tourneur's location-shot films as well as the films with completely artificial sets. *Prunella* (1918), made by Tourneur and Carré for Paramount, provides the most elaborate example of their use of artificial sets. In an oral history transcript at the Margaret Herrick Library, he recalls designing individual layers of the set, often just suggestions of shapes, and positioning them in three dimensions: 'we never used light in the foreground and left them as silhouettes. That pushes the stage further back and by this separation makes it more realistic.' The 'realism' to which Carré refers is the set's illusion of depth, as none of the film is shot on location, and the sets are constructed almost entirely out of flat, painted surfaces rather than built structures. The production stills and extant fragments of the film suggest a strong connection to the fantasy theatre, and yet the fan press (crediting Carré alongside Tourneur) and film manuals discussed the film's scenes in terms of their pictorial effect. Frances Patterson, in one of the moments in which her *Cinema Craftsmanship* overlaps with Victor Freeburg's theories of cinema composition, admired the painterly qualities of *Prunella*'s sets and the compositional emphases of the costumes in relation to the flowers sown into the cloth 'grass'.[15] The composition of the film evoked for her a painterly aesthetic for which Tourneur was becoming known.

Carré's technical background proved compatible with Patterson's aesthetic mission because they each evoked painterly form and tradition. Throughout his oral histories and unpublished memoirs, Carré describes the care in constructing layered scenes just like those in *Prunella*. These scenes move beyond providing a simple frame for the action, they reference a recognisable technique in painting. In his English-language memoir Carré consistently describes how he wanted 'to push back' the set.[16] In his native French, '*repoussoir*' has a much clearer art-historical connotations. Nearly anyone trained as a painter (like Carré and Tourneur) would have known how to use a *repoussoir* to enhance the illusion of depth and to draw the viewer's eye into the composition. And many more people who attended art lectures (including many who wrote reviews of films) would have known this technique from its more famous sources like Caravaggio or Vermeer, precisely the types of paintings with which Tourneur, Carré and prestige critics sought to associate their films.

Their lighting choices within these pushed-back planes of action are just as rich with references to known artworks. When Tourneur, Carré and van den Broek shot static groups of performers, as in a dinner scene or a meeting, they frequently concealed a strong light in the centre of the group. Often below eye level, this dominant light source brightly illuminated the faces of the central figures and silhouetted those figures with their backs closest to the camera. Apparently infatuated with this technique, Tourneur and his collaborators used it in nearly all of his American films, from the scenes at a gypsy encampment in *The Wishing Ring* to the military planning scenes in *The Last of the Mohicans* (1920). The lighting fits with their

Repoussoir in *The Wishing Ring* (1914)

larger project of pictorial stylisation, but its reference is more specific, just like the *repoussoir* technique to which it is related. It references a technique common in the French Baroque paintings that made up a central part of the curriculum at French art schools. These strong contrasts between illuminated central figures and dark peripheries, like those seen in the candle-lit paintings of Georges de la Tour, also circulated in the USA. In American art-education lectures and textbooks, paintings and drawings deploying this technique provided important lessons in the arrangement of light and shade.[17]

My aim in isolating these recycled painterly techniques (which Carré also used on the stage) is less to trace how they become established film techniques and more to show how they help to figure a certain relationship between cinema and art at this time. Considered together, their battery of techniques seem scattered at best. They resist coherent aesthetic pedigrees. What made these techniques not appear inchoate and haphazard, indeed what made them appear to define cinematic aesthetic maturity, were the massive parallel efforts to promote Tourneur as a screen painter. His persona affected the way his films could look, the way they could be discussed and how they could be seen. This frame was just as important in the exchange between cinema and art as the design of Tourneur's and Carré's film techniques.

THE BLUE BIRD: FROM THE YELLOW BOOK TO THE YELLOW PRESS

Tourneur's films would remain in conversation with the other arts more or less throughout his life, even with his later low-budget French genre films like *Justin de Marseille* (1935). His films of the late 1910s, however, mark the high point of his cross-media position within the American film industry. Most of the articles about him as a painter of the screen were written during this period in which Paramount agreed to promote and distribute the films under the Artcraft label. This arrangement allowed Tourneur and Carré to concentrate their pictorial experiments and to explore fantastic themes on a healthy budget. In these films, the kinds of pictorial techniques discussed above reached an intensity. Lighting contrasts grew, sets became more elaborate and they increasingly flattened layers of their compositions to a point that recalled Puvis. They began by inserting some of their early pictorial excesses at climactic moments within films with more straightforward stories, like Mary Pickford's drug-induced hallucination sequence in *Poor Little Rich Girl* (1917). By 1918 they moved into broader allegory and fantasy with films like *Woman, Prunella* and *The Blue Bird*.

The Blue Bird offers a remarkable case here, and not only because it is the most stylised of this cycle and has survived in a relatively complete form. It also stands out among these films as having a particularly rich intermedial history, which follows the path of 1890s decadent aesthetics into American media culture in the late 1910s. The film was an adaptation of the famous play by Maurice Maeterlinck, a Belgian Symbolist whose plays eventually found notoriety among an American audience not too different from those who admired Puvis. In the 1890s, Maeterlinck found his main American admirers among Boston and New York decadents like pictorialist photographer F. Holland Day and Vance Thompson, editor of the influential *M'lle New York*.[18] Day was responsible for publishing the famous 1890s journal *The Yellow Book* in the USA. His close colleague and fan of the yellow 90s, Richard Hovey, became Maeterlinck's main English translator starting with his 1895 edition of *The Plays of Maurice Maeterlinck*. In Hovey's introduction to the volume, he reads Maeterlinck as an unequivocal decadent, setting his Symbolism 'against the masquerade of morality'. For Hovey and his circle, Maeterlinck restricts himself, 'to a single mood. His master tone is always terror – terror too of one type – that of the churchyard. He is a poet of the sepulchre ... His devotion to the wormy side of things may prevent him from ever becoming popular.'[19]

Hovey's prediction about Maeterlinck's popularity could not have been more wrong. A survey of American newspaper databases reveals a swell of interest in Maeterlinck beginning with Hovey's 1890s publications and peaking in the late 1910s with thousands of articles on the author available for each year. By the time Maeterlinck visited the USA in 1920, civic groups were holding parades in his honour, New York socialites were dressing up as peacocks for *Blue Bird* balls and Samuel Goldwyn was hosting him in Culver City in an attempt to persuade him (eventually declined) to write directly for the screen.[20] With this popularity, however, came a major transformation in the reception of his work. As discussion of Maeterlinck surged, 'the wormy side of things' did recede into the background. Like Puvis, Maeterlinck's work adapted to the American scene better than other Symbolists'. It was more his pop mysticism than his amorality, more his dreams of the afterlife than his sepulchral obsessions, that made him a hit with the lyceum crowd. Already by 1902 a critic noted his popularity with 'long hair females' who digressed in lyceums on 'the comprehensibility of what is commonly called the incomprehensible in Maeterlinck'.[21] The description of the 'long hairs' in this audience recalls the decadent tradition that characterised the work of Hovey and Day, but it also shows how Maeterlinck has moved from Day's salons to the educational sphere of the lyceum. It was lyceum mogul James Pond (also Alexander Black's tour manager) who eventually sponsored Maeterlinck's grand tour of the USA. The theatrical run of *The Blue Bird* put Maeterlinckana in particularly high demand, with numerous quasi-educational publications helping to explain the philosophical meaning in its allegories.[22] With *The*

Blue Bird, Maeterlinck's reception in small-scale avant-garde publications continued to spill outward, first to the lyceum and then onto the broader public.

By the time the Tourneur/Artcraft adaptation went into production, American theatre companies, aesthete photographers, critics and public lecturers had already formed a dense and heterogeneous network of references around the story and its characters. Paramount's interest in marketing a Maurice Tourneur adaptation of *The Blue Bird* came at the height of the story's popularity. The opening credits noted Maeterlinck's 'famous masterpiece', and film critics assumed that 'everyone knows the story of *The Blue Bird*'.[23] Tourneur certainly knew the play better than most. It was one of the major productions at the Théâtre Réjane, where he produced shows (including the production of *Alias Jimmy Valentine* starring Émile Chautard). Réjane revived the play three times in the 1910s, and each revival exhibited a familiar taste for stylised sets, celebrity and pop philosophy. The 1911 Théâtre Réjane programme began with an essay explaining the play's philosophical allegory, even before showcasing stars like Séverin Mars (later the celebrated lead actor for director Abel Gance).[24] Zukor essentially contracted Tourneur to import the Réjane production and, box-office returns aside, they received glowing praise for the project. The trade papers, and even the fan magazines, praised the producers alongside Tourneur and Carré. 'For the vision to see the possibilities, the Artcraft executives deserve praise, scarcely second to that which must be accorded to the genius of the play himself – Tourneur.'[25]

Visual analysis of this film has been scarce. The most extensive consideration has been given it by Jan-Christopher Horak, who, in addition to his pioneering scholarship on early art film-makers like Tourneur, has also helped to preserve their films. Horak has observed the way the film revisits early cinema's 'archaic techniques, e.g. tableau images, live action animation, visual metaphors, ... direct address' and costumes reminiscent of Méliès, which 'must be contextualized within [Noel Burch's discussion of] the larger struggle against classical narrative'. Horak's point about early cinema reappearing can be seen throughout the film, and it raises the question of why Tourneur would deploy these techniques at this time. I would contend that what attracted Tourneur and Carré was not early cinema as a marker of cinema's freer past, but rather early cinema's omnivorous inclusivity, its penchant for citation and frame-jumping (discussed in Chapter 2). The turn to antedated techniques contributed to a larger effort to create a film that wore its rich texture of references on its surface. If these references included early cinema techniques, they pointed through them to pictorial traditions in painting, theatre design and illustration.

It makes sense in a film that references the other arts that the *mise en scène* would dominate. Elements of the décor frame each shot more decisively than the camera frame. Editing is minimal throughout the film, and generally limited to cut-ins within composed tableaux. The performers seem to be caught in an uphill struggle to satisfy the compositional needs of the elaborate sets. And not only is the design foregrounded over other elements, it also commands the very structures of the film. Consider the pictorial framing devices. If the arched framings in Tourneur's and Carré's set pieces reference illustration and the lantern as much as the theatre, this referentiality works, beyond single images, in the overall arrangement of the sequences. Like sequential lantern shows or illustrations, the foreground arch could be used intermittently throughout a film, highlighting the distinctions between scenes composed with

Entrance hall of the fairy's palace in *The Blue Bird* (1918) (Courtesy of George Eastman House, International Museum of Photography and Film)

vignettes and those without. In *Poor Little Rich Girl*, the arched framing marks the transition to fantasy and hallucination. In *The Rail Rider* (1916), it marks displays of wealth. In *Trilby*, it accompanies the scenes of hypnotic influence. Tourneur used these pictorial effects to organise the films thematically, and did so increasingly in the late 1910s. With *The Blue Bird*, he employed this thematic organisation throughout the entire film. At its core, the production is really just a collage of framed pictures. Tourneur condensed Maeterlinck's spiritual allegory into sequences of allegorical pictures, each one a self-contained symbol of a different type of joy, or terror, or pleasure. The characters in the story simply move from one picture to the next. From the moment they begin their journey by walking through the Fairy Berylune's palace, Tourneur signals that pictorial framing will be a major guiding element. In this transition scene they move intermittently towards the camera through a *mise en abyme* of architectural frames, pausing inside each frame to mark it off from the rest of the space. Once through this palace and fully inside the fantasy space, they encounter several series of pictures. Each one is structured by one of the three palaces visited on the journey: the Palace of Night, the Palace of Luxury and the Palace of Happiness.

Each palace stamps a differently designed pictorial framing device on its series. In the Palace of Night, tableau vivant statues mark arched doorways that open onto the

Making Movies into Art

shades and terrors (sadly weakened by the triumph of the positivist sciences) represented with the most abstract compositions in the film. Tourneur and Carré frame the Palace of Luxury more chaotically. The characters representing different bodily excesses are pushed together in the same frame, surrounded by arching garlands of flowers and segmented by a 'wipe' effect created, not on an optical printer, but with a curtain of flowers drawn up from the floor. In the Palace of Happiness, van den Broek shot the types of happiness – of air, of loving, of springtime, of watching the stars rise – in an outdoor setting, but with an arched, in-camera vignette. They frame each type of happiness identically and style them similarly. The theme is pastoral, with the happinesses personified by shepherds and young women in Arcadian dress dancing along hillsides. Tourneur marks the transitions from one series of tableaux to the next with transitions in pictorial style, which help to structure these fragmentary scenes like dioramas, illustrations, lantern slide sequences, or sequential paintings in the decorative tradition.

Here Puvis re-enters the frame. During a time when he avidly publicised his work on Puvis's murals in numerous interviews, Tourneur crafted the allegorical tableaux in the *The Blue Bird* in an elaborate gesture towards the fine arts. The palace scenes' connection to early cinema and French theatre cannot be denied, but they did not need to be. Painterly composition worked for Tourneur and for Carré as a kind of unifying concept for their many pictorial references. He was already forming patterns of referencing art history in his lighting and foreground objects. *The Blue Bird* took this painterly pose a step further and spent the greater portion of the resources for a feature film on a series of individually titled compositions. Considering these compositions as a sequence of pictures, it is not difficult to notice stylistic affinities between Tourneur's and Puvis's pictures. Puvis's Boston Public Library murals form a sequence of thematically linked allegorical pictures that symbolise the divisions of human knowledge. If Tourneur had added a Palace of Knowledge to Maeterlinck's story and requested that Carré restage the Arcadian figures from Puvis's Boston murals, the sequence would have fitted seamlessly within the film. The same goes for the style of the Boston murals. Each scene is framed by an architectural arch, and is composed in flat planes rather than in naturalistic depth. The figures seem to occupy multiple two-dimensional planes within three-dimensional space. Puvis famously flattened his figures, so much that cartoons could caricature him, showing him using larger-than-life models made of cardboard.[26] This move towards flattened composition and away from pictorial illusion could easily describe Tourneur's and Carré's approach to layered deep space. To be clear, I am not suggesting that Tourneur learned his specific film-making techniques in Puvis's atelier. It would be safer to describe their aesthetic relationship as affinity rather than appropriation. This affinity is important because of how it was used to promote Tourneur during his rise in the American film industry. To analyse his style by identifying only how his techniques were borrowed from early films or from turn-of-the century stagecraft would miss the way that Tourneur was able to synthesise these various influences as a painter of the screen.

Tourneur's painterly reputation suited Maeterlinck's style. His emphasis on *mise en scène* fitted within a tradition of Symbolist performance theory better than many theatrical adaptations of Symbolist plays. Maeterlinck hyperbolised nineteenth-century physical acting theories by suggesting that actors be treated as puppets and

Stop-motion washbasin and furniture in *The Blue Bird* (Courtesy of George Eastman House, International Museum of Photography and Film)

décor be granted its deserved vitality. 'One should perhaps eliminate the living being from the stage ... Will the day come when sculpture will be used onstage? Will the human being be replaced by a shadow? A reflection? A projection of symbolic forms? Or a being who would appear to live without being alive?'[27] It would already be tempting to suggest the medium of cinema as one answer to Maeterlinck's call for the next generation of Symbolist performance, simply by virtue of its incorporeal shadows and reflections, but *The Blue Bird* film directly invites this temptation. Tourneur's film answers each one of Maeterlinck's suggestions. For starters, he did not use stars. Tourneur had strong working relationships with actors like Mary Pickford and Clara Kimball Young, either of whom could have secured greater financial success for the film. But Tourneur set different priorities for the film, so that his *Blue Bird* remains (next to productions starring Shirley Temple, Jane Fonda and Elizabeth Taylor) the only feature-length American adaptation of the story not to draw on star power. And just as Tourneur avoided recognisable faces, he submerged all of his performances in the heavy pictorial design of each scene.[28] The living performers yield to elaborate costumes, designed sets and trick effects. As requested by Maeterlinck, the Rich Children are seen only as shadows in windows. The Shades and Terrors are diffuse outlines of bodies projected on a scrim. Sculpture and performer merge in the tableaux vivants that guard the entryways to the different chambers in the Palace of Night. If Symbolist aesthetics required de-emphasising the living performer, then Tourneur's pictorial *mise en scène* uses every trick available to enable this transformation of values.

An allegory of the search for spiritual fulfilment, *The Blue Bird* demands that one learn to see the invisible souls inhabiting things. Tourneur turns to the media environment of early cinema as a way to explore this theme. This happens most clearly in the sequence where the main characters in the story emerge, in human form, from the everyday objects and pets inside the children's home. The stop-motion animation in this sequence immediately stands out, as it did to reviewers in 1918. As the magic in the story begins, before Tourneur introduces the human forms

Making Movies into Art

of Fire, Milk, Water, Sugar, Bread and the Cat and Dog, the children see their beds race across the room and the washbasin pirouette around wardrobe. The origin of this stop-motion scene has roots in the studios of the famous animator Émile Cohl. Before coming to work for Éclair, Carré worked with Cohl and helped him to create early animation films like *The Pumpkin Race* (1908). Carré's animated furniture – moving, yes – but also expressing emotion through the suggestion of dancing, recreates the effect from Cohl's *The Automatic Moving Company* (1911). Maeterlinck demanded that Carré embue his furniture with living souls, but Cohl taught Carré's living furniture how to act.

Tourneur's and Carré's dancing washbasin premiered, however, in a very different context than Cohl's animations. This was the same year that proto-surrealist Louis Aragon published 'On Décor', recommending Poe's 'Philosophy of Furniture' as mandatory reading for the student of cinema and singling out Chaplin as a performer with a spiritual sense of décor. 'The elements of décor which surround Charlie participate intimately in the action. ... The décor is Charlie's very vision of the world which, together with the mechanical and its laws, haunts the hero to such an extent that by an inversion of values *each inanimate object becomes a living thing for him, each human person a dummy* whose starting handle must be found.'[29] Aragon admired moments when Chaplin seemed to invert the relationships between performer and object. Tourneur dwelled on these same moments in the animated sequences of *The Blue Bird*. Tourneur's film parallels Aragon's article by updating the Symbolist fascination with the souls in things. This parallelism is even more significant because it was a popular one. If Aragon's reading of the souls in filmed things was intentionally a reading against the grain of mainstream cinema, Tourneur's film brings it into the mainstream. A *New York Times* critic, describing the premiere at the Rivoli with orchestral accompaniment by Hugo Reisenfield, noted the stop-motion.

> Maurice Tourneur, who directed the production of the film, used the art of magic to make the souls appear and act their parts, to show the flight of people and Father Time's ship through the air, to make all sorts of mysteries take place before one's very eyes. There may be some who will talk of fadeaways and superimposing and all of the tricks of the motion-picture trade, but such are the kind of people who don't believe that Things have souls.[30]

The reviewer makes a connection between Symbolist spirituality and a set of film techniques outdated enough to appear conspicuous. Not only do we have recycled early cinema in the scene. We also have a recycling of those charged ideas about cinema that Symbolist writers of the 1890s imagined in the early devices of Lumière and Edison, this time in a mainstream press review of a studio film.

Stop-motion offers one palpable example, but references to early film magic proliferate in the scene's styling of the puppet-characters. The film magic of Georges Méliès in particular appears to influence the film, which does make some sense in a *féerie*, even one produced even as late as 1918. The loaf of sugar grows into a cone-head man with a moving camera superimposition that mimics Méliès's *The Man with the Rubber Head* (1902), and the loaf of bread transforms into an Orientalist sultan who, as Horak notes, brings Méliès's conjurer characters to mind. Tourneur's costumes for Sugar and Bread also directly copy those of the 1911 Théâtre Réjane production directed and designed by Maeterlinck's lover, Georgette Leblanc. Méliès and Leblanc drew, after all, from similar material, and neither of them shied away from what one might call the 'wormier side' of these magical transformations. In the 1918 adaptation, Sugar snaps off his own fingers and Bread slices of his own flesh with a scimitar to feed the hungry mouths around them. If Leblanc's production almost called out for the violent alchemy of Méliès's earlier cinematic tricks, Tourneur's adaptation seems to recognise this and uses tricks from early cinema magic to extend the violent, alchemical spirit of the stage production.

Indeed, Leblanc's production design exposes the threads that join Symbolist aesthetics, early cinema and Tourneur's and Carré's picture craft. The flowing gowns Tourneur and Carré used for the women who play Water, Milk and Night might have more clearly gestured to Symbolist icon Loïe Fuller's serpentine dance, had Tourneur staged his film with more rapid movement. Night's gown in the Théâtre Réjane production comes much closer to Fuller's costumes for her Folies Bergère performances, with dowels to extend the reach of her arms and the span of fabric hanging from them. Stills and descriptions from the production indicate that Night's gown was indeed within the same sphere of influence that produced Edison's many serpentine dance films with Annabelle Whitford and Toulouse Lautrec's paintings of Fuller in frenetic splashes of colour. Carré and Tourneur offer a more direct reference to Fuller's *Fire Dance* with the transformation of the character Fire, whose billowed-fabric movements resemble a serpentine dance projected in reverse, or in reverse gravity. They use a fan to blow the orange-tinted costume upward like flames. If one reads Fuller's performances, as Tom Gunning does, as a Symbolist art of animation that stages the transition between non-human things (like flowers and flames) and moving pictures of the human body, then *The Blue Bird's* transformations fit squarely within this tradition.[31] Tourneur's traces of Fuller's serpentine dance almost literalise the connection that Gunning makes between Fuller, as a Symbolist icon, and early cinema. Tourneur extends this connection into later experiments with art film-making by reconfiguring these early cinema traditions in a 1918 film. He affirms those correspondences between Maeterlinck's philosophy of art and a Paramount feature film.

The Blue Bird looks back to Symbolist art and to early cinema together. The connection with early cinema mediates the way the film works as an art film. Tourneur may have assisted Rodin and painted with Puvis. He may have produced Symbolist plays for the Théâtre Réjane. But to call his films Symbolist in the narrow sense, to see them as simply a type of art film influenced by Symbolist artists, would miss what makes Tourneur's relation to these artistic traditions so compelling. If one considered Symbolist and decadent traditions to be invented by, say, a few painters, and then approximated in moving images, then *The Blue Bird's* stylised *mise en scène* could only bowdlerise Symbolist aesthetics. Clearly, the bowdlerisation argument should be acknowledged, especially given the transformations of decadent aesthetics in the American context. Maeterlinck's popular philosophy did migrate from the amoral salons of Richard Hovey to the YMCA lecture, where he was received as a kind of warmed-over Emerson. Puvis, too, became an icon of aesthetic restraint and an ideal craftsman in contrast to colleagues like Moreau. And Tourneur, with the help of

Watching Fire spring from the hearth in *The Blue Bird* (Courtesy of George Eastman House, International Museum of Photography and Film)

producers like Adolph Zukor, actively courted the American cultural elite in selecting and promoting his films.

But Tourneur's films do not simply mimic the noble themes and restrained styles of respected artists of the end of the nineteenth century. His films are hopelessly tangled collages of references and traditions. They recycle early cinema's tableaux, animations, dances and caricatures with an inclusivity that challenges restraint. With *The Blue Bird*, Tourneur attempts one of his most direct examinations of a specific aesthetic tradition, Symbolism, and yet the film's painterly citations borrow lighting techniques from eighteenth-century oil painting and framing from Victorian illustration – techniques that many Symbolist painters rejected. The film alternates between deep-focus *repoussoir* and its opposite, the cardboard-cut-out staging that resembles his sketches for Puvis. Its mode is inclusive and irreverent, even as it addresses reverent cultural institutions. Lecturers on Symbolist art may have softened the edges of an aesthetic tradition for the lyceum set, but they also reveal this tradition's promiscuous life in American discussions about art. Tourneur's film appeals to these lecturers, but also revels in this promiscuity by bringing Loïe Fuller, Georges Méliès, Émile Cohl and Louis Aragon into renewed contact with Symbolist traditions. The line connecting Tourneur's films to early cinema is not a straight line. It doesn't get to Edison, Méliès, or Lumière without also winding through Symbolist theatre and painting. Tourneur's art cinema succeeded by actively forging these connections.

CONCLUSION: TOURNEUR AFTER 1920

Tourneur's American career moved increasingly towards independence from and eventual disillusionment with the American film industry. He made films in the USA for a few more years and then, in 1926, he returned to Paris and effectively started over making B movies for Pathé. By his last couple of years in Hollywood he was gravitating towards adventure novel adaptations that held out a likelihood of larger audiences. These films, including *Treasure Island* (1920), *The Last of the Mohicans*, *Lorna Doone* (1922) and *The Isle of Lost Ships* (1923), did not reject his pictorial style, but they did seek out ways to merge athletic physical performance with conspicuous style, into a kind of swashbuckling pictorialism. These films are fascinating in the way they hybridise the vigour of the celebrity proponents of the strenuous life with the decadent traditions of atmospheric fantasy compositions, strains of American aesthetic culture that mainstream art and film critics of the time frequently placed in opposition to one another as a way to delimit teachable aesthetic principles. The next chapter continues the discussion of swashbuckling, strenuous pictorialism as it was a prominent defining characteristic for Rex Ingram (his films as well as his adventuring personal life). Ingram's and Tourneur's mutual tendency to combine action with attention to composed pictures was one of the reasons that film critics regularly discussed these two directors, who had no real professional connection to each other, as a pair. To highlight this link between the two directors, let me close with one brief example from one of Tourneur's later American films.

Among adventure novelists, James Fenimore Cooper was known for his interest in picturesque landscape, which was one of the reasons that N. C. Wyeth's illustrations for *The Last of the Mohicans* were so successful.[32] Tourneur's adaptation of the novel clearly bears a rich relationship to Wyeth's illustrations. Following Wyeth but also using his own signature compositions, Tourneur's *Last of the Mohicans* attracted fans of adventure films and pictorially minded critics alike. The film stages battle scenes through the shadowy mouths of caves and alongside picturesque cliffs. Tourneur's heroes stood still, silhouetted and contemplative, in these layered deep compositions, but no less frequently than they wrestled in them with knives drawn. This combination of action and *repoussoir*, of subtle composition and dynamic confrontation, could just as easily describe Wyeth's scenes. There is a similar double movement working in these illustrations, in Tourneur's adaptation and throughout many of the works of early art cinema. But the question of how to parse this painterly influence is trickier than tracing the lineage of techniques.

If Wyeth's illustrations provide a resource for understanding Tourneur's film, it is not just as raw material for citation. It is because, in their respective fields, they were responding to some of the same questions about the role of aesthetics in mass culture. Wyeth was an avid promoter of 'better illustration', and his approach to defining an aesthetics of popular illustration often parallels those promoters of better films.[33] He openly criticised illustration's lower placement in the art school hierarchy relative to

Strenuous pictorialism in *The Last of the Mohicans* (1920)

painting. His views on illustration were simultaneously anxious, in their reaction to the painters he believed to 'hold illustration in contempt', and aspirational in their recommendations for 'growth into the field of painting'.[34] These aspirations and anxieties help to explain why his blockbuster illustrations resisted being illustrations. These were pictures made during the golden age of the illustrated book, pictures that paid for his Pennsylvania estate, where he entertained a steady stream of guests including F. Scott and Zelda Fitzgerald. But instead of wholeheartedly embracing a format efficiently suited to mass production, Wyeth insisted on painting his scenes as large-format oil paintings. These illustrations made use of elements of academic oil painting, but with important revisions. When defining properties of illustration that had an advantage over the painting with which he was familiar, Wyeth continually returned to the term 'virility'. Thus in his own strenuous compositions, he brightened the colour palette and enhanced the physicality of his pictures, but at the same time he continued techniques that would remind viewers of those traditions of painting the waning of which conservative art critics lamented, precisely because of the proliferation of popular illustration. In this way Wyeth's illustrations are relevant for seeing Tourneur's film less in terms of simple influence or adaptation, less as a one-way movement from painting to cinema, than as similar negotiation happening in a neighbouring profession. It is the prevalence of these types of negotiations, happening simultaneously in cinema and popular illustration, that provides a broader context for the techniques shared between painter and director.

The body of work Tourneur made before moving to Europe spans a period of possibility in American art cinema. His approach to film-making became possible during a moment when the styles and themes of European art history, ranging eclectically from academic composition to avant-garde traditions like French Symbolism, were thriving themes within the American press, in exhibits, lectures and also in the studio-backed feature film. Cinema contributed, as only one medium among many, to this broader practice. Illustrators, advertisers and theatre producers recycled these aesthetic traditions alongside film-makers. It is cinema's interaction with this milieu, not necessarily its direct borrowing from painting, that situates the films of Tourneur and his colleagues. The history of Tourneur's pictorial citations, combined with the promotion of the pictorial aspects of his films in print, is part of the history of the American public reception of art. In this larger intermedial context aesthetic influences circulate as dynamically as Loïe Fuller's *Fire Dance* from the Folies Bergère, to Symbolist watercolour, to Edison's Black Maria studio, to Tourneur's Paramount films from the late 1910s.

5
Rex Ingram's Art School Cinema

In the early 1920s, the National Board of Review formed the Exceptional Photoplays Committee to oversee publication of a monthly bulletin that would serve as a mouthpiece for the organisation. As the board members refined their mission to replace the moral evaluation of films with aesthetic evaluation, they held up Rex Ingram's *Scaramouche* (1923) for special consideration, comparing it with Maurice Tourneur's *Last of the Mohicans*. More than a simple example of an exceptional film, *Scaramouche*'s release in September 1923 inspired a discussion of the standards and aesthetic traditions on which the committee based their evaluations. The author of the lead article for the Autumn–Summer [*sic*] 1923 issue of *Exceptional Photoplays* took the occasion of the film's release to break with the traditional review format, to risk being 'distressing to the reader who wants to know what the story is about and who are the actors', and to discuss what might make a film exceptional in the aesthetic sense. The article begins, 'If the art of the motion picture is the art of composition ... then the mechanics of effect must always be paramount in the use of the photoplay medium.' It declares Ingram's films, alongside Tourneur's, to be essential to a cinema of vibrant, composed pictures, 'which is the exact reverse of what is commonly thought to be the nature of pictures in motion'.

> [*Scaramouche*] becomes something other than ['mere narration', 'drama', or 'action'] through that art of composition first mentioned which Mr Ingram really understands – through a knowledge of technique which is born of a feeling for beauty. *Scaramouche* is nearly always beautiful – is primarily aimed at being beautiful – and achieved beauty most often because its unfolding motion crystalizes into periods of signifying and revealing stillness.[1]

   Fused here to this passage's flowery rhetoric of beauty – a mainstay in writing on artistic films – is a notion of composition carried over from art education in the lecture hall and the university. The article starts by defining the art of cinema generally as composition, and it recalls psychological, pictorial aesthetics with its reference to 'effect'. Art lecturers of the time sought out the vital effects of aesthetic composition on the psychology of the beholder. Applied to cinema, this living, engaging composition competes with other vitalities of the medium, such as cinema's mechanical capacity to move and its capacity to tell stories in sequence. It is this less-examined vitality of motion pictures, the argument goes, that distinguishes common motion pictures from a kind of art film. Directors like Ingram and Tourneur constituted a privileged minority because they were able to do the work required to compose scenes in this way. While to many this work seemed at odds with (or even the exact reverse of) the nature of moving pictures, to the Exceptional Photoplays Committee composition offered cinema the promise of mobility into other spheres.

Like Tourneur, Rex Ingram seemed made for the project of defining aesthetically ambitious cinema. Ingram's films often proved more marketable than Tourneur's, but they worked in same vein. As so many reviewers of his films noted, he, too, trained train in sculpture and painting. The task with a director like Ingram is to figure out exactly how this kinship with the other arts functioned at various stages in his career. One way to address this question would be to follow a primarily formal line of enquiry and highlight Ingram's borrowed painterly and sculptural techniques as instances of early Hollywood's ability to absorb visual styles.[2] As in the previous chapter, I am proposing a related but not identical approach that puts intellectual networks and institutional publicity in the foreground. It focuses on how critics and educators helped to create a critical niche for his films' stylistic experimentation. This indirect, or mediated, approach to a director's style applies to Ingram's films even more than to Tourneur's. *The Blue Bird* is a collage of references to be sure, but it retains a strong art-historical thread of Symbolism and other French decadent traditions. Ingram's ties to the artist's studio were just as strong, they were even more avidly publicised, but his separation from specific movements was greater. He framed his influence from the artist's studio in bolder and more abstract terms.

In other words, Ingram's public affinities with the other arts allowed for an array of pictorially stylised techniques (many devised by his cinematographer John F. Seitz) to classify the director as exceptional. Framing Ingram's films in this way not only connects art cinema to educational institutions previously overlooked. It also highlights how the compositions of directors like Ingram differed from early Los Angeles-based peripheral film-makers, such as those mapped by David James in his 2005 book *The Most Typical Avant-Garde*. One could certainly trace significant stylistic similarities between, for example, Dudley Murphy's *Soul of the Cypress* (1921) and several of Ingram's films. But shared influences notwithstanding, Ingram resists classification as a 'minor' film-maker in the way that James uses the term to describe Murphy's work in the early 1920s. The type of art cinema that Ingram represented positioned itself as exceptional, but not marginal or peripheral.[3]

Ingram's releases were perennial favourites in publications devoted to better films. These publications traded in his reputation, much of which he fashioned himself, as a visual artist working in the medium of film. By situating this self-fashioned reputation within parallel movements in aesthetic education it becomes possible to understand how Ingram contributed to a definition of art cinema, not only by adopting techniques of pictorial composition, but also by drawing from traditions of teaching craft and composition and shaping an image of the director around the image of the plastic artist in the studio.

THE OLDEST ART SCHOOL AND THE NEWEST ART

In noteworthy parallel with Tourneur, Ingram's position between cinema and the other arts was built on exceptional myths of origin. Known in the press as a 'sculptor of the screen', his work in film always managed to point back to the 1912–13 academic year that he spent studying sculpture at Yale. This training proved valuable in a number of ways. There were potential financial advantages to Ingram's association with the first university art school in the nation.[4] A critic could read strategy, for both Yale and Metro, in Ingram's statement that, 'As time went on I began to realize how valuable my training in the art school was going to prove.'[5] Film producers could benefit from a director with an Ivy League art education, and college administrators could benefit from alumni in Hollywood. Some evidence supports this position. Yale awarded Ingram the BFA in 1921, with one year of completed course work (three years was the requirement), only after he had become a famous director. Ingram, along with several of his celebrators to be discussed in the section on *Scaramouche*, maintained of course that the value of his association with Yale was in his formal training. 'I had gained an understanding of the laws that govern perspective, composition, balance, construction, form and the distribution of light and shade, thanks to repeated lectures on these subjects.'[6] Rather than seeing these two interpretations as being at odds with one another, it is important to see how both aspects of Ingram's association with Yale's art school were intertwined. Knowledge of light and shade may be useful, but not in itself. Producers and critics had to find ways to frame film techniques so that they registered for audiences as part of film's kinship with the other arts. And even an interpretation of his arts training as a cynical marketing strategy would be lacking if it did not account for how his publicity accessed a tradition of representing the artist's work space and a specific language of composition. In either case, Ingram's myths of origin helped frame the labour of art so that it would include cinema.

While these efforts reached a high point in the early 1920s, they were present at every stage of his career. Ingram often cited a New Haven screening of the Vitagraph Company's quality adaptation of *A Tale of Two Cities* (1911) as his inspiration to enter motion pictures. 'I brought several friends of mine, most of them either students of the art school, or members of the Yale Dramatic Association, the following day to see the picture. … All of us decided thereupon to enter the motion picture field.'[7] This anecdote served him well, as Vitagraph was his first steady employer, and his interest in promoting himself as a sculptor of the screen began there, years before he had the opportunity to direct his art films for Universal's Bluebird brand and then for Metro. This early identity as an artist of the screen was conveyed on screen rather than behind the camera. He seemed to have been seeking out opportunities to show his knowledge of an artist's studio. He gravitated towards artist roles (usually sculptors) in Vitagraph films, including *The Artist's Great Madonna* (1913), *The Spirit and the Clay* (1914) and *Eve's Daughter* (1914). Whether he chose these roles, or they were chosen for him because of his experience, Ingram's study of fine arts provided an uncommon point of entry into cinema.[8] His early work in front of the camera shows the link between the artist stereotypes in fictional illustration and a more material fascination with the trappings and processes of the studio in educational material. Films with aesthetic ambitions made use of both of these popular types of studio imagery. Ingram was not singular among directors in this regard, but he was exceptional in the extent of his familiarity with the artist's studio.

Just as exceptional was Ingram's connection to the craft traditions to which several critics and early art-film directors paid some degree of deference. Fresh out of art

Rex Ingram plays a sculptor in *The Spirit and the Clay* (1914)

school, and eager to combine work in decorative and fine arts, he followed the
teachings of Arts and Crafts educators in an exemplary fashion. In addition to drawing
and sculpting, he studied the decorative arts and Persian poetry. Although never
published, he spent some time in the mid-1910s tinkering with his own translation of
Omar Khayyam's *Rubaiyat*, an aesthete staple. In a 1915 letter to his aunt in Ireland,
after describing his experiences working at Vitagraph, Ingram expresses his great
ambitions to found his own Arts and Crafts colony. 'I'm going to buy an old castle on
the West Coast – I have a number of talented friends – and I would like to start a place
like William Morris where artists, sculptors, writers, designers, interior decorators
could turn out really fine works with the commercial interest – while in good hands –
being of second importance.'[9] He framed this as a desire to help bring the Arts and
Crafts traditions of Morris and Ruskin to the USA, but the movement was already
deeply influencing the art departments at American universities. He was just as likely
to have encountered William Morris's work at Yale than anywhere else. His real
contribution would, of course, be to Hollywood and not to the Arts and Crafts
movement, but this early formulation of what constitutes an arts community still
benefited the industry.

Film studio interest in craft movements was minor, but some silent film companies
incorporated traces of recognisable styles or paid lip service to aesthetic workmanship
as a marker of prestige. These traces are evident in the work of art directors, in
suggestive company names like Artcraft, and in the design of promotional material.[10]
Universal made use of the potential of Arts and Crafts design for branding groups of

Making Movies into Art

films. As part of his analysis of Universal's prestige labels, Mark Cooper notes that Bluebird's brand identity took priority over other elements of its films.[11] Bluebird advertisements avoided pictures of stars and described the film plots only telegraphically. If the Bluebird label sought to distinguish itself by diverging from standard pictorial publicity, its choice of design is revealing. Its style clearly draws on American Arts and Crafts graphics that were taught around the country. The Bluebird logo is prominent in the print ads, but so are the flat, monochromatic clouds and backgrounds sometimes printed in the rich yellows and blues common among Arts and Crafts groups like the Roycrofters. The layout of the ads often seems to replicate the decorative cover designs of the little magazines, which were important venues for the transatlantic circulation of the movement's designs. The Bluebird ad for *Hop, the Devil's Brew* (1916), singled out by Cooper for its distinctive labelling, includes an Arts and Crafts typeface flanked by ornamental poppy seed pods, which were almost clichés of Arts and Crafts design. The designers of Universal's Bluebird ads did not simply differentiate this publicity from the usual trade-paper copy with more decoration. They appropriated some of the Arts and Crafts movement's most recognisable iconography. As Universal increased its institutional reach and industrial organisation, it sought to brand some of its films as craft products. By promoting himself as a student of the movement, Ingram fitted this brand perfectly and became one of Bluebird's regular directors. In this way, albeit perhaps not the way he had originally intended, Ingram did help to bring William Morris's influence to a castle on the West Coast.

As he gained recognition as a director, Ingram actively framed his film work through his apprenticeship in an artist's workshop. He had spent his most valued time at Yale studying with and later assisting Lee Lawrie, the only professor of sculpture and modelling in the department.[12] As an architectural sculptor who would be remembered primarily for his Art Deco figure of Atlas outside the Rockefeller Center, Lawrie offered a model of aesthetic craft labour. Ingram made frequent reference to his mentorship with Lawrie, beginning with his discussions with producers at Bluebird and Metro. The press really began to talk about Ingram's mentorship under Lawrie during the production of *The Four Horsemen of the Apocalypse*. Before the release, journals commissioned artists to review the film, like San Francisco sculptor Edgar Walters, who described why he would have known that *Four Horsemen* was made by a trained sculptor even if he had not known who had made the film.[13] Reviews like these served as a preamble to an elaborate integration of artist's studio and set.

The film represented a significant investment by Metro, and it would quickly become Ingram's most successful film. Adding to the fanfare of a Lyric Theatre premiere, Metro requested not only that Lawrie participate, but also that he create a specially commissioned sculpture of the *Four Horsemen* for the lobby display.[14] The company printed photographs of Lawrie's *Four Horsemen* on the invitations and later used it in publicity material for the film. The public fanfare continued when Ingram presented the sculpture as a gift to Vicente Blasco Ibáñez, who wrote the novel adapted by June Mathis for Ingram (and for Rudolph Valentino).[15] Lawrie also designed cut-out lobby displays for *Four Horsemen*. Images of his sculpture circulated, as did publicity stills of Ingram showing Valentino how to look natural in an artist's studio. Ingram was a sculptor working in film, he featured sculptures in his films, and he exhibited sculpture at his film premieres – all to help convince his audience that he

Invitation to the New York
Premiere of *The Four
Horsemen of the Apocalypse*
(*Metro*, 1921). Lee Lawrie
created the sculpture
featured here and in the
publicity material for the film

made films with a sculptor's sense of form in a space that worked like a fine arts studio.

If Lawrie's cardboard cut-out display suggests the value of his sculptural labour in motion-picture publicity stunts, it is important to remember that the benefits of this connection worked both ways. The publicity surrounding *Four Horsemen* produced not just an air of artiness for films of a certain type of ambition. It also produced an actual degree for Ingram, a BFA from the oldest and most established university arts programme in the country. Yale administrators made clear that this was not an honorary degree. They voted to recognise Ingram's film as work appropriate towards a degree in art.[16] In framing the degree in this way the Yale art programme could go beyond claiming a celebrity alumnus (and the donations that they rightly assumed would result from this recognition) and towards a systematic recognition of aesthetic cinema. The local paper agreed: 'In conferring the degree of bachelor of fine arts on Mr Ingram Yale comes forward as the first university to officially recognize artistic achievement in the art of the silent drama.'[17] The release of *Four Horsemen* staged a moment of institutional contact in which a film studio and a studio art programme looked to each other in search of an expanded aesthetic remit.

Making Movies into Art

Again, this is not to say that Ingram's schooling and mentorship did not have the effect on his visual style that he claimed. Yale had a great art school, and the thirty-year correspondence between Lawrie and Ingram in Lawrie's papers does reveal a wealth of discussion about art. The correspondence includes sustained debate about their aesthetic inclinations and of particular artworks as they exchanged photographs of these works taken during their travels.[18] Ingram did not fabricate his aesthetic training and interest in art history. But this training was not training in film technique, and even his most stylised cinema compositions, while referencing painting, borrow more directly from media with a closer material proximity: from the stage, from photography and even from popular illustration. No matter how much Ingram argued to the contrary, art school was still not a practical first step towards learning the craft of a director. It certainly could be for an art director who worked with paint on set. The fantastic set designer Ben Carré trained as a painter before taking his first film studio job at Éclair, as did Hugo Ballin and Cedric Gibbons, who both attended the Art Students League of New York before they went to work for Goldwyn. But there was little technical advantage for Ingram to begin making films with this schooling.

When critics, former mentors and the director himself mythologised Ingram's formative work as a visual artist they helped to guide products of the film-making profession towards traditions of pictorial appreciation in American universities, lyceums and art institutes. These strategies became increasingly thorough as Ingram took on higher-profile positions at Universal and Metro. The general importance of his background emerged alongside the viability of its exploitation. This publicity generally benefited most of the films he made during this time of growth for his career. But each film had its own idiosyncrasies in its cross-media promotion. The next two sections offer examples of Ingram's film-making techniques and a study of an uncommon film promotion to demonstrate in finer detail the kinds of cultural exchange enabled by someone positioned as a studio artist at work in early Hollywood.

FROM EXCEPTIONAL STYLE TO CROSS-MEDIA APPRECIATION

Ingram depended, as a director working within a frame of art cinema, on a collection of techniques that encouraged viewers and critics to make analogies with painting and sculpture. From his early work in the 1910s on, he included a particularly dense concentration of pictorial techniques that stood out as compositions. He paced films slowly and arranged actors pictorially, in tableaux. When actors moved, he directed their movements less as actions than as composed, moving lines. When he staged scenes in depth, he usually layered their compositions to create an effect, not so much of unified depth, but of overlapping picture planes. These compositions yielded strong foregrounds, which served as pictorial framing devices, arching over the central image in the distance. The lighting choices in Ingram's films further separated these planes and the lavish décor that filled them. He lit from the sides and from below a figure and often used beams of light from lamps and windows to offset parts of the composition. While these techniques may not have formed a foundation for a stylised art-film movement, in Ingram's case they reinforced the larger mythology of the artist-turned-director and allowed some writers of the time to position his films within the discursive field of art appreciation.

Ingram could not really claim priority or ownership for these techniques, as they were in circulation within many European film studios. All the better to compare his work with the imports from Germany and Scandinavia that competed for space in better-films publications. These techniques also circulated within prestige divisions of film companies in the USA. A description of his *mise en scène* techniques for Bluebird might just as easily describe Cecil B. DeMille's Paramount-Artcraft films. Ingram's battery of techniques parallels and most certainly responds to the success of productions like *Carmen*, one of many films DeMille made in collaboration with cinematographer Alvin Wyckoff and art director Wilfred Buckland. The strong shadows and pointed light in Ingram's Bluebirds only gain significance alongside DeMille's self-promotions, in which he claimed (like the long line of art photographers before him) to have singlehandedly brought artificial film lighting to the level of Rembrandt. Ingram's recently rediscovered Bluebird production *The Chalice of Sorrow* (1916) bears evidence of this cross-pollination of techniques among art film-makers. It is perhaps not so much influenced by the techniques imported from the stage by Lasky-Paramount as it is a borrowing of ideas about how to package these techniques. *Chalice* was released a year after *Carmen*, the same year that Chaplin piggybacked on its notoriety with his *Burlesque on Carmen*. Not only did Ingram adapt a similar opera of a diva's tragic death – in this case, *Tosca* – into a screen melodrama, but he also transposed Puccini's story from Italy to Mexico, which allowed him to create scenes that came far closer to DeMille's interpretation of Bizet's settings in *Carmen*. Ingram's penchant for shooting Tosca framed in archways and staging the performances in depth could be generally said to mirror some of the stylistic choices in *Carmen*. But more directly, certain scenes like those shot on a sloped, arid hill with a low horizon line or those in which the diva stands with soldiers in front of a crumbling colonial wall, verge on obvious citation of the Lasky *Carmen*. These were the same iconic locations that Chaplin burlesqued, even poking fun at the film's pictorial style in the process. Whether for satire or for art-film recognition, each film plays with the same network of references.[19]

Ingram developed close and long-lasting working relationships with famous art directors and cinematographers who reinforced the conception of him as an artist of the screen while they shaped what would become known as the director's exceptional style. If DeMille had Buckland and Wyckoff, and Tourneur had Carré and van den Broek, Ingram had the editor Grant Whytcock at Universal and the cinematographer John F. Seitz at the beginning of his tenure at Metro. The prestige picture departments in which Ingram began his career encouraged collaborative teams involving people like Seitz. And while these collaborators' public reputations as screen painters did not reach the same level as the director's – their discussions of the idea of the art film did not circulate much beyond the trade press – Seitz clearly influenced the ways these films addressed the public as fine-art films. In an interview, Seitz described his compatibility with Ingram as instantaneous: 'He liked the way that I worked and the form and modeling he saw in the lighting – as you know he was a sculptor.'[20] Seitz goes on to describe their early acquaintance as a process of looking through hundreds of stills from their previous films and discussing what makes a strong composition. In the films they made together they favoured strong contrasts and side lighting to give dimensionality to sets and faces. This emphasis on modelling, a lighting technique named in analogy to sculpture, superseded other priorities, like showcasing the star. Other directors and cinematographers were more likely to use shadowy close-ups for villains or the supernatural. Ingram and Seitz used them to light leading actors like Ramon Novarro and Alice Terry. They traded lush and flattering star lighting for compositional interest and reference to the other arts. This tradeoff did not escape the notice of other technicians on set. The convention-bound still photographers often corrected Ingram's and Seitz's pictorial excesses. They shot the actors in the tableaux from the films but, more often than Seitz's setups for the actual scenes, they bathed the stars' faces in even light.[21]

In his study of the development of Hollywood lighting, Patrick Keating identifies Seitz, particularly during the time he worked with Ingram, as a central figure in what he calls the 'mechanics-to-artists' narrative that transformed the cinematographer's profession in the late 1910s and early 20s.[22] Seitz had become one of the most famous cinematographers in the world by the early 20s, and this success helped mark a point of divergence from the older 'technicians' towards the rhetoric of artistry in cinematography. Moreover, Seitz stakes this distinction between artist and technician on a hierarchy of genre.

> The Cinematographer in the dramatic field is more of a photographer and less of a cinematographer than the comedy cameraman, his action contains less of the physical and more of the mental, consequently he is concerned less with motion and more with lighting and tone. … [P]erfection can only be attained by men who, through long, patient experience, have gained that fine sensitiveness so necessary to produce the exact tone and quality needed, and this is the cinematographic art.[23]

In this address to his colleagues, Seitz explicitly favoured the drama over other genres like comedy or the actuality, and he implicitly favoured the prestige features through which he and Ingram had established themselves in the industry.[24] Seitz's distinction should be qualified here since, as Hilde D'haeyere demonstrates, several cameramen behind Mack Sennett comedies helped to form the American Society of Cinematographers and thus played an essential role in professionalising the craft of cinematography.[25] The generic distinction between comedy cinematographers and dramatic ones may only have worked for Seitz as a way to mark his professional turf. But whether or not he was successful in moving his favoured genre to the top of the professional hierarchy, his strategy for doing so fell in line with the art-film campaigns that endorsed stylised scenes composed in relation to the other (static) pictorial arts. Seitz's evocation of tone over motion was not so different from the *Exceptional Photoplays* review cited earlier. To promote the narrative of art cinematography Seitz recalled (pictorial) photography, which further recalled the techniques and themes of the paintings circulating in institutions of art education.

Considered together, Ingram's and his collaborators' battery of techniques resist coherent aesthetic pedigrees even more stubbornly than Tourneur's films. And like Tourneur, Ingram's myths of origin and his contact with other arts institutions affected the way his films with Seitz could look, the way they could be discussed and how they could be seen. Here is where the intellectual history of composition, as a kind of craft, reveals the work it could do for cinema. As with several other figures discussed in this book, composition offered a common language, a set of principles that were flexible enough to frame eclectic techniques and irregular institutional collaborations. This language moved freely from art education, to film education, to Ingram's own words. In his 1922 essay on 'Directing the Picture', Ingram uses illustrations of Lawrie's sculptures, including his piece for the *Four Horsemen* premiere, as examples of the properties of composition. Artists like Lawrie, Gustave Doré and John Singer Sargent demonstrate, Ingram suggests, those principles of modelling, line, light and shade that he claimed to translate from clay and paint to film. The essay's conclusions are useful, but not necessarily in a direct way. Ingram's essay recalls the cinema composition manuals of educators and critics, and, like those manuals, it seems to move in two directions at once. He ostensibly advises prospective film workers about 'how to qualify for positions in the film industry's many branches'.[26] But at the same time, he offers an idealised craft-based notion of design appreciation, more-or-less useless from a practical perspective. The essay's publication history also reflects its crossed purposes. Ingram published it twice in 1922: once in a magazine for art appreciation and again under the auspices of the Bureau of Vocational Guidance.[27] The art magazine gave the lie to the manual. Like Arthur Dow's drawing manuals and Victor Freeburg's film 'manual' compiled from his Columbia University lectures, practical guidance functioned better as a ruse for cultivating aesthetic appreciation of workmanship than as a primer for attaining work in the medium. If Ingram's essay had a practical effect, it was with appreciators of cinema. Not only did Ingram make an effort to speak the language of the picture-study tradition in art education, but he also made an effort to enter the debates that sought to link this tradition to cinema. His article on directing is addressed more to participants in these debates (like Freeburg) than to ambitious production assistants. The following year, after the release of *Scaramouche*, Ingram wrote a brief piece for Freeburg himself, to be used as a prefatory note to *Pictorial Beauty on the Screen*.[28] The aesthetic of composition carried real promise for film-maker and critic alike. With its intermedial reach, composition theory aided early art film discourse much in the same way that it aided design education. It suited the reputation of a sculptor at work in Metro's studios.

SCARAMOUCHE, OR CONVERGENCE

By the 1920s, the trajectory of the art film that had launched Ingram's career in the 1910s began to connect very different kinds of institutions. From the perspective of the industry, film companies were increasingly moving from local stunt promotion to a more networked and synchronised form of publicity. The move to the kind of publicity seen, for example, in the tie-in stories that newspapers ran in synchronisation with film serials affected prestige films as well. Successful newspaper tie-ins did not escape the notice of book publishers eager to promote other tie-ins, like photo-illustrated novels. Mass-marketed films with aesthetic credentials could respond to the challenges of some of the earlier, more rigid attempts to market quality films. But pressure was also coming from another direction. From the perspective of educational and evaluative organisations, an aesthetic approach was gaining momentum. Organisations like the National Board of Review (NBR) saw it as their mission to combat censorship in favour of a model of democracy-building through aesthetic education. Again, when these diverse cross-media interests came together and formed committees, they often found a common language in the aesthetics of composition.

Aesthetic reform was a thorny issue for organisations that sought to speak for big films and for mainstream tastes. The NBR's motto was 'aesthetic, not moralistic censorship'. 'For pictures have not sinned morally, as the proponents of censorship would have us think. They have sinned aesthetically.'[29] In making such statements, the NBR had to be careful to define its approach to aesthetics as 'healthy' and 'vigorous'. As this article from the NBR's 1921 *Exceptional Photoplays* newsletter clarifies, 'the trouble is that when the word "aesthetic" is used, it is popularly supposed that one means a quality of pale pink unwholesomeness, or else that one is palely pink and unwholesome for using the word'.[30] The author euphemistically refers to mauve, the colour most clearly associated with late-Victorian decadence, a strain of British aestheticism that had a strong influence on American artists like Richard Hovey and F. Holland Day. Here 'mauve' is a phobic term that refers to a certain type of art as well as to those who would appreciate it. The NBR and *Exceptional Photoplays* sought to keep their aesthetic principles distinct from decadence and its perceived links with epicureanism, excess and same-sex desire.

In this context, a film could prove viable if it could appeal to these two forces that helped define and market the idea of the art film in the early 1920s: to certain organisations formed to market art films as well as to those organisations formed to evaluate better films. *Scaramouche*, it turned out, satisfied these often-conflicted interests better than any of Ingram's other films at Metro. The film does not really stand out as either the most profitable, or the 'mauvest', of his Metro productions. *The Four Horsemen* secured better returns and, in *Trifling Women* (1922), the *New York Times* observed, 'Mr Ingram has surely let his pictorial fancy run free.'[31] But *Scaramouche* created its own kind of sensation. It became a lightning rod for debate, a result of having become a finalist for a $10,000 prize in Adolph Zukor's new legitimacy campaign. Zukor had invited a number of well-known writers and visual artists that summer to participate in the Motion Picture Arts Congress, a symposium on the artistic development of the motion picture. He had been promoting the conference for several months in the popular and trade press, and in these promotions he made gestures to the Royal Academy of Arts in London. The conference would represent, in Zukor's revision of Matthew Arnold's maxim, 'the best in American thought and American taste'.[32] The conference predated the formation of the Academy of Motion Picture Arts and Sciences (AMPAS) by a few years and, although there are more direct precursors to AMPAS in the mid-1920s, Zukor's efforts did respond to a similar need.[33]

The press covered some of the conference proceedings, including audience polls at Paramount theatres, outreach programmes that accompanied the official judging and the search for delegates from Harvard, Yale, Princeton and Columbia.[34] But journalists focused their attention on Zukor's $10,000 cash prize for best literary adaptation. Zukor appointed a committee of judges out of several conference participants including the illustrator Charles Dana Gibson, the novelist Mary Roberts Reinhardt and *Life* magazine film critic Robert Emmet Sherwood. Their task was to apply the principles discussed at the conference to the year's releases and select one film adapted from a novel. The novelist, not the director, would then receive the $10,000 award. *Scaramouche* eventually won, and Zukor held a prize ceremony for the source novel's author, Raphael Sabatini. In the competition for recognition that ensued, Nicholas Schenck, president of Metro, immediately downplayed Sabatini's role and claimed credit for his company. Upon announcement of the prize, Schenck wrote to Zukor to thank him for speaking 'so highly of Mr Ingram's Metro-Goldwyn production of "Scaramouche," which won the award for Mr Sabatini. We are exceedingly proud of the honor you personally and the judges who acted on your behalf conferred to Mr Ingram's picture.'[35]

Conditions of the prize seem oddly planned for a company with such an established history of publicity stunts and appeals to esteemed cultural institutions like Columbia University. The prize was evidently not meant to encourage directors or scenario writers, as the money was given to Sabatini, but neither did it encourage novelists to write with the screen in mind. As film educator and NBR member Frances Patterson complained in the *New York Times*, Sabatini's *Scaramouche* had no real connection to the screen, and the prize did not foster these possible connections for up-and-coming authors. 'Mr Zukor realizes that the true photoplay medium is not wordcraft but picturecraft. ... Here, then was a rare opportunity for the judges to show their appreciation of actual creative effort on the screen. ... "but," say the judges, "the prize is to go to a storyteller."'[36] Moreover, in Sabatini's personal correspondence with Zukor, he admitted (rather arrogantly) to complete ignorance of the fact that his *Scaramouche* was a finalist until he read that he had won the prize in a Paris newspaper.[37] If there was some small potential for coaxing novelists towards the screen, Zukor did not exploit it. The literary community seems to have been left out of the loop. It was an award for a film posing as an award for a novel. Sabatini received the prize money, but Patterson gave Ingram the credit, as the value of the film, she maintained, 'has derived from the beauty of composition and the grace of rhythm that marks all the work of Rex Ingram'.[38]

Zukor's motivation for configuring the award as he did can be explained in part by his increased interest in book publicity in the early 1920s. In a response to antitrust pressure from the Federal Trade Commission, Paramount had moved from distribution strategies like its 'Star Series' form of block booking to a pricing system based purely on the popularity of individual titles, and Zukor and Lasky pursued avenues whereby this title recognition could be established in advance. Zukor announced several tie-in strategies to famous novels in trade journals. A publicised award to a popular novelist could be seen as simply one of these strategies. This tie-in strategy worked for exhibitors and booksellers too. Beginning in the 1910s, several book publishers partnered with film production companies to run novel editions illustrated with production stills from their film adaptations. At the height of this phenomenon in the mid-20s, nearly every possibility for tying a major production to a 'photoplay edition' release was exploited. The publishing company of Grossett and Dunlap led this effort by a large margin.

Sabatini's novels were exceptionally well suited to promotions like Zukor's, which 'celebrate', Vachel Lindsay only half-complained, 'cooperation between vigorous novel

Tie-in book display for *Scaramouche* (1923), at the Fremont Theatre in Ohio (*Moving Picture World*, 15 March 1924)

writing, good film production and hearty bookstore cooperation'.[39] Sabatini's novels worked in this context because they were able to serve both commercial and educational constituencies. They were solid best-sellers, but just as importantly the novels found their way onto the reading lists for high school classes across the USA, diversifying their reader demographics.[40] *Scaramouche* contributed to high school and community lessons in the history of the French Revolution, which no doubt put to good pedagogical use the novel's often ponderous historical details and French idiomatic expressions. As a result, *Scaramouche* ranked among the most successful of Grossett and Dunlap's photoplay editions. It was the only novel (out of the hundreds on the series lists) that Grossett and Dunlap released in two different editions, each with its own set of illustrations taken from the film production.[41] The display of these editions accompanied the exhibition of the film. Bookstores set up displays with production stills from the film, and many offered free tickets to see the film with a purchase of the novel. Likewise, theatre lobbies advertised the film with gigantic display books. In 1923–4, *Moving Picture World* documented these book-themed lobby displays at cinemas from Victoria, British Columbia, to Rio de Janeiro.

Zukor's conference and prize also sustained the attention of the National Board of Review. An editorial in the 1923 Autumn–Summer [sic] issue of *Exceptional Photoplays* entitled 'What Will Be the Result?' aligned the conference with the goals of the NBR to foster intellectual discussion of the cinema.[42] The article expressed some cynicism about the prize's relation to common publicity stunts, but it also recognised how a productive discussion of film aesthetics could happen by way of this particular stunt. The author noted that the 'brisk exchange of ideas overshadowed the publicity aspects of the congress' and concluded that Zukor's prize could work as an experiment to determine the result of some of these ideas on institutions of film-making and film criticism. The editors knew, after all, that the mandates of their journal and of Zukor's prize remained in close step with one another – so close that the same issue that ended with the editorial on the Zukor prize began with the featured review of *Scaramouche*, not entirely coincidentally. The *Scaramouche* review not only predicted the winner of Zukor's competition; it also prefigured the general direction of the prize's critical reception, or 'the result', in its insistence that film art is located in the work of pictorial composition.

The members of the NBR were far from alone in their assessment of Ingram's picture craft. Film critics in New York and across the country ensured that Ingram received the bulk of the publicity surrounding the prize, and they did so by continually returning to his fine-arts background, and to his principles of pictorial composition. Even Robert Emmet Sherwood, who headed the committee that selected *Scaramouche* for Zukor's prize, made several references in his reviews to Ingram's skill at crafting pictures. He said that any still taken from his films 'would be worthy of praise for its pictorial qualities alone'.[43] In Sherwood's book, *The Best Moving Pictures of 1922–23*, he offered a similar assessment of Ingram's *Prisoner of Zenda* (1922), noted the director's fine-arts credentials and lamented that *Scaramouche* came out too late for inclusion in the book.[44] In privileging the film's pictures over its story, Sherwood betrayed the complicated motivations involved in offering the prize to Sabatini.

The critical reception of *Scaramouche* supports my larger claim that pictorial composition and references to the works and work spaces of fine artists went hand in hand. A *Los Angeles Times* review of *Scaramouche* moved beyond Ingram's background and drew associations to other artists, noting that the film's 'attraction is not that of drama but of beautiful and glorious pictures. Individual photographed shots recall the work of dozens of painters and sculptors.'[45] Ingram's films and writings about film art directly reference several painters and sculptors including John Singer Sargent's *Frieze of the Prophets* (1895) and Edouard Manet's *Woman with Parrot* (1866). The films 'recalled', for many critics, the work of dozens more. *Scaramouche* benefited in this respect from the rich history of painting and sculpture about the French Revolution. These images were familiar among those whom Metro wanted to court, and at whom Zukor aimed his Motion Picture Arts Congress. Given this pictorial milieu, Ingram could easily steer pictorial techniques in close-ups and long shots towards traditions of painting and sculpture. The modelling in the film's star close-ups already gestured towards sculpture, but not as directly as the brief cameo close-ups that had no anchor in developing characters. Ingram and Seitz shot the young avant-gardist, Slavko

Slavko Vorkapich's slow turn of the head as Napoleon in *Scaramouche*. Ingram and Seitz used the sculptural metaphor of 'modelling' to describe their close-ups of faces; battle scene from *Scaramouche*

Vorkapich, as Napoleon in this way. They dressed and positioned him to reference the well-known illustrations of Napoleon as a young officer, reprinted in his biographies. He slowly turns his head into the light in a gesture that resembles a contemplative pose from a screen test, bizarrely placed in the middle of a crowded, violent battle sequence. They essentially turn Vorkapich into a modelled bust of a historical figure whose likeness was well known, particularly in the form of busts. Many of the crowd sequences, too, feature Ingram's favoured gestures to the other arts. For references to painting, they use dark foregrounds, centre lighting and smoke in the background. Reviewers made connections from here to the smoke, lighting and foregrounds in famous paintings by artists like Eugène Delacroix and Jacques-Louis David depicting the storming of the Bastille, the executions and the National Assembly.

But to work as an adaptation of a Sabatini novel, and thus to maintain a distance from associations with epicurean decadence, *Scaramouche* also needed to register as an adventure film. Sabatini wrote action stories, subtitling this one 'a romance of the French revolution'. Sabatini's source material seemed to be the only major rival to Douglas Fairbanks's ubiquity in the adventure genre. Beyond *Scaramouche*, Sabatini had also provided the source novels for *The Sea Hawk* (1924) and *Captain Blood* (1924), and when the trade papers promoted the 'picture values' of Sabatini's novels, they were mainly referring to their action plots.[46] They affirmed that the author's generic preferences happened to lean, as was true of Hollywood at this time, towards swashbuckling scenes that were exciting to watch. But the swashbuckler (one of the least 'mauve' genres) and pictorialism were not necessarily considered mutually exclusive. For early film theorists and film-makers with a sustained interest in the pictorial aspect of cinema, the composition of the moving body on screen ranked among the most important concerns in their work. This was certainly the case with Vachel Lindsay, for whom Fairbanks represented a type of film-making that spoke directly to these concerns. Following the announcement of *Scaramouche* as the winner of the prize, Lindsay began his second book of film criticism from a hotel room in Spokane, as an open letter to Zukor and Sherwood and as a song of praise to Douglas Fairbanks.

Climactic duel staged within
a pictorial frame and
photographed from a
distance in *Scaramouche*

Ingram never made a film with Fairbanks, but in this adaptation of a Sabatini story, he comes closer to Lindsay's pictorial requirements than the Fairbanks-focused Lindsay would admit. He carefully overlays pictorial composition with active physical performance, but he does so in a way that likely disappointed Lindsay's fetish for the individual star's body.[47] Ingram and Seitz shot the climactic revenge swordfight in *Scaramouche* in a wide shot through two nested archways of a Gothic cathedral. They place the camera even further away than in the opening fight, which sets up the revenge plot. Instead of using frequent cut-ins, they enclose the duel within a pronounced, static frame, highlighting Ramon Novarro's action by having him step back through the archway, into the path of the light, as he dodges each lunge. Ingram and Seitz would repeat this fight-scene staging and lighting in later films like *Mare Nostrum* (1926). In each case, just at the climactic confrontation, they place the camera further back and set the action within a static frame. In each case the films attempt to merge climactic, athletic performance with conspicuous style into a kind of strenuous pictorial composition. It is this approach to composition that made *Scaramouche* the focus of the *Exceptional Photoplays* article mentioned at the start of this chapter. The reviewer claimed that each film 'becomes something gripping beyond mere narration, ... other than "drama" melted down to glycerine tears and "action" that blows up in frenzy'.[48]

Not exactly Lindsay's prescription. Ingram and Seitz's approach is much closer to Victor Freeburg's theory of cinema composition. By putting the action within, and as part of, the pictorial composition, by not relegating composition to the status of ornament, it is as if they were directly responding to Freeburg's rather impractical hope that great art films would eventually synchronise their climactic moments with their most artfully composed scenes. Freeburg thought that DeMille's *Carmen* left this hope unfulfilled. He wanted *Carmen*'s dramatic denouement to have been staged as a long-shot composition rather than as a series of edited medium shots. Ingram's films showed that Freeburg's prescription was possible. It does not seem surprising, then, that Freeburg mentions Ingram's films in his *Pictorial Beauty on the Screen* more

Making Movies into Art

frequently than any other director's. Nor that Ingram wrote the prefatory note for Freeburg's book, in which the director reminds readers of the imperative 'pictorial qualifications, such as form, composition, and a proper distribution of light and shade'.[49] Ingram's work had influenced Freeburg's analysis, and it appears that Freeburg had some influence on him. While brief, the prefatory note does indicate at least some familiarity with Freeburg's work. The timing is right, too. Ingram completed his introductory note to *Pictorial Beauty on the Screen* on 5 August 1923. This was while he was completing *Scaramouche*, two months after the Motion Picture Arts Congress, just as the committee was beginning to deliberate on which films to consider for Zukor's prize.

Taken together, these diverse appropriations of Ingram's *Scaramouche* show that it is remarkable both for its conspicuous style, and for the way it was introduced to the public. Or, more to the point, the film's inclusive pictorial style in many ways made its exceptional public debut possible. *Scaramouche*'s style may have restricted its mass marketability in one sense. Its references to the pictorial history of the French Revolution, framed fight sequences and crystallised 'periods of signifying and revealing stillness' may have stifled the film's blockbuster appeal. But these elements were precisely what made the film so productive within the networks of educators, critics, producers, committees and bookstores that did celebrate it.[50] It was a bulky swashbuckler only because it was such a rich intermedial film. How else could it have succeeded as a point of convergence for a spectrum of interests broad enough to include Patterson, Freeburg, Gibson, Sherwood, Lindsay, Zukor, Schenck, the NBR and Grossett and Dunlap, among others? These representatives from such varied corners of American film needed a film that could adapt and move from one sphere to another. *Scaramouche*'s framing as a Rex Ingram art film made it adaptable and mobile.

CONCLUSION: THE LIMITS OF EXCEPTIONAL FILMS

Ingram's films staged a productive conversation between early Hollywood and art education, but this period of productivity did not last. He fared well for a while, but his career was marked by gradually souring relationships with the studios. After 1926, Ingram started his own studio in Nice, bringing stars and crew with him and continuing to distribute his films through MGM. While he clearly made an important break from Hollywood, and soon from film-making altogether, it would be inaccurate to characterise his pull away from Metro as a clash between an artist and his compromised employers. His often costly films, with their studied compositions and deliberate pacing, may have tested Metro's bottom line, but to the extent that they were also testing the possibilities of prestige film-making they proved quite compatible with the wishes of these studios. To insist on their incompatibility would obscure how his standout style, critical reputation and company affiliation worked together in the years before many of the lasting institutions of prestige cinema had taken root.

While the films' visual experiments and excesses were exceptional in the sense that they were not the norm for the companies in which Ingram worked, they were also exceptional in the NBR's sense of 'exceptional photoplays'. They stood out, but they were also somehow representative. The films hovered above non-exceptional films and thus avoided challenging their norms from the margins. The problem was never really that Ingram was minor or peripheral, but that his exceptional status as a master of picture craft, part of his authorial identity from his time making Bluebirds for Universal, gradually became less useful to the changing business models of the studios for whom he worked and which distributed his films. During the period encompassing exceptional films like *The Chalice of Sorrow* and *Scaramouche*, his art-film-maker status was productive and useful. It was not resisted but rather cultivated with the help of people like Seitz.[51] He succeeded in Hollywood for over a decade not *despite* being a sculptor of the screen. Just the opposite, he remained relevant in Hollywood *as* a sculptor of the screen, if only for a time.

To consider Ingram's films as early Hollywood art cinema is to search for a cultural apparatus that rendered their impurities productive. Ingram assembled his techniques from numerous sources, but he staked his films' ambitions on discourses of craft and picture. To stand out, as an exceptional director of early Hollywood, he placed the motion picture studio in conversation with 1890s artists. He linked his craft, his assortment of techniques, with art studios of the past. More important than any direct imitation of painterly style, he fitted within an aestheticist approach to form, which valued pictorial composition and its mechanics of effect above all else in art. It was this move that prompted critics of the National Board of Review to write about the vitality in his still compositions, and to use his films as evidence of an underlying aesthetic quality that defines the 'exceptional' in *Exceptional Photoplays*.

Conclusion: Moving Forward from the Slow Movie

What happened to the array of critical and creative practices that formed early American art cinema? It is a delicate task to discuss the afterlife of an aesthetic tradition that rarely seemed content in its own time. The very questions of the past and future of moving-image art preoccupied each of the figures in this book in ways that, even they knew, defied practicality. They were ever looking forward beyond the practical future and looking back, from the early 1920s to 1890s visual culture, with a lingering gaze. Their imaginative works stand as testimony to intricate possibilities of early art cinema while at the same time inviting a lament that many of these practices were living on borrowed time. Black's picture plays retired from the lecture circuit when he did. Triart pictures, and Hiller's film-making career, ended after a handful of films. Freeburg's and Patterson's curriculum did not directly grow into an academic discipline. Tourneur and Ingram both left Hollywood in search of other possibilities in France. These projects, in their unusual institutional alliances as much as their creative output, posed questions more than they established foundations. They were provocative, if not always viably innovative, during a period of uncertainty. The discourses of art discussed in this book find their strongest period of imaginative possibility before the more viable institutions of art cinema took shape towards the end of the silent era and into the 1930s. They mark a period of experimentation before what Steven Neale, in his foundational essay on the institutions of art cinema, has described as the moment when 'the configuration of forces inside and outside the cinematic institution began to fracture that unity [of entertainment, experimentation and art] into a set of distinct spheres of practice, circulation, discussion and activity'.[1] A few years later, the Little Cinema movement improved alternative programming and the Amateur Cinema League established a specialised category of artistic experimentation. Soon after that, journals like *Close-up* and *Experimental Cinema* began to define the field, and the Museum of Modern Art opened its doors to movies. The organisations and practices that preceded these stable institutions dealt in imagined possibilities for moving-picture art. They looked forward to an art cinema not yet realised and back to earlier aesthetic thought about the pictorial arts.

Recognising this uncertainty as part of the archive of early art cinema makes it possible to focus on traditions that, while lesser known in film studies, are prominent within this array of practices. The figures that anchor each chapter are not part of a single defined movement, but considering the frequency with which they reappear from one chapter's context to the next, neither are they isolated cases. They did not all pay dues to a single, driving organisation; the very point was to function in multiple contexts and cultivate connections among organisations. To make sense of these persistent linkages I have pursued an archive not typically consulted in histories of silent cinema: that of American art education. Aesthetic thought from the lyceums and the art schools threads through this broad range of work. It provides a context for the film critics and -makers who advocated for aesthetically ambitious moving pictures that are deliberately crafted. The principles of picture composition, and the theories of its psychological effects, offered a crosscurrent to the literary and dramatic definitions of moving-picture art. In this formulation, production design, décor and on-screen bodies could showcase their integrated plastic aspects. Verisimilar acting styles and realistic elements of décor were not the focus of those who felt that the moving image should take advantage of its opportunities to charm, to magically transform and to explore affinities with the arts of painting and sculpture.

These are unabashedly aesthetic definitions of art cinema, and they have rarely managed to generate the energy or cultural authority that they did during the first quarter-century of American cinema history. But this does not mean that these processes of imagining, and making, movies as pictorial art cannot be pursued in later incarnations. If this book has argued against a tendency to overlook the composed pictures of early art cinema, how might this historical attention to aesthetics inform current assumptions about later art cinemas? Rosalind Galt's expansive *Pretty*, which came out as this book was in its final stages, makes a strong case for re-evaluating the 'structural devaluation of the decorative image in cinema' and modern aesthetic theory, in which craft is characterised as manipulation and stylised images encounter suspicion as 'cunning tricks'.[2] Writing an aesthetic history of picture craft in silent American cinema means engaging with the early aesthetic roots of these tendencies. In the studies of silent art cinema and recent art cinema alike, the pictorial often confronts, abashedly, serious cinematic art's iconoclasm. Indeed, there is still a kind of awkwardness in teaching pictorial aesthetics in relation to art cinema. Much of the scholarship on art cinema, because of the prominence of later periods, from neo-realism through the global new waves, has sidelined pictorial traditions. The post-World War II trajectory tends to emphasise alternatives to causal narrative, images that remain open or ambivalent and anti-pictorial theories of *mise en scène* that value moments in which the object world, recorded by the camera, resists the preconceptions of film-maker and viewer alike.[3] As early as the 1930s in the USA, the suspicion of the plastic image permeates scholarship on the art of cinema in the leftist writings of Lewis Jacobs and Seymour Stern. These frameworks of cinematic distinction have at least one thing in common: they could not be further from traditions of pictorial composition and craft that value the object world precisely for its ability to be worked-over. From the perspective of these later intellectual traditions it makes sense to bracket the alien early configurations of aesthetic cinema. But this history could prove useful in the effort to understand the experiments and minor configurations in later art films that then seem out of place in established accounts of art cinema. Is pictorial cinema a road not taken in later years, or has the continuing suspicion of composed pictures obscured crosscurrents? If 'slow movies' informed by aesthetics of pictorial composition have persisted in some form, then where might we begin looking to see how have they fared in later economies of prestige?

wordery
your online bookshop

Your Details

Order date:	10/03/2020
Order reference:	AMSUS-56036856
Dispatch note:	20200307520801

Your Order

ISBN	Title	Quantity
9781844576951	Making Movies into Art Picture Craft ...	1

For returns information visit wordery.com/returns. Please keep this receipt for your records.

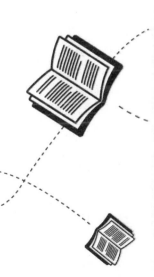

Thank you for your Wordery order. We hope you enjoy your book #HappyReading

wordery
your online bookshop

20200307520801

Some of the uncertainties of the future of pictorial cinema begin right where the book leaves off, at the moment where art-cinema discourse comes into focus with its own exhibition venues and publications. In the late 1920s, the International Film Arts Guild put art-cinema exhibition into practice. It mobilised progressive and modernist sentiments to create a space for viewing art films on the margins of mainstream exhibition, either due to their age or to their lack of broad box-office appeal. The Guild managed the struggle involved in fostering a new distribution and evaluative network, and its efforts would energise the Little Cinema movement in the following years. The Guild's persuasive director, Symon Gould, led the initiative, but he depended on a network of art-cinema advocates including producers, screenwriters, exhibitors and critics to revisit older films worthy of artistic consideration.[4] The critical discourse surrounding these programmes infused intellectual life into earlier features. Their first director-focused series, of D. W. Griffith's work, prompted critics to look back from 1926 to *The Birth of A Nation*, *Intolerance* (1916) and *Broken Blossoms* (1919) as a way to define art cinema. On the occasion of the revival, John Cohen of *The New York Sun* declared Griffith 'better copy than ever before', and a number of high-profile critics, including Carl Sandberg and Robert Sherwood, took the opportunity to make oeuvre-like career assessments. Pictorial aesthetics faced new challenges in this context as art cinema began to develop its own identity in exhibition and the related critical discourse, but it also persisted in unexpected places.

Of all the critics who took on the task of assessing the aesthetics of Griffith's earlier work in pictorial terms during the revival, Seymour Stern stands out as one of the most prominent but also one of the most surprising, given the context in which his work is most commonly remembered. Indeed, to think of Stern as a proponent of aesthetic cinema, let alone pictorial cinema, is already an unsettling thought, as he is best known as one of the intellectuals who established the leftist, avant-gardist definition of cinematic art in the 1930s and 40s. Co-editing the influential journal *Experimental Cinema* with Lewis Jacobs, Stern helped to deliver Soviet aesthetics to the American scene. Thus his interest in Griffith makes more sense to film historians when it highlights the links between Charles Dickens and Sergei Eisenstein. He certainly made these links later in his pioneering *Index to the Creative Work of D. W. Griffith*. His indices, released over a few years in the mid-1940s, have circulated in discussions of Griffith's work ever since. In them Stern identifies Griffith as 'the real beginning of the Soviet film', going so far as to claim that 'Griffith's *Intolerance* was to the Soviet cinema what Marx's *Capital* was to the Bolshevik Revolution – the creative inspiration and ideational source.'[5] To make this claim he stressed Griffith's contribution to film language and montage. So it would seem counterintuitive, at the very least, to link Stern with other aspects of aesthetics, to the pictorial, to the intermedial, to aesthetic restraint. To link Stern with the pictorial, using Griffith of all directors as an example, makes even less immediate sense.

But when Stern took part in the lectures and publications surrounding the Film Arts Guild's Griffith revival, even this future editor of *Experimental Cinema* called for pictorial composition and aesthetic restraint. At his lecture on 'film aesthetics' in October of 1926, a well-publicised event scheduled around the Griffith revival and the new release of Griffith's *Sorrows of Satan*, Stern returned to themes I have been tracing among intellectuals and film critics throughout this book. Stern gave the talk at the

Grub Street Club, a more bohemian venue than the typical lecture hall.[6] He framed his lecture, eccentrically, as commentary from a time-travelling Martian landing on earth in 1914 to explain where cinema was headed in the 1920s. Looking forward and back at the same time, this Martian would explain to prewar film fans, Stern hypothesised, that the cinema of the next generation will have made stunning advances, but the 'mechanical development ... would be all out of proportion with the aesthetic development'.[7] He cites the critical and popular perception of 'the master' as a 'failure to keep pace' with 'German technique' and the 'advanced, and more distinctly cinematic ideas' of Lubitsch, von Stroheim, Seastrom, Dupont and Murnau. German technique is properly cinematic because of its aesthetic dimension, and Stern searches Griffith's work for this dimension. It was too early for Stern to lecture about the Soviets, but someone familiar with Stern's later writing might still assume that his early lecture would have discussed the pioneering of film language. His lectures roughly coincided with the first publication of the historical study, *A Million and One Nights*, in which Terry Ramsaye's praise of Griffith as a screen-syntax pioneer fed into the enduring and ever-transforming narrative of Griffith's cinematic paternity.[8] But at this point Stern had not yet turned his interest away from Griffith's other aesthetic interests. While Griffith formed the centrepiece of Stern's lecture, the topic of Griffithian language found him less enthusiastic. He describes the director's race-to-the-rescue trademark 'through the alleys of Paris or the valleys of America' as part of '[t]he trouble with Griffith'. This advancement of film language is for Stern 'a formula, and true artists generally don't bother with formulae'.[9] Stern asked his fellow critics to consider *The Birth of A Nation*, not for its hieroglyphic clarity, but rather for its minor moments of restraint, such as the shot of Henry Walthall in which 'nothing else is seen; just his back, slightly stooped, and his terrible, trembling, grasping arm. There are no faces.'[10] Stern favours the moment when Griffith, whom he identifies as 'essentially a lyricist', avoids a grand screen utterance using editing or close-ups. He draws out the moment when these inventions give way to a pictorial shot, referencing his earlier discussion of films like *Varieté* (1926), in which actors perform with their backs to the camera and without facial close-ups.

With these criteria guiding his analysis, Stern's criticism at this time is closer to *Exceptional Photoplays* than to *Experimental Cinema*, closer to the better-films movement than to even his own later cinema manifesto for *The Left*.[11] In a move that would run contrary to many critics of the 1930s, who favoured an aesthetic largely defined in opposition to the pictorial, he saw in pictorial composition and restraint something that could counter cinema's technical accomplishments invented, he believed, for their own sake. For Stern in 1926, the dangers of colour, stereoscopic cinema and even advances in editing threatened to overshadow their aesthetic possibilities. And this puts him into conversation with other early attempts to delimit and describe art cinema. His approach recalls pictorially oriented critics such as Lindsay and Freeburg in its call for an aesthetic cinema alongside fast-paced rescue sequences. This aesthetic would resist the narrative charge of a crowd scene and appreciate it as Lindsay's famous architecture-in-motion, or in Freeburg's terms, the 'moving texture' of 'a mob of people' resembling 'the stately coiling of clouds, and the majestic weaving of ice floes in the river'.[12] Although they incubated their ideas in separate intellectual circles – Stern in bohemian Greenwich Village, Freeburg at

Making Movies into Art

Columbia University and the upscale National Arts Club and Lindsay in a series of itinerant encounters from New York to Spokane – these early writers on film aesthetics encircled similar conclusions. That Stern's first contributions to this conversation coincided with Freeburg's and Lindsay's last, and that he would soon go on to denounce pictorial aesthetics as manipulative spectacle, suggests a shifting terrain of art cinema worth pursuing in all of its contradictions.

These networks continue on, and the debates intensify, in the following decades. From major studio directors to minor film-makers on the periphery of Hollywood, tracing influences from the figures discussed in this book can reveal occulted traditions. Josef von Sternberg, a film-maker not always effusive about those who came before him, had only kind words about his first mentor in directing:

> [Working as an assistant director] placed me in a position to observe how little some of the directors I assisted knew about the elements of their craft. A notable exception, however, was the first director I ever served. He not only was well qualified to direct but was a gracious teacher, never failing to explain precisely what he was doing and why. His name was Émile Chautard.[13]

While Chautard himself had trouble advancing from the periphery of the American film industry, he was a significant mentor and influence on Maurice Tourneur and Sternberg alike. In Sternberg's account of learning the director's craft, Chautard's attention to the details of a composition 'alerted me to inspect everything before the camera through the lens and soon paved the way for me to appraise the dimensional impact of everything in front of the lens, including the value of light and shadow'.[14] This is an account of an education in composition from one of the most compositionally focused Hollywood directors. Sternberg's films resist editing-focused definitions of film aesthetics. They give primary attention to lighting and shade, to the plastics of the body in the frame, to composed superimpositions and to a *mise en-scène* that seems to overflow with layers of fine objects. These were major, aesthetically ambitious Hollywood productions, and their aesthetics provoked strong reactions from those who favoured montage or realism in their definitions of the art of cinema. The pages of Stern's and Jacobs's *Experimental Cinema* were less than kind to Sternberg in the 1930s. They assessed his films as primary examples of 'the degenerate ideology [of] pictorialism for its own sake'.[15] Stern himself uses a language of decadence to describe why he felt Sternberg was 'one of the worst American directors'. He criticises Sternberg's 'inter-melting' dissolves as 'an extreme misuse of a false method' that betrays a 'perverse idea of the cinema'.[16] Such strong condemnations, especially in the context of Stern's earliest criticism, show how dramatically the stakes of composed pictures could shift in a short time. Considering these changes and Sternberg's early influences, it is clear that his films' aesthetic adornments are better understood in context with the discourses of pictorial composition from the preceding period.

This aesthetic context also links the sound stages of Paramount with the underground as Sternberg mentored his own aesthetes along Hollywood's periphery.[17] Curtis Harrington's films and writings seem made to provoke the curiosity of someone interested in an art cinema that never quite fits its time. Harrington possessed a deep interest in film history, specifically in the work of Ingram and Tourneur.[18] In his article

'Ghoulies and Ghosties' he praises *The Blue Bird*, *Prunella* and *The Four Horsemen of the Apocalypse* for their pictorial style and for their fantastic qualities. Harrington claims that 'Other American directors during the 'twenties dealt with the fantastic from time to time as their story material demanded, but Tourneur and Ingram were perhaps the two most consistently interested in using films to present fantasy rather than reality.'[19] Around this time, while he was making his own underground shorts, Harrington wrote some of the first studies of Sternberg's films. He called out critics like Lewis Jacobs and Paul Rotha, praising Sternberg's roots in 'the romantic and decadent movements of the latter half of the nineteenth century'.[20] In Harrington's view Sternberg's insistence that 'cinema is a plastic medium' presaged both European art cinema and American experimental cinema.[21] Harrington's own film work pursued these same connections. It intersected with the avant-garde plastics of Kenneth Anger when Harrington worked on *Puce Moment* (1949) and performed, as Cesare the somnambulist, in *Inauguration of the Pleasure Dome* (1954). His art-film first feature *Night Tide* (1961) draws from both Sternberg and Anger, triangulating them around aesthetic fantasies of the 1890s. It shows the influence of Sternberg in its slow rhythms, its composition of bodies, its dense *mise en scène*, its fatal woman and its obsession with the sea and carnivals as sites of upheaval. But *Night Tide* also takes on the occultism and fevered eroticism of Anger's films. The seaside carnival setting is a site of danger, and a young Dennis Hopper as a sailor on shore leave encounters these dangers through ominous tarot readings and sweaty nightmares. The mermaid painting at the entrance to the carnival attraction, created by Anger collaborator Paul Mathison, stands as the primary pictorial omen. The mermaid stares out from the picture through a reflection in a hand mirror, and Harrington repeats this moment of composed direct address at the end of the film. In a fever dream, the sailor walks towards his beloved who is sitting along the rocks at the water's edge. He sees her distressed face momentarily in a hand mirror. A reverse shot through the mirror frames the face of a water witch, a fleeting glimpse of occultist Marjorie Cameron, before he is pulled into the ocean. The combination of *mise en scène*, and somnambulistic pacing make *Night Tide* an unusual kind of art film for the 1960s. It emerges from Harrington's avant-garde interests only to find that its fantastic elements do not quite fit within a tradition of unadorned art-film features. It takes an alternative path as an art film, one nourished by the pictorial aesthetics of silent cinema. If a film like *Night Tide* was out of place in postwar art cinema, it might find more productive meaning in relation to other traditions. Tracing an aesthetic lineage through Tourneur and Ingram keeps someone like Harrington, whose aestheticism placed him between the film industry and the avant-garde, from slipping through the cracks of histories of art cinema.[22]

And, finally, leaving these networks aside, a richer understanding of early pictorial art cinema can contextualise global outliers from more recent years. There is no shortage of art-film anomalies made in the past fifty years that make use of painterly intermediality, in which painting is not only referenced, but also integrated into the films as a way to explore the pictorial qualities of the moving image. The saturated tableaux in Sergei Parajanov's *The Color of Pomegranates* (1968), the labyrinth of linked pictures in Raúl Ruiz's *Hypothesis of the Stolen Painting* (1978), Terrence Malick's citations of Andrew Wyeth in *Days of Heaven* (1978), Eric Rohmer's green-screen recreations of French painting in *The Lady and the Duke* (2001) and Peter Greenaway's study of Rembrandt in *Nightwatching* (2007) operate in different national, technological and historical contexts, but they each provoke curiosity as art films due in part to their pictorial intermediality. Indie directors that students typically understand as creators of art films, like Todd Haynes, Sofia Coppola and Wes Anderson, rely heavily on the aesthetic experience of *mise en scène* to create their alternative affects. The generic revisionism in *Far From Heaven* (2002) is comprehensible only through its colour-saturated 1950s décor, and the aesthetic dandyism of *Marie Antoinette* (2006) and *The Grand Budapest Hotel* (2014) works best when the characters merge with the long takes of cluttered spaces and designed surfaces. This shift in perspective could also benefit the study of certain non-western new waves that are arguably the most vital sites of production in contemporary art cinema. Abbas Kiarostami has received so much attention globally that his work sometimes stands as shorthand for all Iranian cinema. His films, from the neo-realism of his early festival success *Where is the Friend's Home?* (1987) to the layered reflexivity of *Certified Copy* (2010), clearly take on recognisable features of other postwar new waves. By reconsidering the history of pictorial art cinema one might ask what is excluded by this tendency to see Iranian art cinema as a realist, reflexive new wave with Kiarostami as its spokesman.[23] This discourse on Iranian art cinema outside of Iran has obscured the significance of film-makers such as Ali Hatami, whose colour musicals animated Persian paintings with tableaux and costumes he created, or Bahram Bezai, whose composed images draw from his scholarly interest in the history of Iranian visual culture. Even well-known Iranian art-film-makers reveal new aspects with a shifted perspective. When the Cannes Film Festival awarded Samira Makhmalbaf jury prizes for *Blackboards* (2000) and *At Five in the Afternoon* (2003), critics were not wrong to highlight the politicised realism of these works about precarious Kurdish and Afghani lives. But Makhmalbaf continually emphasises the pictorial movements of blackboards and blue parasols that turn together, frame faces, diffuse light and reconfigure bodily movements. One-dimensional attention to the neo-realism of the New Iranian Cinema might miss how, in her films, compositional style is not a picturesque frame for realist stories. It manifests right at the point where the marginalised subjects of the films interact with the physical world. While the discourse on contemporary global art cinema has expressed significant interest in the political meanings of Makhmalbaf's films, there is still more to be gained from a discussion of her aesthetic choices in depicting these realities. While these examples, from Parajanov to Makhmalbaf, draw from reference points as varied as Persian miniaturists, Dutch masters and American landscape painters, they each call attention to the pictures in their art films. And this idea of the pictorial as an enduring component of the aesthetic experience of cinema has a long history.

American silent cinema's pictorial splendour, rooted in the aesthetic theories of the 1910s and the craft traditions that came before them, offers a historical starting point for considering how film has been conceived in relation to the other arts. As a production history it marks early attempts to collaborate with cultural organisations and make prestigious movies. As an intellectual history, it forms part of a longer tradition of debates about the value of the aesthetic in motion pictures. To the extent that this intellectual history of picture composition intermingled with emergent film scholarship, from the first film theories of the 1910s to canons of film art formed in the 30s, it contributed to the process of reflection on the critical categories that continue to shape the discipline of film studies. In this way it can, I hope, raise curiosity about the odd moments pictorial splendour in other moments in history: from a largely forgotten lecture associated with an art-house revival of D. W. Griffith films in 1926, to Dennis Hopper's fever dreams in a macabre avant-garde hybrid feature in 1961, to the animated paintings and backlit parasols obscured by the more recognisable features of the global new waves.

Notes

INTRODUCTION

1. Herbert Beerbohm Tree, 'The Worthy Cinema', *New York Times*, 30 January 1916.
2. In his early work as well as in his most recent reflections on art cinema, Dudley Andrew describes the term as a mode of ambition. It defines certain films that achieve exceptional status and, through this status, circulate in less proscribed ways than standard fare. Such films spill over national and cultural borders more easily, using their distinction to gain entry into spheres closed off to the majority of motion pictures produced within a given national industry or for a certain predictable audience. Dudley Andrew, 'Foreword', in *Global Art Cinema: New Theories and Histories*, ed. Rosalind Galt and Karl Schoonover (Oxford: Oxford University Press, 2010). See also Dudley Andrew, *Film in the Aura of Art* (Princeton, NJ: Princeton University Press, 1984).
3. Juliet Goodfriend, 'National Art House Theater Operations Survey', Art House Convergence Conference, Sundance Institute, Park City, January 2014.
4. Two of these foundational works, representing the institutional and the aesthetic/formal approaches respectively, are Steve Neale, 'Art Cinema as Institution', *Screen* vol. 22 no. 1 (1981); David Bordwell, 'The Art Cinema as a Mode of Film Practice', *Film Criticism* vol. 4 no. 1 (1979).
5. See Mark Betz, *Beyond the Subtitle: Remapping European Art Cinema* (Minneapolis: University of Minnesota Press, 2009).
6. For a lucid and compelling account of new-wave art cinema in the context of global modernity, see James Tweedie, *The Age of New Waves: Art Cinema and the Staging of Globalization* (New York: Oxford University Press, 2013).
7. Galt and Schoonover primarily refer to post-World War II art cinema, but impurity also figures historically for them in what they describe as 'the mongrel nature of art cinema's prehistory'. Galt and Schoonover, *Global Art Cinema*, p. 6.
8. This disintegrated approach to early art cinema has in some ways become a defacto standard, whether explicitly advocated or not. Jan-Christopher Horak's *Lovers of Cinema* traces some coherent early art-film movements but its richness lies in its openness to the range of projects explored by the book's contributors. David James's examination of minor cinemas in *The Most Typical Avant Garde* has a similar structure. Bruce Posner's *Unseen Cinema* video series and book construct a picture of the early art cinema that includes shorts and feature fragments spanning genres and periods. Jan-Christopher Horak, *Lovers of Cinema: The First American Film Avant-Garde, 1919–1945*, Wisconsin Studies in Film

(Madison: University of Wisconsin Press, 1995); David E. James, *The Most Typical Avant-Garde: History and Geography of Minor Cinemas in Los Angeles* (Berkeley: University of California Press, 2005); Bruce Charles Posner *et al.*, *Unseen Cinema: Early American Avant-Garde Film, 1894–1941*, Blackhawk Films Collection (New York: Anthology Film Archives, 2005).

9. See Alain Carou and Béatrice de Pastre (eds), *1895: Le Film D'art & Les Films D'art En Europe (1908–1911)*, vol. 56 (Paris: AFRHC, 2008); Jon Burrows, *Legitimate Cinema: Theatre Stars in Silent British Films, 1908–1918* (Exeter: University of Exeter Press, 2003).

10. For the fusion of sculptural posing and physical culture, see Eugen Sandow, *Strength and How to Obtain It* (London: Gale and Polden, 1897). For an authoritative discussion of the interaction between stage stars and cinema in this period, particularly of the work of Beerbohm Tree, see Burrows, *Legitimate Cinema*, especially pp. 141–79.

11. Alec Issigonis, *British Vogue*, July 1958.

12. See pp. 4–9 of Galt and Schoonover, *Global Art Cinema*, and also p. 6.

13. See André Gaudreault and Philippe Marion, 'A Medium Is Always Born Twice ...', *Early Popular Visual Culture* vol. 3 no. 1 (2005), pp. 3–15.

14. This shift in perspective has brought film historians together at recent conferences sponsored by organisations like Domitor and GRAFICS. Recently established journals such as *Early Popular Visual Culture* and *Kintop* have similarly given considerable attention to early cinema's relation to other media.

15. This is evident from foundational new media work by Lev Manovich through more recent work by scholars such as Mark Hansen. Some of the exciting projects in this vein have been structured around concepts that promote conversation across historical periods. For one recent example of a special issue structured in this way, around questions of the 3-D image, see *Film Criticism* vol. 37/38 no. 3/1 (Spring/Autumn 2013).

16. Dana B. Polan, *Scenes of Instruction: The Beginnings of the US. Study of Film* (Berkeley: University of California Press, 2007); Peter Decherney, *Hollywood and the Culture Elite: How the Movies Became American*, ed. John Belton, Film and Culture (New York: Columbia University Press, 2005); Haidee Wasson, *Museum Movies: The Museum of Modern Art and the Birth of Art Cinema* (Berkeley: University of California Press, 2005).

17. '[T]he true drama woven on a solid framework of history is likely to have a power of impression far deeper and therefore to be of incalculable value in education.' Tree, 'The Worthy Cinema'.

18. 'Michael Angelo', in volume 12 of Ralph Waldo Emerson, *The Complete Works of Ralph Waldo Emerson*, 12 vols (Cambridge: Riverside Press, 1903).

19. See Peter Betjemann, *Talking Shop: The Language of Craft in an Age of Consumption* (Charlottesville: University of Virginia Press, 2011).

20. Benvenuto Cellini and John Addington Symonds, *The Life of Benvenuto Cellini Newly Translated into English*, 2nd edn, 2 vols (London: J. C. Nimmo, 1888).

21 For a famous how-to lantern manual see Thomas Craddock Hepworth, *The Book of the Lantern* (London: Hazell, Watson and Viney, 1899).

22. Louis Reeves Harrison, *Screencraft* (New York: Chalmers, 1916); Epes Winthrop Sargent, *The Technique of the Photoplay* (New York: Moving Picture World, 1913); Frances Taylor Patterson, *Cinema Craftsmanship* (New York: Harcourt, Brace and Co., 1920); .

23. Glenn Adamson, *The Craft Reader*, English edn (Oxford; New York: Berg, 2010), pp. 9–39.

24. Mary Ann Stankiewicz, 'A Picture Age: Reproductions in Picture Study', *Studies in Art Education* vol. 26 no. 2 (1985).

25. Mary Ann Stankiewicz, 'From the Aesthetic Movement to the Arts and Crafts Movement', *Studies in Art Education* vol. 33 no. 3 (1992).

26. Arthur W. Dow, *Composition*, 3rd edn (New York: Baker and Taylor, 1900); Arthur W. Dow, *Theory and Practice of Teaching Art*, 2nd edn (New York: Teachers College, Columbia University, 1912).

27. For example, the picturesque, as Giorgio Bertellini has shown, had a direct influence on shaping modern racialised depictions of Italy in American cinema. Giorgio Bertellini, *Italy in Early American Cinema: Race, Landscape, and the Picturesque* (Bloomington: Indiana University Press, 2010).

28. Cinema and photography are as much extensions of printing technologies as they are new media, and thus are connected to the history of design.

29. In my characterisation of intellectual traditions that make use of the tableau, I draw on work in art history and theatre history influenced by Michael Fried and Martin Meisel. For Fried, the notion of the tableau came to denote a new absorptive relation between picture and beholder as he demonstrates in the paintings of Greuze and Chardin. I return to a pictorial notion of absorption, de-emphasising questions of film narrative, in my discussions of 'instantaneous tableau' (Chapter 1), mesmerism and a figure for absorption (Chapter 2) and the pictorial absorption of early feature-film theory (Chapter 3). My second-chapter discussion of 'frame jumping', where one medium appears to step out of another, revises Meisel's concept of realisation to make it more appropriate to moving pictures. Michael Fried, *Absorption and Theatricality: Painting and Beholder in the Age of Diderot* (Berkeley: University of California Press, 1980); Martin Meisel, *Realizations: Narrative, Pictorial, and Theatrical Arts in Nineteenth-Century England* (Princeton, NJ: Princeton University Press, 1983).

30. On Stickley's labour politics, see T. J. Jackson Lears, *No Place of Grace: Antimodernism and the Transformation of American Culture, 1880–1920* (Chicago: University of Chicago Press, 1994 [1981]), pp. 70–95.

31. See Mabel Emery and Stella Skinner, *How to Enjoy Pictures, with a Special Chapter on Pictures in the Schoolroom* (Boston: Prang Educational Co., 1898).

32. See John C. Van Dyke, *Studies in Pictures* (New York: Scribner's, 1907). John LaFarge, *Great Masters* (New York: McLure, Phillips and Co., 1903).

33. Emery and Skinner, *How to Enjoy Pictures*, pp. 260–75

34. For a discussion of the modernisation of craft labour in the university outside the domain of art education, see Christopher Newfield, *Ivy and Industry: Business and the Making of the American University, 1880–1980* (Durham, NC: Duke University Press, 2003).

35. Minnie Hays, 'Appreciation', *School Arts* vol. 9 (1910).

36. For a discussion of the movement-image's divergence from the 'order of the pose', see Gilles Deleuze, *Cinema 1: The Movement-Image* (Minneapolis: University of Minnesota Press, 1986), pp. 4–8.

37. See 'Girls and Crisis', in Siegfried Kracauer, *The Mass Ornament: Weimar Essays*, trans. Thomas Y. Levin (Cambridge, MA: Harvard University Press, 1995).

38. Theodor W. Adorno, 'Transparencies on Film', *New German Critique* vol. 24/25 (1982). See also Theodor Adorno, 'Functionalism Today', *Oppositions* vol. 17 (1979).

39. Garrett Stewart, *Between Film and Screen: Modernism's Photo Synthesis* (Chicago: University of Chicago Press, 1999), especially chapters 3 and 7.

40. Walter Benjamin, 'One-Way Street', in *Walter Benjamin: Selected Writings Volume 1, 1913–1926*, ed. Marcus Bullock and Michael Jennings (Boston: Harvard University Press, 1996), p. 476.

1 MOVING-PICTURE ART BEFORE CINEMA

1. The last year of travelling exhibition in Black's ledger at the New York Public Library is 1904. The decline in the frequency of his tours was gradual. They had tapered off by this point.

2. Terry Ramsaye, *A Million and One Nights: A History of the Motion Picture* (New York: Simon and Schuster, 1926), p. 91.

3. Black's work was often compared to such famous illustrated poems as 'Little Jim'. See 'On Black's Picture Plays', *Photogram* vol. 3 no. 36 (1896), pp. 287–8. His audiences would have known the life model sets, in which actors were posed for serial photographs by companies like Bamforth in the UK and Scott and Van Altena in the USA. These practices became particularly viable in the form of the illustrated song, which developed alongside the picture plays and became a staple of nickelodeon shows. Black was occasionally compared to illustrated song pioneer Charles K. Harris. Black even claimed credit for the invention of the illustrated song. See 'An Interview with Alexander Black', *Kalamazoo Telegraph* (1901), New York Public Library. While invention is too strongly put, influence is not. Edward van Altena saw Black's New York shows before he became one of the largest producers of illustrated songs. In a private letter written in 1959 Van Altena claims to remember two of Black's 1890s performances well, Marnan Collection, Minneapolis. Not entirely comfortable being grouped with these popular amusements, Black tried to align his work with the activities of artistic and literary circles. There were others at this time who, like Black, had careers in loftier circles and sought these kinds of audiences. The most notable of these was probably Hubert von Herkomer, whose staged pictorial music shows outside London helped him transition from painting to making films. See Ian Christie, 'Before the Avant Gardes: Artists and Cinema, 1910–14', in Leonardo Quaresima and Laura Vichi (eds), *The Tenth Muse* (Udine: Forum, 2001), p. 374.

4. See Gilles Deleuze, *Cinema 1: The Movement-Image*, trans. Hugh Tomlinson and Barbara Habberjam (Minneapolis: University of Minnesota Press, 2003), pp. 1–11; Friedrich Kittler, *Gramophone, Film, Typewriter* (Stanford, CA: Stanford University Press, 1986), pp. 154–82.

5. 'New Darkroom Opened at Last Night's Meeting of the Department', *The Brooklyn Eagle*, 13 November 1889, p. 4.

6. See Peter Cherches, 'Star Course: Popular Lectures and the Marketing of Celebrity in Nineteenth-Century America', PhD, New York University, 1997. On the working-class origins of the lyceum, see pp. 35–50.

7. *Yearbook of the Brooklyn Institute of Arts and Sciences* (Brooklyn Institute, 1893).

8. See George Ehrlich, 'Chautauqua 1880–1900: Education in Art History and Appreciation', *The Art Bulletin* vol. 38 no. 3 (1956). Brooklyn Museum director William Henry Goodyear wrote many of the books used for the correspondence courses. See William Henry Goodyear, *The Debt of the Nineteenth Century to Rome: A Syllabus of a Course of Six Lecture-Studies*

(Chicago, 1897); William Henry Goodyear, *A History of Art: For Classes, Art Students, and Tourists in Europe* (New York: A. S. Barnes Co., 1896); William Henry Goodyear, *Roman and Medieval Art* (New York: Flood and Vincent, 1873).

9. See Pierre Bourdieu, *Photography, a Middle-Brow Art* (Stanford, CA: Stanford University Press, 1990).

10. See George Santayana, *The Genteel Tradition: Nine Essays*, ed. Douglas Wilson (Cambridge: Harvard University Press, 1967). Santayana targeted Brander Matthews among others as the worst of the genteel tradition. Matthews was Alexander Black's longtime acquaintance and Victor Freeburg's dissertation advisor.

11. Charles Musser and Carol Nelson, *High-Class Moving Pictures: Lyman H. Howe and the Forgotten Era of Traveling Exhibition, 1880–1920* (Princeton, NJ: Princeton University Press, 1991), p. 79. I have found no documents that specifically detail Black's relations with Edison during this demonstration, but his position at the institute makes it a safe assumption.

12. *Yearbook of the Brooklyn Institute of Arts and Sciences*, vol. 11, 1898–9, pp. 177–8, 260.

13. Alexander Black, 'The New Photography', *The Century Magazine* vol. 64 no. 6 (1902). Black wrote this essay, alongside an essay by Alfred Stieglitz, as a conversation among a painter, a photographer and an aesthetic philosopher. Their conversation is written in the spirit of the debates that went on in the lecture halls of the Brooklyn Institute.

14. For a discussion of the development of the lyceum, see Cherches, 'Star Course'.

15. Chase was interested in many of the same issues of art education that interested Black. He was also known for his use of colour in his landscape paintings. For a thorough account of Chase's career (unfortunately without colour illustrations), see Keith L. Bryant, *William Merritt Chase, a Genteel Bohemian* (Columbia: University of Missouri Press, 1991).

16. Black's two-part article with Alfred Stieglitz explores the possibilities of pictorialist photography. While Stieglitz laid out the tenets of the Photosecession, the characters in Black's eclectic lyceum-style debate entertained the position of the Photosecession among other definitions of photographic art.

17. Paul Spencer Sternberger, in his recent study of the transition from amateur photography to institutionalised art photography in late nineteenth-century America, identifies interrelated currents in this period of pictorialist photography and what he calls 'the photographic aesthetic'. In contrast to pictorialist manipulations of exposure, focus and printing, proponents of the photographic aesthetic based their conception of photographic art on the sharp realism of the photograph combined with a knowledge of rules of composition. He attributes this current to a suspicion of European pictorial models and to distinctly American 'positivist tendencies and a willingness to embrace technology'. Sternberger's characterisation helps to uncover aspects of American amateur photography often overshadowed by Stieglitz and other pictorialist photographers during this period. It helps to indicate important aspects of Black's work as well. There is a positivist dimension just as much as a pictorialist dimension in Black's celebration of the amateur. In the case of embracing technology, the case should be stated more strongly for Black. Paul Spencer Sternberger, *Between Amateur and Aesthete: The Legitimization of Photography as Art in America, 1880–1900* (Albuquerque: University of New Mexico Press, 2001), pp. 72–8.

18. Handbill for 'Ourselves as Others See Us', Alexander Black Clipping File, Billy Rose Theatre Collection, New York Public Library.

19. Alexander Black, *Captain Kodak: A Camera Story*, 3rd edn (Boston: Lothrop, 1899), p. 21.

20. For a discussion of the pleasures of manipulating technology motivating film aesthetics of Douglas Crockwell, see Tom Gunning, 'Machines That Give Birth to Images', in Jan-Christopher Horak (ed.), *Lovers of Cinema* (Madison: University of Wisconsin Press, 1995).

21. For a discussion of Black's experiments with amateur film-making later in his life, including an address at the inaugural meeting of the Amateur Cinema League in 1926, see Kaveh Askari, 'Early 16mm Color by a Career Amateur', *Film History* vol. 21 no. 2 (2009).

22. *Captain Kodak* was published ten years after Black began travelling with his detective lectures and fictionalises many of the themes and photographs accumulated during his years on the lecture circuit. Most of the 100 images used to illustrate this story of a camera club are taken directly from Black's photographic contributions to his lectures. For this reason, I read *Captain Kodak* in conjunction with Black's nonfiction lectures. The book provides a more complete set of photographs from the lectures than the surviving slides. It also gives useful commentary on these images in the absence of a surviving script or outline of the lecture. I would like to thank Carl and Annetta Black, who have worked diligently to preserve and catalogue their family archive. Their generosity and willingness to discuss this material has made this project possible.

23. By 1897 Alfred Stieglitz, happy that the hand camera fad was coming to a close, was eager to promote the advantages of the hand camera for making art. Alfred Stieglitz, 'The Hand Camera: Its Present Importance', *The American Annual of Photography* (1897).

24. X. Theodore Barber, 'The Roots of Travel Cinema: John L. Stoddard, E. Burton Holmes and the Nineteenth-Century Illustrated Travel Lecture', *Film History* vol. 5 no. 1 (1993).

25. 'Life through a Camera', *The Brooklyn Eagle*, 14 February 1889.

26. See Lynne Kirby, *Parallel Tracks: The Railroad and Silent Cinema* (Durham, NC: Duke University Press, 1997); Charles Musser, 'The Travel Genre in 1903–1904: Moving Towards Fictional Narrative', *Iris* vol. 1 (1984).

27. Phillip Prodger has argued for considering instantaneous photography as a coherent '*vernacular* movement – a grassroots upheaval, organized around a singular wish: to freeze motion in time'. From his broad archive, Prodger notes that street scenes and marine views were the main categories of instantaneous photograph until Eadweard Muybridge made the photography of bodies in motion a famous subject. Phillip Prodger, *Time Stands Still: Muybridge and the Instantaneous Photography Movement* (Oxford: Oxford University Press, 2003).

28. I am indebted here to James Lastra's work on the material basis of diegesis. See James Lastra, 'From the Captured Moment to the Cinematic Image: A Transformation in Pictorial Order', in Dudley Andrew (ed.), *The Image in Dispute: Art and Cinema in the Age of Photography* (Austin: University of Texas Press, 1997).

29. From a handbill in the Billy Rose Theatre Collection, New York Public Library.

30. Maren Stange, *Symbols of Ideal Life: Social Documentary Photography in America, 1890–1950* (New York: Cambridge University Press, 1989), p. 17.

31. A picture of a woman sitting at the side of the street crying accompanied some of the publicity material.

32. From a poster in the Billy Rose Theatre Collection, New York Public Library.

33. See Tom Gunning, 'New Thresholds of Vision: Instantaneous Photography and the Early Cinema of Lumière', in Terry Smith (ed.), *Impossible Presence: Surface and Screen in the Photogenic Era* (Chicago: University of Chicago Press, 2001).

34. 'A Lecture by the Picture Play Author before the Institute', *The Brooklyn Eagle*, 18 December 1896.

35. See André Gaudreault, 'The Diversity of Cinematographic Connections in the Intermedial Context of the Turn of the 20th Century', in Simon Popple and Vanessa Toulmin (eds), *Visual Delights: Essays on the Popular and Projected Image in the 19th Century* (Trowbridge: Flicks Books, 2000).

36. 'As Mr Black Sees Us', *The Brooklyn Eagle*, 28 December 1896.

37. For a discussion of the relation between illustration and dramatic picturing, see Martin Meisel, *Realizations: Narrative, Pictorial, and Theatrical Arts in Nineteenth-Century England* (Princeton, NJ: Princeton University Press, 1983).

38. Italics in original. Alexander Black, 'The Amateur Photographer', *The Century* vol. 34 no. 5 (1887), pp. 723–4.

39. See Peter Galassi, *Before Photography: Painting and the Invention of Modern Photography* (New York: Museum of Modern Art, 1981).

40. 'It was a capital audience to show pictures to, for they were prompt to notice and commend attractive compositions, felicitous or characteristic groupings, [and] forcible light and shade.' *The Brooklyn Eagle*, 6 May 1890.

41. Alexander Black, 'Art and the Camera', *New York Times*, 18 December 1892.

42. For an extension of Galassi's claim to film theory, see Jacques Aumont, *L'oeil Interminable: Cinéma Et Peinture* (Paris: Librarie Séguier, 1989).

43. Handbill from the Billy Rose Theatre Collection, New York Public Library. Italics original.

44. Alexander Black, *Time and Chance: Adventures with People and Print* (New York: Farrar & Rinehart, 1937), p. 70.

45. This painting also known as *The Fairman Rogers Four-in-Hand*.

46. Black, 'The Amateur Photographer', p. 723.

47. 'New Books Acquired', *The Brooklyn Eagle*, 16 November 1888; Ramsaye, *A Million and One Nights*, p. 94.

48. Black, 'The Amateur Photographer', p. 723.

49. Alexander Black, *Photography Indoors and Out: A Book for Amateurs*, 4th edn (Boston: Houghton Mifflin, 1894), p. 214.

50. Edward Gregory, 'On the Galloping Horse in Art', *The Century* vol. 26 (1883). Rodin, quoted in Hollis Frampton, *Circles of Confusion: Film, Photography, Video Texts 1969–1980* (Rochester: Visual Studies Workshop Press, 1983), p. 91.

51. 'Life through a Camera'.

52. Black, *Captain Kodak*, p. 87.

53. This inevitability of certain pictured instants was often used for dramatic effect. Augustus Egg, in his well-known *Past and Present* (1858), uses the instantaneous effect of a falling house of cards for heavy symbolism.

54. I refer to it as Black's picture in the tradition of attributing authorship to the lecturer. The actual photographer of this picture is J. S. Johnston. Since Black used it for the covers of multiple handbills, he obviously saw it as representative.

55. 'In the first photograph, I was shown at the very moment of entering the water, and my face reflected all too clearly the sensation of the first contact with the cold sea-water. Really, one would not approach a lady with such gestures in the shore.' 1886, quoted in Tom Gunning, 'Embarrassing Evidence: The Detective Camera and the Documentary Impulse', in Jane Gaines and Michael Renov (eds), *Collecting Visible Evidence* (Minneapolis: University of Minnesota Press, 1999), p. 57.

56. Victor Oscar Freeburg, *Pictorial Beauty on the Screen* (New York: Macmillan, 1923), pp. 50–1.

57. William Abney, *Instantaneous Photography* (New York: Scovill and Adams, 1895), p. 2.

58. See Kirsten Gram Holmström, *Monodrama, Attitudes, Tableaux Vivants: Studies on Some Trends in Theatrical Fashion 1770–1815* (Uppsala: Almqvist and Wiksells Boktryckeri, 1967).

59. François Delsarte, mostly through his Anglophone disciple Genevieve Stebbins, was highly influential in connecting acting styles and the athletic physical culture of the nineteenth century. See Delaumosne *et al.*, *Delsarte System of Oratory*, 3rd edn (New York: E. S. Werner, 1887); Genevieve Stebbins, *Delsarte System of Dramatic Expression* (New York: E. S. Werner, 1886).

60. The early instances of Swedish and German acrobats engaged in 'fancy diving' at the turn of the nineteenth century coincides with the development of actors presenting their bodies as sets of posed pictures for an audience. The sport gained a new popularity right at the time that the diver became a subject of instantaneous photography. The first modern diving competitions were held in England in the 1880s, and the sport became an Olympic event in 1904. George Rackham, *Diving Complete* (New York: Faber and Faber, 1975).

61. For a discussion of tableau vivant culture and Eakins's Arcadian works, see Kathleen A. Foster and Mark Bockrath, *Thomas Eakins Rediscovered: Charles Bregler's Thomas Eakins Collection at the Pennsylvania Academy of the Fine Arts* (New Haven: Yale University Press, 1997).

62. His interest in the juxtaposition of recognisably modern nude bodies and Arcadian settings cost him his commission and eventually his position at the academy in 1886, an unfortunate event that Black laments in his autobiography.

63. The photographic modernity of the painting was noted in the first reviews of the painting. See 'At the Private View, First Impression of the Autumn Exhibition at the Academy of Fine Arts', *Philadelphia Times*, 1885.

64. Marta Braun, *Picturing Time: The Work of Étienne-Jules Marey (1830–1904)* (Chicago: University of Chicago Press, 1992).

65. Mary Ann Doane, *The Emergence of Cinematic Time: Modernity, Contingency, the Archive* (Cambridge, MA: Harvard University Press, 2002).

66. Braun, *Picturing Time*, p. 246.

67. From a handbill from the Billy Rose Theatre Collection, New York Public Library.

68. 'The whisper began in the clutter of pictures which I had been displaying with the screen talks. When I found parallels and sequences not only in action, but in likeness, when the bit of story in one snapshot began to join quite naturally with the bit of story in another snapshot of differing origin, the whisper became a shout. Why not use a chosen group of people in a variety of situations?' Black, *Time and Chance*, p. 129.

69. Alexander Black, 'The Camera and the Comedy', *Scribner's Magazine* vol. 20 (1896), p. 607.

70. Alexander Black, 'Photography in Fiction: "Miss Jerry," the First Picture Play', *Scribner's Magazine* vol. 18 no. 3 (1895), p. 348.

71. 'Sort of Big Kinetoscope,' *Boston Herald*. Undated clipping (1896?) from St Lawrence University Library Special Collections.

72. Slides from Princeton University Library, Department of Rare Books and Special Collections. Script from the New York Public Library Rare Books and Manuscripts.

73. This is slide change number 102 in the script at St Lawrence University Special Collections.

74. Black, *Time and Chance*, p. 137.

75. Thomas Craddock Hepworth, *The Book of the Lantern* (London: Hazell, Watson and Viney, 1899), p. 282.

76. Black, *Time and Chance*, p. 129.
77. Slides 113–15 in Princeton University Special Collections.
78. See 'Dioramic Effects', in Lewis Wright, *Optical Projection* (New York: Longmans, Green and Co., 1891).
79. Alexander Black, 'How to Give a Picture Play', *Ladies' Home Journal* vol. 15 no. 11 (1898).
80. Alexander Black, *A Capital Courtship* (New York: Scribner, 1897). Illustration facing p. 24.
81. Gaudreault, 'The Diversity of Cinematographic Connections in the Intermedial Context of the Turn of the 20th Century'.
82. Programme from the Billy Rose Theatre Collection, New York Public Library.
83. 'Sort of Big Kinetoscope'.
84. Musser and Nelson, *High-Class Moving Pictures*, p. 166.
85. Black, 'The Camera and the Comedy'.
86. 'An Interview with Alexander Black', *Kalamazoo Telegraph*, 1901.
87. 'Making the First Picture Play', *Harper's Weekly* vol. 38 (1894).
88. Freeburg, *Pictorial Beauty on the Screen*, p. 36.
89. See Gunning, 'New Thresholds of Vision'.
90. Christine Gledhill, 'Introduction', *Nineteenth Century Theatre* vol. 25 no. 2 (1997).
91. For a graphic comparison to the filmstrip, see Black, 'The Camera and the Comedy'. The illustrations are presented in a single vertical row on each page to invite comparison to celluloid.
92. Tour ledger, New York Public Library Special Collections, Alexander Black Collection.
93. Harriet Underhill, 'Unreeling the Past of the Motion Picture', *New York Tribune*, 9 November 1919, p. 3.
94. New York Public Library clipping from *Picture Play Weekly*, 2 October 1915, pp. 25–8; italics mine.
95. Letter from Zukor to Black, dated 8 October 1919. Black family collection.
96. Ramsaye, *A Million and One Nights*, pp. 100–1.

2 MOVING PICTURES IMAGINE THE ARTIST'S STUDIO

1. Browsing examples of historical educational slides from the collections of major American art schools, the setting of the workshop increases in prominence as historical scenes are recycled, from common stories translated from sources like Vasari's *Lives of the Artists*, to nineteenth-century academic paintings, to chromolithographs and then to lantern slides. These scenes of the studio were scattered throughout art-educational slide collections, and occasionally were produced in slide series, like the 'Arts in History' series created by prominent American slide producer C. W. Briggs. The slides were designed to illustrate lectures about old masters, and were sourced from mid-century French academic artists with whom such subjects were popular. The selection of images foregrounds the workspaces for Briggs's educational markets. Consider the picture of Benvenuto Cellini. As Renaissance art historian Janet Cox has shown, the typical mid-century depiction of Cellini's time in France foregrounds the cult of Francis I as the grand patron of Renaissance art, and de-emphasises Cellini's role as a craftsman. By the end of the nineteenth century in the USA, Cellini had of course become a key figure of the Arts and Crafts movement thanks to the best-selling translations of his self-promoting autobiography. In the Briggs slide, the

patrons take a seat, Cellini hops onto a bench and reveals his sculpture of Jupiter with a pile of tools and props still cluttering the foreground. The series frames Raphael in his studio with his *Madonna della Sedia*, apparently unfinished, as he begins work with a life model on the *Sistine Madonna*. Raphael's famously efficient and productive workshop is in motion, as his patrons (probably Pope Julius II) look on, his craftsmen collaborate on a cartoon for a fresco and another model waits for her work to begin. Like the other slides, this is taken from a lithograph of a mid-century French academic painting, and again its themes cut against the grain of the more common pictures following romantic traditions in which Raphael is used to glorify Francis I or the iconic pictures that depicted Raphael's relations with models outside of the work they did together. The groupings in the Briggs series would have been far more effective as edifying tableaux about the multiple steps involved in creating a composition. Briggs Collection, George Eastman House.

2. Neil Harris, *Humbug: The Art of P. T. Barnum* (Chicago: University of Chicago Press, 1981).

3. A 1904 slide from the School of the Art Institute of Chicago showcases how art educators used altered images of the studio space to teach art appreciation. This rendition of the *Painter in his Workshop* (1663), the iconic self-portrait by Adrian van Ostade, modifies the work of an artist already famous for depicting the studio space in its cluttered detail. The lithographer transforms the original by bringing the apprentice figure, grinding pigments, out of the dark background and adding a second worker behind the first. While the slide recreates the painter's style (indeed it is labelled as the artist's work), it inverts the solitary tone of the original oil painting into a more social space of work. Art Institute of Chicago slide, collection of the author.

4. Eadweard Muybridge sold prints of his scientifically rigorous motion studies to artists as extensions of the life room. Companies like Aurora and Norwood Studio specialised in photographing classically posed models and thus bringing life classes to an even larger audience through correspondence courses. They advertised in the art-education magazines with photographs of models and testimonials by Arts and Crafts correspondence education specialists. The company regularly published a testimonial by E. L. Koller, Principal of the Arts and Crafts division of the International Correspondence Schools, who wrote in to praise 'the great diversity of poses and postures' for use by 'the student of figure drawing as well as the professional commercial artist'. *Arts and Decoration*, September 1914, p. 397. The testimonial was used in Aurora advertisements for years.

5. See Sarah Burns, *Inventing the Modern Artist: Art and Culture in Gilded Age America* (New Haven: Yale University Press, 1996), pp. 277–99.

6. See Susan Waller, *The Invention of the Model: Artists and Models in Paris, 1830–1870* (Burlington: Ashgate, 2006).

7. In his seminal intellectual history of art education, Stuart Macdonald treats *Trilby* as more of a studio memoir of the 1870s than as a popular fantasy of the 1890s. Stuart Macdonald, *The History and Philosophy of Art Education* (London: University of London Press, 1970).

8. Roy Fleming Notebook, Kellen Design Archives, Parsons, 1905.

9. For an account of the lightning sketch at Chautauqua, see Isabella Pansy, *Four Girls at Chautauqua* (Boston: D. Lothrop and Co., 1876), pp. 361–75.

10. Charles Musser, 'A Cinema of Contemplation, a Cinema of Discernment: Spectatorship, Intertextuality and Attractions in the 1890s', in Wanda Strauven (ed.), *The Cinema of Attractions Reloaded* (Amsterdam: Amsterdam University Press, 2006).

11. As Malcolm Cook has noted, often these transformations in chalk would be accompanied by filmic trick transformations such as the sudden animation of the drawing or an image of an actual overlaying the drawn one. Malcolm Cook, 'Performance Times: The Lightning Cartoon and the Emergence of Animation', Domitor Conference, Brighton, June 2012.

12. The term 'metalepsis' is more appropriate to narratology, but the way is it often used to explain intermedial texts suggests that it could be usefully imported to discuss the jump from one medium to another. For a recent theorisation of the term in narratology, see Debra Malina, *Breaking the Frame: Metalepsis and the Construction of the Subject* (Columbus: Ohio State University Press, 2002).

13. Lynda Nead, *The Haunted Gallery: Painting, Photography, and Film around 1900* (New Haven: Yale University Press, 2007), pp. 45–106.

14. David Mayer and Gwendolyn Waltz have most consistently use the term 'frame-bursting' in their work on theatre/film hybrid performances, which has helped to form strong connections between historical study of film and of theatre. See Gwendolyn Waltz, 'Embracing Technology: A Primer of Early Multi-media Performance', in Leonardo Quaresima and Laura Vichi (eds), *The Tenth Muse* (Udine: Forum, 2001).

15. Giorgio Vasari, *Vasari's The Lives of the Artists* (New York: Dover, 2005), pp. 61, 225.

16. Some of the items included in the mania for Trilbyana were plays, paintings, dances and films, as well as items for more literal consumption such as Trilby sausages and ice cream in the shape of the title character's foot. The *Harper's Monthly* edition of the novel appeared from January to August 1894. The book was released by Harper and Brothers in September of that year, and a revised version appeared the following year. For detailed evidence of Trilbymania, see *Trilbyana: The Rise and Progress of a Popular Novel* (New York: Critic Co., 1895), p. 26. The following description of the ice cream is from an undated clipping in the Billy Rose Theatre Collection of the New York Public Library: 'The congealed sweetness is packed into the molds, which are surrounded by broken ice until the hour of service, when a dainty foot, a model of a foot, the very apotheosis of a foot is turned onto the plate in all its virginal whiteness and plump seductiveness.'

17. Three Edison burlesques of the story were made in 1895: 'Trilby Hypnotic Scene', 'Trilby Death Scene' and 'Trilby Quartette'. The description for 'Trilby Death Scene' states that, 'The dramatis personae of this act are made up in exact imitation of the illustrations given in Du Maurier's book.' In Charles Musser, *Edison Motion Pictures, 1890–1900: An Annotated Filmography* (Gemona, Italy: Le Giornate del Cinema Muto; Smithsonian Institution Press, 1997). In November 1896 Biograph made a kiss film, 'Trilby and Little Billee', following the popularity of the play as well as the popularity of 'The May Irwin Kiss' made earlier that year. See Kemp R. Niver and Bebe Bergsten, *Biograph Bulletins, 1896–1908* (Los Angeles: Locare Research Group, 1971), pp. 12–19.

18. A cartoon from a clipping file at the Billy Rose Theatre Collection shows A. M. Palmer, producer of Potter's *Trilby*, defending his Trilby on a platform against a line of imitation Trilbys of every shape and size. On one of their aprons is written, 'Try Trilby Flour'. On legal issues, see also Emily Jenkins, 'Trilby: Fads, Photographers, and "Over-perfect Feet"', *Book History* vol. 1 no. 1 (1998), pp. 241–4.

19. An undated clipping from the Billy Rose Theatre Collection contains a photograph of a woman in the 'Wistful and Sweet' pose from the novel with the caption, 'Society girl posing as Trilby on a pedestal'. See also *Trilbyana*, p. 19. Three months before the first New York production of Paul Potter's play, Pape threw this benefit performance for the New York

Kindergarten Association comprised of twelve tableaux accompanied by twelve songs. Programme from the Billy Rose Theatre Collection.

20. Joseph W. Herbert, 'Thrilby' (New York, 1985).
21. Carleton S. King, 'Fun in an Artist's Studio: Musical Comedy Sketch', in Rare Books and Special Collections Division, Library of Congress, Washington, DC, 1897.
22. According to Daniel Pick in *Svengali's Web: The Alien Enchanter in Modern Culture* (New Haven: Yale University Press, 2000), this film was also known as 'Svengali and the Posters'.
23. See Alison Winter, *Mesmerized: Powers of Mind in Victorian Britain* (Chicago: University of Chicago Press, 1998).
24. For a discussion of the origins of a concept of pictorial absorption in the neo-classical rejection of Rococo, see Michael Fried, *Absorption and Theatricality: Painting and Beholder in the Age of Diderot* (Berkeley: University of California Press, 1980).
25. The pictorial strain in Münsterberg's theory is evident in sections of *The Photoplay*: 'The Means of the Various Arts' and 'The Means of the Photoplay'. He ends the latter section with the claim that every film frame should be treated with 'the respect of the pictorial artist for the unity of forms'. Hugo Münsterberg, *The Photoplay: A Psychological Study and Other Writings* (New York: Routledge, 2002), p. 138.
26. Ibid., pp. 96–8 107–8, 134–8.
27. Ibid., p. 98.
28. See also Münsterberg's analogy between film frames and the droplets of water from a fountain. He moves from frames to cuts here as well. Ibid., p. 135.
29. Ibid., p. 97.
30. Vachel Lindsay, *The Art of the Moving Picture ... Being the 1922 Revision of the Book First Issued in 1915* (New York: Macmillan, 1922), pp. 85–6, 100–1.
31. For his praise of Fairbanks as Hollywood's proponent of Roosevelt's 'strenuous life', see Vachel Lindsay, *The Progress and Poetry of the Movies*, ed. and with commentary by Myron Lounsbury (Lanham, MD: Scarecrow Press, 1995 [c. 1925]), p. 173.
32. Ibid., p. 224.
33. Roy Fleming Notebook, Kellen Design Archives, Parsons, 1905.
34. Ibid.
35. Hiller Clipping File, 1920, Visual Studies Workshop, Rochester, NY.
36. Roy Fleming Notebook, Kellen Design Archives, Parsons, 1905.
37. Billie Scott, 'The True Story of an Artist's Model', *Star*, London, Hiller Clipping File, Visual Studies Workshop, Rochester, NY.
38. 'The meteoric rise of more than one little model offers an inspiration that the debs find difficult to resist. This coupled with a fair amount of pay and the glamour of what they think is bohemia, has attracted much resisted amateur competition.' 'Girls in Society Pose for Artists as Picture Models', Hiller Clipping File, Visual Studies Workshop, Rochester, NY.
39. Lejaren à Hiller, Proposal for Never-told Tales Series, 1919, pp. 1–2. Visual Studies Workshop, Rochester, NY.
40. The cast included Helen Gardner, Templer Sexe, Hiller, Peggy O'Neil and Marc Connley (who also helped Hiller with the script).
41. Hiller Collection, Visual Studies Workshop, Rochester, NY.
42. Underwood and Underwood had established itself in the nineteenth century, selling lantern slides and stereocards, but was now, with Hiller's help, making photographic advertising their main business.

43. For a discussion of Hiller's work in advertising, see Elspeth H. Brown, *The Corporate Eye: Photography and the Rationalization of American Commercial Culture, 1884–1929*, Studies in Industry and Society (Baltimore: Johns Hopkins University Press, 2005).

44. 'In the News Net', *New York Times*, 13 June 1920, Hiller Clipping File, Visual Studies Workshop, Rochester, NY.

45. *Exhibitor's Trade Review*, Hiller Clipping File, Visual Studies Workshop, Rochester, NY.

46. Hiller Collection, Visual Studies Workshop, Rochester, NY.

47. For more information on the series, and for a discussion of the films in the series I do not address here see, D. John Turner, 'Lejaren à Hiller and the Cinema', *Film History* vol. 19 no. 3 (2007).

48. Hiller Collection, Visual Studies Workshop, Rochester, NY. Indeed, the only surviving copies of these films are 16mm prints struck several years after the initial release, presumably for educational markets.

49. One interesting attempt to publicly frame these films was a contest that the board members planned to announce in *Ladies' Home Journal* to pick the star of the next film. The plan was aborted, but it had the enthusiastic support of each of the board members and the illustrator and editor of *Ladies' Home Journal*, N. C. Wyeth. Hiller Collection, George Eastman House.

50. Hiller Clipping File, Visual Studies Workshop, Rochester, NY.

51. Foster Gilroy, 'Vera Royer, St Petersburg Girl, Aids US Film Screen to Make Artistic Answer to Demand for Better Pictures', *St Petersburg Times*, Sunday, 5 February 1922.

52. Hiller Clipping File, Visual Studies Workshop, Rochester, NY.

53. See Susan Lasdun, *Victorians at Home (a Studio Book)* (New York: Viking, 1981).

54. Henry Clay Frick Papers, Frick Collection.

55. Frick Collection records indicate that Frick loaned the painting to the Metropolitan Museum for exhibition as *Portrait of a Young Man* during the Fulton-Hudson celebration of 1909.

56. See Ernst Gombrich, 'Rembrandt Now', *New York Review of Books*, 12 March 1970.

57. A new assessment and cleaning of the painting confirms the brushes in the background. See Joanna Sheers, 'Portrait of a Young Artist', in *Rembrandt and His School: Masterworks from the Frick and Lugt Collections*, ed. Colin B. Bailey (New York: Frick Collection, 2011).

58. Hiller may have read any of the monographs on Rembrandt, but he definitely read one by Edinburgh art historian George Baldwin Brown, which devotes a section to the artist's studio interior and to his pupils. Hiller gave Brown's book a cameo appearance in his film, and used the same young self-portrait in the film's prologue that Brown used in his biographical chapter.

59. See Carl Chiarenza, 'Notes on Aesthetic Relationships between Seventeenth-century Dutch Painting and Nineteenth-century Photography', in Van Deren Coke (ed.), *One Hundred Years of Photographic History* (Albuquerque: University of New Mexico Press, 1975).

60. Svetlana Alpers, *Rembrandt's Enterprise: The Studio and the Market* (Chicago: University of Chicago Press, 1995), p. 83. For a discussion of Rembrandt's thematic engagement with the workspace, see chapter 3 'A Master in the Studio', pp. 58–87.

61. In a similar manner, schools often noted their borrowings from Paris. The brochure for the Eric Pape School of Art, another frequent advertiser in art magazines, makes clear Pape's intention to 'carry out the great but simple principles of the art academies of Paris. ... Students begin at once to draw from the nude' and upon enrollment 'obtain free entrance

cards to the Museum of Fine Arts and may work in the art rooms of the Boston Public Library', studying from the murals of Pierre Puvis de Chavannes and John Singer Sargent. Pape's school, while it taught courses in modern applied arts, sought to simulate the Parisian system already outstripped by the influence of Impressionism. These borrowings made Pape's staging of tableaux from Trilby seem like less of a coincidence. *Pape School Brochure*, The Internet Archive.

3 CINEMA COMPOSITION

1. See Richard Koszarski, *An Evening's Entertainment: The Age of the Silent Feature Picture, 1915–1928* (Berkeley: University of California Press, 1994); Myron Lounsbury, *The Origins of American Film Critisicism, 1909–1939* (New York: Arno Press, 1973).
2. Dana B. Polan, *Scenes of Instruction: The Beginnings of the US Study of Film* (Berkeley: University of California Press, 2007).
3. Peter Decherney, *Hollywood and the Culture Elite: How the Movies Became American* (New York: Columbia University Press, 2005).
4. This foundational work is particularly important in this case. Compared with an early film theorist like Hugo Münsterberg, whose writing on film follows clear and self-contained logical steps, one finds it much more difficult to disentangle Freeburg and Patterson's aesthetic ideas from their practical origins in the classroom.
5. See Peter Smith, 'The Ecology of Picture Study', *Art Education* vol. 39 no. 5 (1986); Mary Ann Stankiewicz, 'A Picture Age: Reproductions in Picture Study', *Studies in Art Education* vol. 26 no. 2 (1985).
6. Henry Rankin Poore, *Pictorial Composition and the Critical Judgment of Pictures: A Handbook for Students and Lovers of Art* (New York: Baker and Taylor, 1903). Poore's influence comes late in this intellectual history. Poore continued to develop a systematic paradigm for art education that had already reorganised art curricula across the country. I will save my discussion of Poore's reflections on pictorialism and modern art for later in order to begin with the earlier and more foundational influence of Arthur Wesley Dow.
7. See Arthur W. Dow, *Theory and Practice of Teaching Art*, 2nd edn (New York: Teachers College, Columbia University, 1912).
8. See Arthur W. Dow, *Composition*, 3rd edn (New York: Baker and Taylor, 1900), pp. 7–20.
9. Dow, *Theory and Practice of Teaching Art*, pp. 1–8. Italics original.
10. See John Dewey, *Interest and Effort in Education* (Boston: Houghton Mifflin Co., 1913).
11. *Yearbook of the Brooklyn Institute of Arts and Sciences*, vol. 18, 1905–6, p. 192.
12. *Yearbook of the Brooklyn Institute of Arts and Sciences*, vol. 24, 1911–12, pp. 229–33. See also Marianne Fulton *et al.*, *Pictorialism into Modernism: The Clarence H. White School of Photography* (New York: Rizzoli, 1996).
13. See Thomas Bender, *New York Intellect: A History of Intellectual Life in New York City, from 1750 to the Beginnings of Our Own Time* (New York: Knopf, 1987).
14. See David Levine, *The American College and the Culture of Aspiration, 1915–1940* (Ithaca: Cornell University Press, 1986).
15. See John Angus Burrell, *A History of Adult Education at Columbia University* (New York: Columbia University Press, 1954); Milton J Davies, 'University Social Service', *The Chautauquan: A Weekly News Magazine* vol. 72 no. 3 (1913); 'Democratizing Education:

Columbia, with Other Universities of the Country, Is Revolutionizing Its Policies to Reach the Masses', *New York Times*, 25 April 1915.

16. Minutes from the administrative meetings at the Brooklyn Institute indicate that Davies worked as supervisor of lectures between 1903 and 1905. Brooklyn Museum Archives.

17. In his letter outlining his official plan for the Columbia Institute to Director James Egbert, Davies notes that the plan is, 'Not an Experiment: The Brooklyn Institute of Arts and Sciences has very successfully applied the same methods for a number of years and its membership is now over six thousand.' Milton Davies folder, Columbiana Archive, Columbia University.

18. See Ernest Francisco Fenollosa and W. H. Ketcham, *The Masters of Ukioye: A Complete Historical Description of Japanese Paintings and Color Prints of the Genre School* (New York: Knickerbocker Press, 1896). Fenollosa's influence on the pictorialists is less famous than his influence on modernists like Pound. See Ezra Pound, *Instigations of Ezra Pound* (New York: Freeport, 1967).

19. For an emphasis on the narrative dimensions of Freeburg's work, see Noel Carroll, *Theorizing the Moving Image* (Cambridge: Cambridge University Press, 1996); Kristin Thompson, 'Narrative Structure in Early Classical Cinema', in John Fullerton (ed.), *Celebrating 1895: The Centenary of Cinema* (New Barnet: John Libbey, 1998).

20. Victor Oscar Freeburg, *The Art of Photoplay Making* (New York: Macmillan, 1918), p. 26.

21. Ibid., p. 70.

22. Vachel Lindsay, *The Art of the Moving Picture ... Being the 1922 Revision of the Book First Issued in 1915* (New York: Macmillan, 1922).

23. Freeburg, *The Art of Photoplay Making*, back matter.

24. Frances Taylor Patterson, *Cinema Craftsmanship* (New York: Harcourt, Brace and Co., 1920).

25. Syllabus for intermediate course in Frances Patterson folder at the Columbiana Achive, Columbia University.

26. See Freeburg, *The Art of Photoplay Making*, pp. 7–25.

27. Dow, *Theory and Practice of Teaching Art*, p. 1.

28. Frances Taylor Patterson, 'The Swedish Photoplays', *Exceptional Photoplays* (1922).

29. Ibid.

30. On the exhibition of casts in museums, see Lawrence Levine, *Highbrow/Lowbrow: The Emergence of Cultural Hierarchy in America* (Cambridge: Harvard University Press, 1988), pp. 146–60.

31. Frances Taylor Patterson, *Scenario and Screen* (New York: Harcourt, Brace and Co., 1928), p. 206.

32. See the photographs of the Hall of Greco-Roman Sculpture, *Yearbook of the Brooklyn Institute of Arts and Sciences*, vol. 11, 1898–9, pp. 185–6.

33. Goodyear wrote extensively on repose in classical sculpture. He took a particular interest in the *Laocoön*. See William Henry Goodyear, 'Laocoön', *Brooklyn Museum Quarterly*, 1917.

34. Gotthold Ephraim Lessing, *Laocoon, or, the Limits of Poetry and Painting* (London: J. Ridgway & Sons, 1836).

35. Henry Fuseli, *Lectures on Painting, Delivered at the Royal Academy* (London: Luke Hansard, 1801). For a discussion of Fuseli's legacy in British aesthetic history, see Martin Meisel, *Realizations: Narrative, Pictorial, and Theatrical Arts in Nineteenth-Century England* (Princeton, NJ: Princeton University Press, 1983). For a discussion of German critical history, including Lessing, Winckelmann, Herder, Moritz and Goethe, see Simon Richter,

Laocoön's Body and the Aesthetics of Pain: Winckelmann, Lessing, Herder, Moritz, Goethe (Detroit, MI: Wayne State University Press, 1992).

36. See Phyllis Keller, *States of Belonging: German-American Intellectuals and the First World War* (Cambridge: Harvard University Press, 1979).

37. See Vernon Lee, *Beauty and Ugliness and Other Studies in Psychological Aesthetics* (New York: John Lane, 1912); Vernon Lee, *The Beautiful: An Introduction to Psychological Aesthetics* (New York: Putnam, 1913). For a discussion of the German origins of these aesthetic theories and their relation to cinema, see Scott Curtis, *The Shape of Spectatorship: Art, Science, and Early Cinema in Germany* (New York: Columbia University Press, forthcoming).

38. Ethel Puffer, *The Psychology of Beauty* (Boston: Houghton Mifflin, 1905).

39. Freeburg, *The Art of Photoplay Making*, p. 28.

40. Mary Ann Doane, *The Emergence of Cinematic Time: Modernity, Contingency, the Archive* (Cambridge, MA: Harvard University Press, 2002), p. 108.

41. Note that Freeburg's understanding of the theatrical tableau is already once removed from the common usage of the tableau as it is outlined by Brewster and Jacobs. Brewster and Jacobs show how these significant moments traditionally happened at narrative climaxes; they freeze action while communicating character relations essential to the development of the plot. Freeburg suggests that tableaux should fall at pictorially expressive moments rather than narratively significant moments. He emphasises composition over dramaturgy. Tableaux of pictorial beauty heighten the aesthetic effect of compositions that would otherwise pass too quickly. See A. Nicholas Vardac, *Stage to Screen: Theatrical Method from Garrick to Griffith* (North Stratford: Ayer Co., 1949) and B. Brewster and L. Jacobs, *Theatre to Cinema: Stage Pictorialism and the Early Feature Film* (Oxford: Oxford University Press, 1998).

42. Freeburg, *The Art of Photoplay Making*, p. 31.

43. Ibid.

44. Freeburg's language, here and elsewhere, comes close to Bergson's in *Creative Evolution*. Henri Bergson, *Creative Evolution*, trans. Arthur Mitchell (New York: H. Holt and Co., 1911). It is likely that his familiarity with Bergson went beyond his documented encounter through Henry Poore's writing. Ubiquity of *Creative Evolution* aside, Freeburg was a graduate student at Columbia during Bergson's blockbuster lecture series on campus.

45. Freeburg's analysis depended in large part on the physical availability of the stills that companies were willing to provide. I have already noted Paramount's relationship with Columbia, and Cecil B. DeMille himself even sought to develop relations with his father's alma mater. Sumiko Higashi, *Cecil B. Demille and American Culture the Silent Era* (Berkeley: University of California Press, 1994).

46. See Lea Jacobs, 'Belasco, Demille, and the Development of Lasky Lighting', *Film History* vol. 5 no. 4 (1993).

47. See Jan Olsson, 'Trading Places: Griffith, Patten, and Agricultural Modernity', *Film History* vol. 17 (2005).

48. Cecil B. DeMille and Donald Hayne, *The Autobiography of Cecil B. Demille*, Cinema Classics (New York: Garland, 1985).

49. Freeburg, *The Art of Photoplay Making*, p. 256

50. Ibid., p. 43.

51. Ibid.

52. Ibid., p. 42.

53. In another passage Freeburg claims that the cinema has greater opportunities for suggestion because of the abstraction of the drama onto the celluloid medium. Film's mediated nature extends theatre's capacity for suggestion. This is interesting because it is the exact opposite of the argument A. Nicholas Vardac would make a generation later, when he claims that it was film's capacity to record real spectacles that extended theatre audiences' increasing appetite for realistic spectacle on the stage. Vardac, *Stage to Screen*.

54. For a discussion of how mainstream cinema fuses the movement of the apparatus with the movement of the narrative, see Doane, *The Emergence of Cinematic Time*, pp. 20–33.

55. Freeburg does not use the term 'innervation', but he states clearly that his understanding of the psychology of pictorial perception comes from Ethel Puffer, who does use the term. I reiterate the term in the context of Freeburg's work because of the importance the term has gained in Miriam Hansen's readings of Walter Benjamin's theories of cinema, mass culture and modernity. See Miriam Bratu Hansen, 'Benjamin and Cinema: Not a One-way Street', *Critical Inquiry* vol. 25 no. 2 (1999).

56. Victor Oscar Freeburg, *Pictorial Beauty on the Screen* (New York: Macmillan, 1923), p. 10.

57. This is not to simply say that emphasis should go hand in hand with narrative. 'Guiding the attention of the spectator properly helps him to understand what he is looking at, but it is still more important to help him feel what he is looking at.' It is clear that Freeburg does not ignore the dramatic effect of the film, but he subsumes it within the concept of pictorial feeling. Bad pictorial composition and sequencing of pictures uses up the spectator's limited emotional energy before he or she can feel into the shot or sequence properly. Ibid., p. 12.

58. Ibid., p. 42.

59. The economic orientation of *Pictorial Beauty on the Screen* comes remarkably close to the more recent discussions of narrative economy, cinema's management of attention and cinema's training of photographic contingency – all of which have been primarily editing based. But this early theory of film spectatorship gives priority to pictorial economy. More important than standardised narration is the notion of feeling into the form. More primary than the flashback's or the close-up's power of narrative suggestion (Münsterberg) is the suggestion of form in two-dimensional space. The cinema composer does work against the contingencies of the apparatus ('the camera is positively stupid, because it always shows more than is necessary'), but these contingencies are managed through attention to line and composition more than the progression of narrative cuts. This is not to say that Freeburg's work should cause us to question recent models of narrative absorption. My point is rather that we can and should trace plural models of absorption at work in these early mainstream art films. It enriches our understanding of cinema's management of the spectator's attention to pursue intellectual traditions that place film's inexorable forward narrative movement in productive collaboration with seemingly opposing forces.

60. Freeburg, *The Art of Photoplay Making*, p. 256.

61. The fact that cinema was excluded further underscores Freeburg and Patterson's efforts to redefine cinema as a medium. Movement presented a set of aesthetic issues that did not need to be addressed so long as cinema's relation to the theatre business outstripped its potential relation to museum culture and institutions of art education. Still photography had a connection to the model of gallery exhibition, but cinema did not. Freeburg and Patterson foregrounded these other venues for the discussion of film because their courses positioned them between film-making practices and an art-education programme derived

from Dow's method. In their unique position they confronted the aesthetic questions traditionally excluded from the intellectual traditions in which they were trained.

62. Paul Souriau, *The Aesthetics of Movement*, trans. Manon Souriau (Amherst: University of Massachussets Press, 1983 [1889]), p. 78.

63. Souriau notably uses *Winged Victory* in a similar argument to Patterson's about aesthetic movement and sculpture. Ibid., pp. 119–20.

64. He suggests that as Hogarth ascribes beauty to the balanced oscillation of an 's' curve, a film should look for those moments the oscillating surface of the sea inscribes the same pattern into a filmstrip. See William Hogarth, *The Analysis of Beauty* (New Haven: Yale University Press, 1997 [1753]). Freeburg, *Pictorial Beauty on the Screen*, pp. 77–8.

65. Freeburg, *Pictorial Beauty on the Screen*, pp. 9–10.

66. See the Jesse Lasky papers, Margaret Herrick Library.

67. Letter dated 10 April 1923, Jesse Lasky papers, Margaret Herrick Library.

68. *Motion Picture News*, 10 March 1923.

69. *Morning Telegraph*, 20 May 1923.

70. Beginning in 1903, after the publication of his *Pictorial Composition*, Poore's writing stood among the most widely received work on the subject. *Pictorial Composition* (in its tenth edition by 1915) and Dow's *Composition* circulated more extensively in American art departments than any other textbooks. Poore's books were often discussed as counterpart to Dow's. He provided philosophical elaborations on many of Dow's practically oriented concepts. For a discussion of Dow as a figure who combined modernism with pictorial idealism, see James L. Enyeart, *Harmony of Reflected Light: The Photographs of Arthur Wesley Dow* (Santa Fe: Museum of New Mexico Press, 2001).

71. Henry Rankin Poore, *The New Tendency in Art* (Garden City: Doubleday, 1913), p. 17.

72. Ibid., pp. 51–2.

73 Henry Rankin Poore, *The Conception of Art* (New York: Putnam, 1914).

74. For a discussion of the movement in the locks of hair in classical sculpture, see C. Anstruther-Thomson, *Art and Man: Essays and Fragments* (New York: E. P. Dutton and Co., 1924).

75. For Freeburg's discussion of Poore, see Freeburg, *The Art of Photoplay Making*, pp. 55–6. Patterson includes Poore's book amoung her course materials, the bibliography for which is listed in the appendix of *Cinema Craftsmanship*.

4 PAINTING WITH HUMAN BEINGS

1. Dorothy Nutting, 'Monsieur Tourneur: Otherwise Accurately Called "the Poet of the Screen"', *Photoplay* (July 1918), p. 55. Nutting goes on to describe his work with famous artists, his textile designs and his book illustrations as contributing to his film style. See also 'Tourneur of Paris and Fort Lee: His Methods and His Artistic History', *Photoplay* vol. 9 no. 2 (1916). Frances Wood, 'Tourneur: A Weaver of Dreams', *Picture Play*, June 1918.

2. See Mark Garrett Cooper, *Universal Women: Filmmaking and Institutional Change in Early Hollywood* (Champaign: University of Illinois Press, 2010); Jane Gaines, 'Of Cabbages and Authors', in Jennifer Bean and Diane Negra (eds), *A Feminist Reader in Early Cinema* (Durham, NC: Duke University Press, 2002); Shelly Stamp, 'Lois Weber, Progressive Cinema, and the Fate of "the Work-a-Day Girls" in *Shoes*', *Camera Obscura* vol. 19 no. 2 (2004).

3. Frances Taylor Patterson, *Scenario and Screen* (New York: Harcourt, Brace and Co., 1928).

4. Charles Emerson Cook, 'Maurice Tourneur Paints with Human Beings', *Exhibitors Herald*, 9 June 1917.

5. It is worth noting that the archive at the Musée Rodin possesses detailed records of the assistants who worked in the studio, but there is no record of the young Tourneur (then Maurice Thomas) in the studio. Likewise, the archival records at the Boston Public Library and the Musée d'Orsay neglect to mention Tourneur's work on the murals. When these stories of his artistic origin circulated, they did so by Tourneur's own agency, and he would continue to tell these stories into the 1940s to groups like Germaine Dulac's cinema salon. Maurice Tourneur clipping file, BiFi, Paris.

6. Judith Cladel, *Rodin*, trans. James Whitehall (New York: Harcourt, Brace and Co., 1937), p. 328.

7. See Aimée Brown Price, 'Puvis De Chavannes and America', in Serge Lemoine (ed.), *From Puvis De Chavannes to Matisse and Picasso: Toward Modern Art* (London: Thames and Hudson, 2002).

8. See Arthur W. Dow, *Composition*, 3rd edn (New York: Baker and Taylor, 1900).

9. Sadakichi Hartmann, 'Art and Artists: Pierre Puvis De Chavannes', *Musical America* vol. 1 no. 6 (1898).

10. Henry Adams, 'Letter of September 8, 1896 to Mabel La Farge', in *Henry Adams and His Friends, a Collection of His Unpublished Letters* (Boston: Houghton Mifflin, 1947).

11. On Puvis's atelier, see Aimée Brown Price and Pierre Puvis de Chavannes, *Pierre Puvis De Chavannes*, 2 vols (New Haven: Yale University Press, 2010).

12. Josef von Sternberg also remembers observing the two together. 'In [Chautard's] heyday there were many prominent French directors working in Fort Lee on the Hudson, where the film studios were concentrated, and whenever possible I watched them at work. There were Mercanton, Blaché, Capellani, and the best known of them all, Maurice Tourneur, whose *Prunella* and *The Blue Bird* were notable excursions into fancy'. Josef von Sternberg, *Fun in a Chinese Laundry* (New York: Mercury House, 1988), p. 44.

13. Newspaper publicity photograph, clipping file, Bibliothèque de l'Arsenale, Paris.

14. From Carré's unpublished memoir, Special Collections, Margaret Herrick Library.

15. Frances Taylor Patterson, *Cinema Craftsmanship* (New York: Harcourt, Brace and Co., 1920).

16. Ben Carré, unpublished memoir, Special Collections, Margaret Herrick Library.

17. For a Boston example, see Boston Art Student's Association, *The Art Student in Paris* (Boston: Museum of Fine Arts, 1887).

18. His work was also published in the influential Green Tree Library series representing 'the new movement in literature', namely, decadent works.

19. Maurice Maeterlinck and Richard Hovey, *The Plays of Maurice Maeterlinck*, The Green Tree Library (Chicago: Stone & Kimball, 1894).

20. Discussion of the *Blue Bird* balls can be found in the Maeterlinck files in the Rondel collection at the Bibliothèque de l'Arsenale, Paris. For Goldwyn's relationship to Maeterlinck, see 'Picture Plays and People', *New York Times*, 8 February 1920.

21. Cited in Elspeth H. Brown, *The Corporate Eye: Photography and the Rationalization of American Commercial Culture, 1884–1929*, Studies in Industry and Society (Baltimore: Johns Hopkins University Press, 2005).

22. See Henry Rose, *Maeterlinck's Symbolism: The Blue Bird and Other Essays* (New York: Dodd Mead, 1911).

23. *New York Times* review of *The Blue Bird*.

24. Programme and production notes Bibliothèque de l'Arsenale, Paris.
25. In Harry Waldman, *Maurice Tourneur: The Life and Films* (Jefferson, NC: McFarland & Co., 2001), p. 75.
26. Undated cartoon in the Puvis de Chavannes clipping file, Musée d'Orsay.
27. 'Small Talk, the Theater', in Henri Dorra, *Symbolist Art Theories: A Critical Anthology* (Berkeley: University of California Press, 1994).
28. This is in contrast to the way that Artcraft tried to promote the film. The posters showcased the child actors to give a sense that this would be a kind of children's movie.
29. Italics mine. Cited in Richard Abel, *French Film Theory and Criticism: A History/Anthology, 1907–1939* (Princeton, NJ: Princeton University Press, 1988), p. 167.
30. *New York Times*, 1 April 1918, p. 9.
31. Tom Gunning, 'Loie Fuller and the Art of Motion', in Richard Allen and Malcolm Turvey (eds), *Camera Obscura, Camera Lucida: Essays in Honor of Annette Michelson* (Amsterdam: Amsterdam University Press, 2003).
32. See Blake Nevius, *Cooper's Landscapes: An Essay on the Picturesque Vision* (Berkeley: University of California Press, 1976).
33. N. C. Wyeth, 'For Better Illustration', *Scribner's Magazine*, November 1919.
34. Ibid.

5 REX INGRAM'S ART SCHOOL CINEMA

1. 'Scaramouche', *Exceptional Photoplays* vol. 3 no. 7 and 8 (1923), pp. 1–2.
2. This approach has been pursued brilliantly, for example, by Kristin Thompson in relation to some of Ingram's colleagues. See Kristin Thompson, 'The Limits of Experimentation in Hollywood', in Jan-Christopher Horak (ed.), *Lovers of Cinema: The First American Film Avant-Garde, 1919–1945* (Madison: University of Wisconsin Press, 1995), pp. 67–93; Kristin Thompson, 'The Sorrows of Satan', in Paolo Cherchi Usai (ed.), *The Griffith Project Volume 10: Films Produced in 1919–46* (London: BFI, 2006), pp. 193–200.
3. For James, 'minor' is not simply a question of film funding. He instead defines productive minor cinemas that typically counter the film industry but remain networked with the industry's resources and its geographies in greater Los Angeles. David E. James, *The Most Typical Avant-Garde: History and Geography of Minor Cinemas in Los Angeles* (Berkeley: University of California Press, 2005).
4. Ingram's association with Yale was a standard biographical note in articles about his films, even after he left to make films in France. For local discussion of this association in the *New Haven Register* and the *New Haven Journal Courier*, see the clippings in Box 1165, Alumni Files, University Archives, Yale University.
5. Cited in Richard Koszarski, *Hollywood Directors, 1914–1940* (New York: Oxford University Press, 1976), p. 87.
6. Ibid.
7. Ibid., p. 86.
8. Later, as a director, he returned to this theme, often including artist characters and studio scenes in films like *The Four Horsemen of the Apocalypse* and *The Magician* (1926). His screen characters served as another venue for the cultivation of a cinema that references the plastic arts.

9. Cited in Liam O'Leary, *Rex Ingram: Master of the Silent Cinema* (Dublin: Academy Press, 1980).

10. The list of suggestive film company names of the 1910s and 20s also includes the Film Craft Corporation and the Cinema Arts and Crafts Corporation of San Francisco. Among art directors whose work bears traces of Arts and Crafts styles, Hugo Ballin stands out, but they can be found elsewhere. Lucy Fischer observes traces of these familiar styles, as late as 1929, alongside the primarily Art Deco style of Cedric Gibbons's sets for *The Kiss* (1929). Lucy Fischer, *Designing Women: Cinema, Art Deco, and the Female Form* (New York: Columbia University Press, 2003), pp. 106–13.

11. Mark Garrett Cooper, *Universal Women: Filmmaking and Institutional Change in Early Hollywood* (Champaign: University of Illinois Press, 2010), pp. 104–6.

12. On the formation of the art school and the hiring of Lawrie, see Theodore Sizer (ed.), *The Recollections of John Ferguson Weir: Director of the Yale School of the Fine Arts, 1869–1913* (New York: New York Historical Society, 1957), pp. 67–91.

13. Walters was invited to the Metro studio to see the rushes of the film. His article applauds the attention to composition saying that Ingram's art training was clear in the film. 'Sculptor Praises Production', 26 March 1921. Alice Terry Scrapbook, Margaret Herrick Library.

14. Correspondence among Ingram, Lawrie and Ibáñez about this sculpture can be found in the Lee Lawrie Papers, Library of Congress.

15. The sculpture arrived at Ibáñez's home in the late summer the following year. He wrote to Lawrie to tell him that he had placed the grouping by his work desk, 'so that when I write, every time I lift my eyes, I see your wonderful work, and I think of you, marvelous sculptor and of my co-worker Rex Ingram'. Correspondence dated 2 September 1922, Lee Lawrie Papers, Library of Congress.

16. The alumni registrar at Yale even took on the task of correcting those who mistakenly referred to his degree. 'The statement has been frequently made in the public press that the degree granted was an honorary one but this is not the case. Mr Ingram was a student at Yale during 1912–13, but did not complete his work for the degree until 1921.' Correspondence dated 14 December 1923, Alumni Files, University Archives, Yale University.

17. 'Yale First University to Recognize Art of Picture Screen', *New Haven Register*, 19 January 1922, Alumni Files, University Archives, Box 1165, Yale University.

18. The biggest topics of discussion were art and the gifts (money and a growing collection of rare pipes) from Ingram to Lawrie. Lee Lawrie Papers, Library of Congress.

19. DeMille was clearly another director with a strong investment in pictorial composition, but it is worth noting here that he also introduced suspicion about how much attention a director should give to these techniques. His famous joke with Samuel Goldwyn about exhibitors paying double for 'Rembrandt lighting' indicates some of this suspicion. In an editorial illustrated with stills from Ingram's *Scaramouche*, DeMille singles out Ingram with a similar critique. 'It is a pity that so many of our promising younger directors become so engrossed in creating individual charming pictures on the screen that they forget to create that clash of characters, that procession of situations, which is the sole and only thing that can hold the attention of an audience through a feature photoplay.' Cecil B. DeMille, 'Pictures Secondary in Cinema Success', *Los Angeles Times*, 18 July 1923, WF5. Thanks to Ruth Barton for bringing DeMille's criticism of Ingram to my attention.

20. In O'Leary, *Rex Ingram*, p. 65.
21. A selection of these images can be found in the collection of 8x10in production stills at the Margaret Herrick Library.
22. Patrick Keating, *Hollywood Lighting from the Silent Era to Film Noir*, Film and Culture (New York: Columbia University Press, 2010), pp. 15–29.
23. John F. Seitz, 'Can a School Teach Cinematography?', *American Cinematographer*, 5 July 1923.
24. O'Leary, *Rex Ingram*, p. 66.
25. Hilde D'haeyere, 'Stopping the Show: Film Photography in Mack Sennett Slapstick Comedies (1917–1933)', University College Ghent, 2012.
26. Rex Ingram, 'Directing the Picture', *Opportunities in the Motion Picture Industry* (Los Angeles: Photoplay Research Society, 1922), pp. 27–33.
27. Rex Ingram, 'Directing the Picture', *Art Review* (February 1922), pp. 12–13, 27. Clipping from Lee Lawrie Papers, Library of Congress.
28. Rex Ingram, prefatory note to Victor Oscar Freeburg, *Pictorial Beauty on the Screen* (New York: Macmillan, 1923), p. vii.
29. 'Aesthetic vs Moralistic Censorship,' *Exceptional Photoplays*, June 1921, p. 8.
30. Ibid.
31. 'The Screen: Pictorial Fancy Runs Free', *New York Times*, 4 October 1922.
32. 'Zukor Plans Big Conference to Consider Screen's Artistic Advance', *Moving Picture World* (1923), p. 761.
33. For precursors to AMPAS, see Peter Decherney, *Hollywood and the Culture Elite: How the Movies Became American*, ed. John Belton, Film and Culture (New York: Columbia University Press, 2005).
34. 'Motion Picture Arts Congress Called Here: Prizes for Development to Be Feature of Convention under Auspices of Author's League', *New York Times*, 26 April 1923.
35. Nicholas Schenck to Adolph Zukor, 13 December 1924, Paramount Pictures Collection, Margaret Herrick Library.
36. Frances Taylor Patterson, 'A Prize Paradox', *New York Times*, 25 January 1923.
37. Raphael Sabatini to Adolph Zukor, 26 February 1925, Paramount Pictures Collection, Margaret Herrick Library.
38. Patterson, 'A Prize Paradox', X5. Ingram agreed to be one of the guest speakers in Patterson's Photoplay Composition course at Columbia University the following year.
39. Vachel Lindsay, *The Progress and Poetry of the Movies*, ed. and with commentary by Myron Lounsbury (Lanham, MD: Scarecrow Press, 1995), p. 158.
40. The National Council of Teachers of English frequently recommended the novel for English or History classes. See 'News and Notes', *The English Journal* vol. 11 no. 7 (1922).
41. See Arnie Davis, *Photoplay Editions and Other Movie Tie-in Books: The Golden Years, 1912–1969*, 1st edn (East Waterboro, ME: Mainely Books, 2002).
42. 'What Will Be the Result?', *Exceptional Photoplays* vol. 3 no. 7 and 8 (1923), p. 5.
43. Robert Emmet Sherwood, 'The Four Horsemen of the Apocalypse', *Life Magazine*, 24 March 1921, p. 432.
44. Robert Emmet Sherwood, *The Best Moving Pictures of 1922–23* (Boston: Small, Maynard and Co., 1923), pp. xix, 19–23. It is also worth noting that in the preface to this book (and throughout its sections) Sherwood echoes the sentiment of the *Exceptional Photoplays* review of *Scaramouche*. 'The Motion Picture is just what its name implies. It is a pictorial

rather than a literary form of expression. It makes its impression on the mind by way of the senses' (p. xi).

45. Undated clipping in Alice Terry Scrapbook, Margaret Herrick Library.

46. Fairbanks and Sabatini were also sought out by educational publications. In 1925, the *World Review*, a Chicago-based scholastic publication for high school students, featured an adventure story by Sabatini in its first issue and an article by Fairbanks on physical fitness in the second. See 'Publications for High School Pupils', *The School Review* vol. 33 no. 9 (1925), p. 647.

47. And Lindsay's fetishes were legendary. While he was writing this book in the Davenport hotel in Spokane, he insisted on having two life-sized dolls accompany him to dinner. After some argument, the hotel manager agreed to sit him with his dolls behind a screen in the back corner of the hotel dining room to avoid disturbing the other guests. See Tony Bamonte and Suzanne Bamonte, *Spokane's Legendary Davenport Hotel* (Spokane, WA: Tornado Creek, 2001).

48. 'Scaramouche', *Exceptional Photoplays* vol. 3 no. 7 and 8, p. 1.

49. In Freeburg, *Pictorial Beauty on the Screen*.

50. Even Buster Keaton references the film in *Sherlock Jr* (1924). Sweeping outside the cinema ticket booth, the silent film clown gestures to an art film about a stage clown from the commedia dell'arte. It also probably did not hurt that that Keaton was working for Metro at the time.

51. Seitz experienced none of the career damage that befell Ingram. He stayed productive in Hollywood for decades as one of the most respected figures in his field.

CONCLUSION

1. Steve Neale, 'Art Cinema as Institution', *Screen* vol. 22 no. 1 (1981), p. 29.

2. Rosalind Galt, *Pretty: Film and the Decorative Image* (New York: Columbia University Press, 2011), p. 7.

3. On realist film practices against causal narrative, see David Bordwell, 'The Art Cinema as a Mode of Film Practice', *Film Criticism* vol. 4 no. 1 (1979). On the open and ambivalent images in world cinema, see Shohini Chaudhuri and Howard Finn, 'The Open Image: Poetic Realism and the New Iranian Cinema', *Screen* vol. 44 no. 1 (2003).

4. The letterhead of the Guild listed each member of the board with his or her institutional affiliation. The list is long, but it marks a set of institutional connections that has remained largely unmapped. Major board members, with their affiliations, as provided in the letterhead, included: Robert Sherwood of *Life*, Quinn Martin of the *World*, Anita Loos, Robert Flaherty, Ralph Block of Famous Players, John Cohen Jr of the *New York Evening Sun*, Benjamin de Casseres, John Emerson, Fannie Hurst, Jay Kaufman of the *New York Evening Telegram* and Sidney Olcott, director. The board of directors was located in New York, and the advisory council included members in fifteen cities across the country.

5. Seymour Stern, 'An Index to the Creative Work of David Wark Griffith', in *Special Supplement to Sight & Sound: Index Series*, ed. Sight & Sound (London, 1944).

6. Henry Harrison, who ran the Grub Street Club as well as the *Quill*, organised the event to bring together critics and many of the revival organisers at the Film Arts Guild. Harrison sent a personal invitation to Griffith, assuring him that his name 'will be elaborated on appreciably'. Letter from Harrison to Griffith, 4 October 1926, D. W. Griffith Papers.

7. Seymour Stern, 'Kaleidoscopia', *Greenwich Village Quill* vol. 19 no. 4 (October 1926), p. 32.

8. Terry Ramsaye, *A Million and One Nights: A History of the Motion Picture* (New York: Simon and Schuster, 1926).

9. Stern, 'Kaleidoscopia', p. 39.

10. Seymour Stern, 'Great Moments From Cinemas that Will Linger in the Memories of Spectators', *The New York Sun*, 14 October 1926. D. W. Griffith Papers.

11. Seymour Stern, 'A Working-Class Cinema for America', *The Left* vol. 1 (1931).

12. Freeburg uses Griffith as his main example of a director with an eye for moving texture. Victor Oscar Freeburg, *Pictorial Beauty on the Screen* (New York: Macmillan, 1923), p. 91.

13. Josef von Sternberg, *Fun in a Chinese Laundry* (New York: Mercury House, 1988), p. 41. After Chautard had retired as a director, he continued to make a living as an actor in Hollywood. Sternberg cast him in such films as *Morocco* (1930) and *Shanghai Express* (1932).

14. Sternberg also comments on Tourneur's work in this same section, describing him – in the context of the French émigrés working in Fort Lee, New Jersey, in the 1910s – as the 'best known of them all'. Ibid., p. 44.

15. B. G. Braver-Mann, 'Josef von Sternberg', *Experimental Cinema* vol. 5 (1934), p. 19. In this article, Braver-Mann launches a sustained attack on Sternberg's style by comparing him with the Soviets and by using the language of decadence. The article begins with a description of a photograph of Sternberg wearing 'a richly ornamented black velvet coat and his arms are outstretched as if offering a benediction'. Ibid., p. 17.

16. Seymour Stern, 'Hollywood and Montage: The Basic Fallacies of American Film Technique', *Experimental Cinema* vol. 4 (1932), pp. 46–52.

17. I am using the term 'aesthete' in reference to the recently published volume, Curtis Harrington, *Nice Guys Don't Work in Hollywood: The Adventures of an Aesthete in the Movie Business* (Chicago: Drag City, 2013).

18. This interest spanned from the 1940s to the 80s, when he had plans to write an index on Ingram, followed by one on Tourneur. Undated letter, Curtis Harrington Papers, Josef von Sternberg correspondence: 1964–99, Margaret Herrick Library.

19. Curtis Harrington, 'Ghoulies and Ghosties', *Quarterly Review of Film and Television* vol. 7 no. 2, Winter 1952, p. 193. Anger, too, was deeply interested in the pictorial traditions of silent cinema, especially when they looked back to the decadent 1890s or made use of fantastic *mise en scène*. He even toured with Rex Ingram's films.

20. 'The Dangerous Compromise', printed in the programme notes for Curtis Harrington, *The Films of Josef von Sternberg: A Film Cycle Presented by the Committee on Arts and Lectures* (Santa Barbara: University of California, 1965), pp. 2–7.

21. Ibid., p. 1.

22. Harrington is typically only mentioned in passing in histories of the American avant-garde. One exception is David E. James, *The Most Typical Avant-Garde: History and Geography of Minor Cinemas in Los Angeles* (Berkeley: University of California Press, 2005), pp. 180–91.

23. Even encountering Kiarostami's films narrowly, as realist art films, elides his (almost compulsive) interest in picturesque landscapes. Composed pictures of natural beauty with lone trees and winding roads brand his films and his exhibitions of still photography at galleries around the world. See also his own documentary about these photographs, *The Roads to Kiarostami* (2005).

Index

Page numbers in **bold** indicate detailed analysis; those in *italics* denote illustrations; *n* = endnote.

LIST OF ILLUSTRATIONS

While considerable effort has been made to correctly identify the copyright holders, this has not been possible in all cases. We apologise for any apparent negligence and any omissions or corrections brought to our attention will be remedied in any future editions.

Miss Jerry, Alexander Black; *The Eternal City*, Madison Productions; *The Sleep of Cyma Roget*, Lejaren à Hillier Productions; *The Beggar Maid*, Triart Picture Company; *The Young Painter*, Triart Productions Inc.; *Audrey*, Famous Players-Lasky Corporation; *The Hand of Peril*, Paragon Bioscope Company; *Carmen*, William Fox; *The Covered Wagon*, Famous Players-Lasky Corporation; *The Wishing Ring*, World Film Corporation/Shubert; *The Blue Bird*, Famous Players-Lasky Corporation/Artcraft Pictures Corporation; *The Last of the Mohicans*, Associated Producers Inc./Maurice Tourneur Productions; *The Spirit and the Clay*, Vitagraph Production; *The Four Horsemen of the Apocalypse*, Metro Pictures Corporation; *Scaramouche*, Metro Pictures Corporation.